SIMPLE SCALING

Hi Bo,

I hope you enjoy the
book and may it inspire
you to continue to scale
with Purpose

Best Wishes,

Brendan

SIMPLE SCALING

TEN PROVEN PRINCIPLES TO 10X YOUR BUSINESS

BRENDAN McGURGAN

CLAIRE COLVIN

HOUNDSTOOTH
PRESS

Hardcover ISBN: 978-1-5445-2590-7

Paperback ISBN: 978-1-5445-2589-1

eBook ISBN: 978-1-5445-2591-4

*This book is dedicated to all of the fantastic clients of
Simple Scaling, our ScaleX™ Tribe.
Thank you for giving us the honor and privilege of serving you.*

CONTENTS

THE SCALEX™ FRAMEWORK

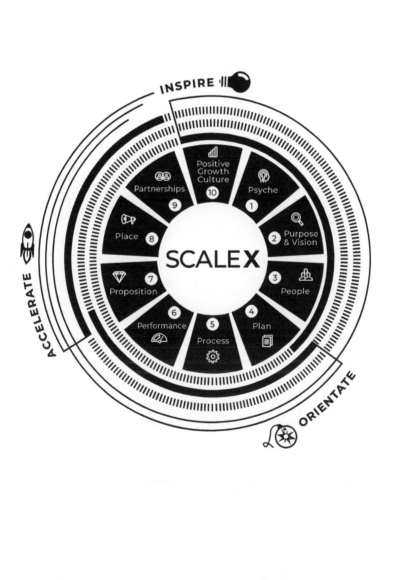

NOTE ON COAUTHORSHIP

THROUGHOUT THIS BOOK, BRENDAN AND CLAIRE SPEAK IN THE first person, delivering insights and revealing lessons learned from their combined experience. Brendan's expertise derives from his many years as an award-winning CEO, while Claire's perspective is that of a high-caliber talent leader with a successful career across a range of business sectors. In a small number of episodes, names and personal information have been changed to preserve anonymity. A number of exchanges are re-created from memory. We have rendered them to the best of our ability.

PO

INTRODUCTION

—BJ McGurgan & CEJ Colvin, August 2021

"Everything should be made as SIMPLE as possible, but not simpler."

—Albert Einstein

THIS BOOK HAS BEEN WRITTEN IN RESPONSE TO A FAILURE AT THE heart of the small and medium enterprise (SME) sector. Only a tiny percentage—estimated at between 2 percent and 4 percent—ever achieve scale.

Think about that.

The vast majority of founders and entrepreneurs, despite making great strides forward in the early years, hit a brick wall and stagnate, denying themselves, their teams, and their communities a golden opportunity to create something special. A ScaleUp Institute report found that if the number of scale-ups in the UK rose by just 1 percent, 150,000 net jobs would be created by 2034, generating an additional £225bn GDP.[1] And that's just the UK!

What is the reason for this failure? Why do so many otherwise excellent, high-potential startups end up treading water?

Another UK ScaleUp report cited "lack of ambition" as the number one impediment to scaling success.

We disagree.

It's not ambition that's missing; it's the know-how required to scale successfully. The reality is that traditional thinking and long-established conventions are no longer serving us. To break through the ceiling and shoot for long-term scaling growth calls for a new set of principles.

Our company, Simple Scaling (simplescaling.com), exists to enable the success of would-be scalers, to allow them to deliver immense value to themselves, their shareholders, their team, their communities, and to society at large. Our ScaleX™ Accelerator is an exclusive program delivered across the globe to CEOs and managing directors of SMEs who have the ambition to scale with purpose.

Just to be clear on exactly what we're talking about here, the Organisation for Economic Co-operation and Development (OECD) defines a scale-up business as one that has seen average annualized growth of at least 20 percent over three years and that has ten or more employees at the start of the observation period.

This is the world Claire and I have been immersed in for over twenty years. The company in which we met grew from a workforce of fifteen in a small business park in Northern Ireland to employ 700 people across six continents. In fifteen years, we went from being a locally focused company to being a global industry leader. Along the way, we won a host of awards: the Deloitte Best Managed Company for twelve years running, and the Sunday Times Profit Track 100, to name just two.

We were not a tech unicorn. We were not one of those business-world lottery winners, the ones who make sensational business news headlines.

We created a moonshot vision in which we would become the number one company in our industry in every country in the world. Then we went on to develop a plan to make that happen. Was it plain sailing? Hardly. Not only did we navigate 9/11, the dot-com collapse, and the global financial crisis, we also made bags of mistakes and took a lot of wrong turns. But we were a "win or learn" company, and that mindset was critical to keeping our vision in focus when things went wrong.

This book, in addition to our ScaleX™ Accelerator Program and our *ScaleX™ Insider Podcast* show, speaks to the 400 million leaders of SMEs out there who wrestle with their businesses day and night in hopes that things will get a little easier and that sustainable growth can happen. These are SME artisans who dream of greater success but can't drag themselves from the everyday slog of their businesses or are paralyzed by the fear of growth. Like so many others, I graduated to the CEO position and immediately felt pressure to provide inspiration, direction, and a plan. Our ScaleX™ Framework is a playbook of sorts, one that I would dearly love to have had when I stepped into the CEO role all those years ago.

We have packed this book with clear calls to action, techniques, and real-life stories that will help you scale your organization. What's more, our website, simplescaling.com, features a range of tools and templates that will support you on each step of your journey.

According to the Herrmann Whole Brain model, I'm blue brained: rational, logical, analytical, fact based. Claire brings a red brain to the table. She's a champion and lover of people: expressive, supportive, and emotional. One thing we both share, however, is the love of a good framework!

We have combined our perspectives to create the ScaleX™ Framework. This puts a logical, intuitive order on the scaling journey. We want you to learn from our many mistakes. We want to simplify the wonderful scaling journey that lies ahead.

What's more, we want you to take this journey with joy, flow, and ease.

As performance guru Enda McNulty, whom we talk to in *P6 Performance*, asserts, reading the book is not enough. You need to take what's here and put it into practice. Don't just read the material; be the material.

A NEW MINDSET

Growing up in the '70s and '80s, LEGO (a great scale-up case study, by the way) was my go-to request for birthdays and Christmas. I would tear open the box, carefully unseal the plastic bags full of bricks and sort them into different bowls, which I had taken from the kitchen cupboard. With everything laid out in front of me, I would open the instructions, and moving slowly from page to page, I would work through them, watching the model evolve and grow. I wasn't the kid who abandoned the instructions and built a dinosaur from what should have been a fire engine. Those dinosaur builders are the startup entrepreneurs, the creatives, and the igniters. We need those people—badly—but when it comes time to scale, a different mindset is required. You need discipline, structure, and a large dose of stick-to-it-iveness. One thread you'll find running through this book is this: what got you this far won't get you the rest of the way.

As you move from startup to scale-up, the focus is less on experimentation and more on establishing, refining, and standardizing the processes, which enable repeatable, scalable, and profitable business. It is about embedding the right level of governance to manage those processes and putting in the performance metrics that will help validate their efficacy and success. Scaling happens when your gains begin to outpace your losses. It's about moving from the potholed laneway where you could only trundle along, and turning onto the scale-up freeway. It's about moving smoothly up through the gears without losing a wheel in the process.

This book was created by business leaders for business leaders. Although there are other books out there that take in elements of what we've created, none provide a comprehensive, holistic, down-to-earth guide to all of the challenges you'll meet as you set out to scale your business. We walk with you through each stage of the scaling process.

HOW TO USE THIS BOOK

The ten principles (10 Ps) are discrete and independent, which means you can reference each separately if you wish. Taken together, however, they represent an integrated framework for scaling success—the ScaleX™ Framework.

They are divided by three actionable themes. Beginning with the Inspire section, P1 Psyche focuses on developing the mindset needed to successfully scale a business. P2 Purpose and Vision is all about creating an inspirational vision of the future, one that is rooted in a strong purpose. Once crafted, it is time to bring the "who." P3 People looks at those you will need to get you where you need to go.

In the Orientate section, we zero in on P4 Plan, which plots a course toward the vision. P5 Process explores how you develop a template for repeatable success, while P6 Performance looks at how you execute.

Last, we deal with how you Accelerate your scaling ambitions. This begins in P7 Proposition with a clear articulation of your value proposition. To scale significantly, you will need to take your product or service beyond your borders into a new region and/or industry. We discuss this in P8 Place. Next comes P9 Partnerships, where we look at the broader business ecosystem that will play a part in achieving your vision.

Finally, we return to the beginning and Inspire once again with P10 Positive Growth Culture and look at how establishing the right culture holds the entire framework and indeed the entire scaling organization together.

By understanding how to navigate the growth phases that all SMEs go through and by implementing a more predictable, repeatable cadence across your business, you will be on your way to building a successful, profitable, and sustainable business. You will be on the road to realizing your vision.

Scaling is not easy.

There is no magic formula for delivering exponential revenue growth without exponential increases in costs, but the truth is that every Fortune 500 company began where you are.

There will always be things that lie outside your control. Technological advancements, such as virtual reality, blockchain, robotics, biometrics, and so on, have given us a world in constant flux. Changes in consumer behavior, employment trends, new product development, competitor activity, and government policy have to be captured and assimilated. You must adapt or die.

In all of this, there is one thing you can control: the fundamental principles on which your business is built. They will secure the foundation for your growing business and provide the basic truths to guide your decision making, behavior, and processes. They will allow you to cultivate the culture for sustainable growth and prosperity. In times of volatility and uncertainty, the ScaleX™ Framework will be there to focus you.

In addition to our own experience, we have incorporated the testimony of a host of experts and SME leaders who have also successfully scaled their businesses: Vishen Lakhiani of Mindvalley, Cameron Herold of COO Alliance (previously of 1-800-Got-Junk), JT McCormick of Scribe Media, and Brendan Mooney of Kainos, to name just four.

The most important piece of advice that we can offer on this challenging journey is to keep it simple, keep it honest, and keep it real. Being able to share complex matters in a simple (but not oversimplified) way requires a level of maturity and clear understanding of the situation.

Beware, however. Simple does not mean easy.

Simplicity can often require the most advanced thinking. Make it part of your business's DNA. Once you embed it in your culture, you will move mountains.

As Henry Ford once said, "Whether you think you can or you think you can't, you're right." If you believe you can, you will. We believe that with the right levels of ambition and belief, these ten principles will get you where you want to go.

THEME 1
INSPIRE

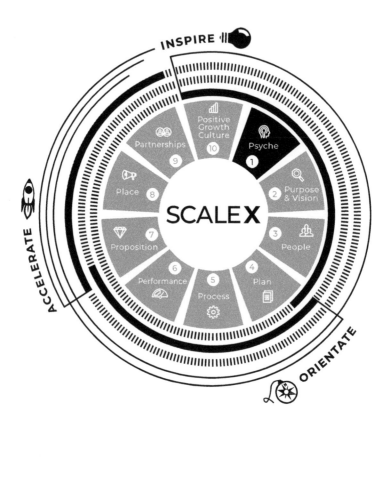

P1

PSYCHE

"What man actually needs is not a tensionless state but rather the striving and struggling for some goal worthy of him. What he needs is not the discharge of tension at any cost, but the call of a potential meaning waiting to be fulfilled by him."
—**Victor Frankl**

IT ALL STARTS IN YOUR MIND. THE SUCCESS OR FAILURE OF YOUR scaling journey starts with the thoughts you think. What you *believe* you can achieve sets the limit on what you *will* achieve. To become a successful scaler, you will need to work on your mindset. Don't underestimate the extent of that inner work. And don't underestimate the magnitude of the challenge you face. Successful scaling is incredibly challenging.

But the rewards are also immense.

Before we delve into the operating principles of scaling your organization, you must first decide if scaling is a journey you truly wish to embark on. Before business scaling, you must be committed to *personal* scaling. You must *level up* in order to scale up.

As it stands, your business may be delivering a certain level of comfort. You've graduated from startup school or have taken over the reins from the founder and are now running a successful SME. Turnover is in the seven figures; you have a small team of capable people delivering decent results. After years of hard work, there's cash in the bank, and you're finally able to stop and enjoy the view. You have a nice lifestyle: the car, the holidays, the home—perhaps even a second home. Maybe you're finally able to engage in some philanthropic activity, giving you a certain standing in your community.

Do you want to stay in this zone and maintain what has become a lifestyle business? Nothing wrong with that. Maintaining the status quo when things are in constant flux is challenging in its own right. But if that is your decision, be clear about it. Be deliberate.

Or are you feeling stuck? Trapped by the constant demands of the day-to-day business, unable to lift your head and work out where you want to go next?

Or maybe you are dissatisfied. Uneasy. Do you have a sense that there's a greater purpose out there? Something that goes beyond simply maintaining a standard of living? Something that will allow you to work *on* rather than *in* the business? Do you feel passionate about your proposition and the value you deliver to your customers? Have you relished the challenges you've faced and overcome to date? If so, you now have a responsibility to scale. You're standing at what I call Scaleverest base camp.

Remember, many SMEs have got to this point before, but according to UK research, only between 2 percent and 4 percent ever go on to scale successfully.[2] An OECD study asserts that companies that grow rapidly represent "a tiny fraction" of all startups.[3]

Before you set out to scale your business, you need to take an unflinching look at your lifestyle, your habits, and your mindset. You need to conduct an honest appraisal, and ask yourself if you are ready to make the fundamental changes necessary to help you get where you need to go.

Nor is it all about finding the drive and the self-belief to join the elite. Other facets of the CEO mindset have to shift, too.

For instance, if you're at the helm of a successful startup, you're probably in control of every aspect of the business. When the business begins to scale, it becomes impossible to exercise that level of control. So many CEOs we've worked with have struggled with letting go and trusting others in the business to deliver what they can no longer deliver on their own. Attempting to do so is a sure path to burnout.

Imposter syndrome is also an issue; the sense that you'll never be good enough, that you'll be found out at any minute. We've worked with many CEOs who feared that they weren't smart enough, or prepared enough, or strong enough to succeed.

Simply shifting your mindset to one of exponential growth from one of incremental growth requires an altered perspective—a reconfigured mindset. You have to do something different, not more of the same.

Do you wish to lead yourself, your team, and your business to the top? If the answer is yes, then your commitment must be unshakeable. If you're only half-committed, you will fail. It's that simple.

So let's look at what getting to the scaling summit entails.

1.1 SCALE WITH A BRUCE LEE MINDSET!

"If you always put limits on everything you do, physical or anything else, it will spread into your work and into your life. There are no limits. There are only plateaus, and you must not stay there; you must go beyond them."
—**Bruce Lee**

I've been practicing martial arts for more than twenty-five years and have always been fascinated by the importance of mindset in performance and the many parallels between performance in elite sport and elite business. Take tae kwon do, the martial art that I've concentrated on. It is based on five principles: courtesy, integrity, perseverance, self-control, and indomitable spirit. You could just as easily ascribe these values to that of any successful scaling organization.

Growing up, Bruce Lee was my hero. His many films inspired my big vision: achieving a black belt. In practice, tae kwon do is a mix of self-defense, competitive sparring, patterns, physiology, the Korean language, and structure. With practice, desire, and focus, you can secure a colored belt every three to six months over a four-year period. I loved how these mini goals allowed me to measure my progress toward the ultimate ambition. At the age of forty-one, having attained my third-degree black belt, I took part in my last competition, the Northern Ireland Championships. By then, I was accompanied by my two daughters, who were competing at junior level that same weekend. After three bouts of competitive sparring, I made it through to the final, where my opponent was five inches taller and half my age. That day, I had to concede that this was a younger person's game, and I proudly accepted my silver medal.

"Giving back" is part of tae kwon do's admirable tradition. Since achieving my black belt, I have coached the sport in my local community. I've noticed, over that time, just how many students quit at green belt stage. Progressing from white through yellow to green is, well, easy. You can secure your grading and be awarded your belt even if you miss classes, fumble your patterns, and get pummeled in sparring. To progress to blue, red, and black, however, requires so much more: discipline, dedication to a vision, the ability to listen, perseverance, desire, faith, an unwavering attitude, and a willingness to learn. Not everyone has this mindset.

Progressing to the later belts—and the black in particular—is very much like the choice facing entrepreneurs who are deciding whether to try to hold what they have or to scale.

It's fifty years since the untimely passing of Bruce Lee—or "The Dragon" as he was known. He was only thirty-two when he died, an age at which many of us have not figured out what we want. Yet, in those short years, he made a huge impact, not only on sport but also on film, on philosophy, and the study of mindset. Bruce was passionately connected to something that was much bigger than himself. It wasn't just about being rich and famous.

The scaling entrepreneur needs the Bruce Lee mindset:

- A "can do, will do" attitude.

- A "win or learn" mentality; mistakes are an opportunity for self-improvement and adaptation.

- Being "formless," that is, not stubborn. As Bruce put it, "flexible like water."

- An insatiable appetite for learning as the sustenance of personal growth.

- Make your best effort each day: "Do just a little more than what's required."

- Take personal responsibility for the outcome.

- Be a source of uplift. Your positive attitude and positive energy will raise those of your team.

The obstacles we think are impeding our progress are almost always self-imposed. We focus energy on the problem, not potential solutions. To knock down those walls, we need to adopt the Bruce Lee mindset—the growth mindset.

1.2 IGNITE THE POWER OF "YET"

"I am also defined by my curiosity and thirst for learning. I buy more books than I can finish. I sign up for more online courses than I complete. I fundamentally believe that if you are not learning new things, you stop doing great and useful things."
—Satya Nadella, CEO, Microsoft

I had just finished a meeting in the business lounge of my hotel in Dubai when my coauthor, Claire—then talent director of the company we both worked at—called with bad news. A crucial member of our team had handed in his notice. He had been leading a business unit delivering revenues of nearly £10 million ($15 million), one that we had grown almost from scratch. He had been progressing steadily through the company and had been appointed to this role only six months before.

I hung up and called the guy right away. In the course of an emotional conversation, he told me that he was broken. Despite having cleverly disguised the fact for some months, he was completely overwhelmed by the job.

"I feel suffocated by it," he said. "I've bitten off way more than I can chew. I can't do it, Benny."

Things had gotten so bad that as far as he was concerned, his only choice was not only to leave the role but to leave the company as well.

As we talked through his experiences over the previous six months and the heady mix of emotions he was still going through, it emerged that he still wanted to do the job. The passion and ambition to make it work remained, but he felt he just couldn't do it anymore. I agreed with him. He couldn't do it.

Yet.

We talked on for about half an hour and agreed that he would take time out from the business. Then he could return to a different, less-pressurized role and take it from there. Three years later, the same position became available. He went for it again and got it. I called him up after a couple of months to see how he was getting on and, more particularly, how he was feeling.

"Like Robocop," he said. "It's great. I'm loving it. Couldn't be better."

What had generated this transformation in ability?

He used his time off to develop his mindset and transformed his energy levels. By doing the inner work and taking on different roles in the company, he built his competence, confidence, and capability to the point where, when the opportunity arose again, he was ready to seize it with both hands. And this time, he was more than equal to it.

Mindset

In her now-famous 2007 book *Mindset*, Stanford psychologist Carol Dweck created a new psychology of success. Following decades of research, Dweck proved that a small psychological change in how we approach challenges can dramatically impact outcome. She identifies two mindsets: the fixed mindset and the growth mindset. Students who have a fixed mindset believe their intelligence, basic abilities, and talent are unchangeable. They are predetermined. If you have a fixed mindset, you tend to avoid challenges so that you don't have to deal with failure, because failure, as far as you're concerned, means you're stupid. By contrast, if you have a growth mindset, you believe that you can develop your talents and abilities through effort, good teaching, and persistence. You believe that with the proper focus, you can learn anything. You embrace challenges because you see them as an opportunity to learn and improve. Effort is worthwhile because it is seen as a path to mastery. Getting things wrong and receiving feedback is seen as positive because it guides further improvement.

In one famous experiment, students attending a high school in Chicago who would otherwise be issued with a failing grade were instead given a grade of "Not Yet." The clear implication was that they were on a learning curve. The grade might not be right, but the trajectory was, and knowing that dramatically improved these students' perseverance, application, and ultimately their success.

If we don't engage the power of "yet," our ability to dream becomes impeded; our desire to explore the what-ifs is neutralized. A fixed mindset doesn't look for solutions; it only seeks validation.

The Warrior Academy

The Warrior Academy is an international business developed by Sebastian Bates, one of the many successful scalers who generously contributed to this book. The academy offers martial arts classes to children, courses designed to develop kids' confidence, conduct, and concentration. The story of how he drove the growth of that business is fascinating in its own right, but right now, I want to say something about how he reacted when the COVID-19 pandemic struck at the beginning of 2020.

In late February, he was on a business trip to South Africa. He had just landed in Johannesburg when he turned on his phone to a message from his wife—then seven months pregnant—to say that the academy had been shut down. They had over 400 students in Dubai alone, where he and his wife were based, but as and from that day, all children's activities ended summarily.

"The problem—well, one of the problems," he explains, "was that they shut us down on payday. We were expecting £180,000 ($270,000) in end-of-term fees, and we had a lot of checks going out. So we pivoted, very, very quickly."

Sebastian got back to Dubai on one of the last planes to leave Johannesburg, and in the ten days that followed, he spent twelve hours a day filming. He and the team at Warrior Academy filmed every single class, from white through to black belt. Within two weeks—just as the most severe lockdown restrictions were announced—Warrior Academy went online.

The COVID-19 pandemic struck so quickly that most of us were left standing like deer in headlights, but Sebastian's quick thinking and tremendous drive meant that his business didn't skip a beat. That's the growth mindset in action.

Breaking Up Negative Self-talk

What is perhaps most profound about Carol Dweck's research is that mindset itself can be changed and that this change can happen in *either* direction. She has found, too, that simply being conscious of the two mindsets can prompt a shift in how you think.

How many times do we look in awe at the achievements of others and think, "I couldn't do that!" Our minds shift automatically to justification mode.

"I could *never* run a marathon, but Tommy was always a great runner at school. I'm not surprised he's training for that."

"Bill's company just topped $10 million in sales? That's no surprise. Didn't his father give him the money to start that business in the first place?"

Think of all the stories we tell to keep ourselves locked, comfortable, and unchallenged. As Dr. Jim Loehr, the world-renowned performance psychologist and executive coach, puts it, "The power broker in your life is the voice that no one hears. How well you revisit the tone and content of your private voice is what determines the quality of your life. It is the master storyteller, and the stories we tell ourselves are our reality."[4]

Simply recognizing that you're adopting a fixed mindset in these scenarios can be enough to jolt you toward growth. Next time you think "I couldn't do that," don't just accept this instinctive, thoughtless assessment. Challenge it. Challenge all negative self-talk. Journaling is a great way of focusing attention on that insidious negative voice. Write down your most prominent negative thoughts and then critique them. Hold them up to the light of day. Are they really based on fact? Are they just negative interpretations? Engage the power of "not yet," and if there are gaps in your skillset, find a way to fill them.

Now, while activating your growth mindset, ask yourself the question, "Do I want to scale my business?" You may not have everything in place to scale *yet*—in fact, you almost certainly won't—but if you think resolutely with a growth mindset, you can and you will. Remember, many, many people have stood where you're now standing. There is a ready repository of help and support for those who genuinely wish to scale. In advance of our scaling journey, we made so many benchmarking visits to companies that had been there before. Throughout the journey, we called on all of the help we could possibly call on to speed us on our way.

If you hear yourself saying, "But I've explored all the options and it simply can't be done," or "I just can't trust my team to deliver these ambitious goals," or "I'll never be good enough or smart enough," recognize the fixed mindset for what it is.

There is always a way.

1.3 MANAGE YOUR MIND

"The greatest accomplishment that you can achieve is the stillness of the mind. It is only when your mind is still that you can go from external to internal programming. In the absence of thoughts, this stillness aligns your feelings with your innermost being, reflecting the true self in a direct mirror...The limit is not the sky: the mind is. It is on the edge of our limits that we find the greatest growth. On this edge you can choose to quit or go beyond what you thought was impossible."

—Wim Hof

Let's be clear. Your health and well-being throughout this scaling adventure should be nonnegotiable. Optimizing your own personal operating system will ensure you maximize your energy levels, which will enable you to not only take your scaling journey but to also enjoy the ride. Skip the inner work and at some point, one or more of the many obstacles you'll face as you scale will derail you.

There are heated debates in the entrepreneurial community about everything related to personal growth, but one practice has come in from the fringes and found widespread acceptance.

Meditation. There is no shortage of successful athletes, entrepreneurs, and executive coaches celebrating the benefits of some form of meditation. When Ray Dalio, founder of the world's largest hedge fund and author of the book *Principles*, says that meditation is the single biggest thing he can trace back to his success, we should all sit up and listen...or maybe sit back and close our eyes for a few minutes.

I was a late convert, but five years ago, after a family trauma, I gave it a try and haven't looked back.

What I've found is that meditation, preceded with a daily ritual of Wim Hof breathing, allows me to become wholly conscious of the thoughts that pass through my mind during the day. It allows me to arrest the negative thoughts that can—if you don't pay attention—swamp you and drain your energy. Time and again, I've seen the truth of the assertion that where thoughts go, energy follows. Understand this: What you consciously think about and allow to take root in your subconscious mind (your emotional mind) will determine how you act and ultimately the results that you achieve. It's simply cause and effect. Your thoughts create the results you achieve.

One of the most compelling studies on the benefits of mindfulness was conducted by New York psychologist Amishi Jha. Her work with US Special Forces demonstrated that fifteen minutes of daily meditation enhanced working memory, clarity of thought, and the ability to focus under extreme pressure.[5] There is also ample scientific evidence to demonstrate the positive impact of meditation on emotional intelligence and even blood pressure.

Meditation isn't about chanting. You don't have to burn incense or sit cross-legged at the feet of the Buddha. It is in fact an umbrella term that covers many things. At its very simplest, it means taking some time out to be still and quiet your mind. There's no great trick to it.

Meditation

Go find a comfortable place to sit, a place where you won't be disturbed. Then begin. Shut your eyes and concentrate on your breath. I recommend starting with simple "box breathing" (an exercise adopted by the US Navy SEALs to create calm during times of high stress). With your eyes closed, take four seconds to inhale through your nose (engage your diaphragm; your belly should expand on the inhale), hold your breath at the top for four seconds, take four seconds to exhale through your mouth, and then hold your breath at the bottom of the cycle for four seconds. Then repeat. Try it now—right now—where you sit.

The focus should remain on the breath. When other concerns, thoughts, and emotions bubble up and force their way in, don't become frustrated. Just let them go again. Refocus on your breathing, and keep that focus for four or five minutes. When you're finished, reset your mind. Visualize what you are going to do. What does your perfect business look like when scaled? Picture your HQ, your team buzzing around the office, and the full, car park. Set your intention. Positively affirm it. Scan your body to see how you feel when you envisage the scaled business. It should excite and scare you in equal measure. Most of all, you should feel alignment; you should feel a strong sense of *rightness* in your intention.

Perform this little ritual regularly. Make it part of your daily routine, but don't think of meditation as another thing to add to your to-do list. It is, rather, a practice that goes hand in hand with cultivating a growth mindset. Start with just two minutes in the morning, or before a meeting, or prior to bedtime. It should be like brushing your teeth—a simple thing that you do regularly without thought, drama, or resentment.

Meditation won't give you instant Zen-like superpowers, but regular practice will bolster your ability to cope with anxiety and fear.

And make no mistake about it. Fear will consume you at different stages. Legendary boxing coach Cus D'Amato, trained Mike Tyson to become the youngest-ever heavyweight world boxing champion. He once said, "Fear is the greatest obstacle to learning in any area of life…It's like a fire. If you control it, as we do when we heat our houses, it is a friend. When you don't, it consumes you and everything around you."

Meditation significantly improves focus, resilience, and performance under stress. We can all remember times when we reacted in the heat of the moment, only to regret our words and behavior. Meditation helps to make me aware of what I'm experiencing. It allows me to catch the first bubbles of emotion before that emotion has a chance to take over.

And so it allows me to extend the time between the stimulus and the response so that I don't get hijacked by those emotions.

There are plenty of great meditation and mindfulness resources out there. The CALM app has a range of simple, guided meditations that I've used consistently for the last four years—be it during a turbulent plane journey or in the back of a beaten-up taxi navigating the chaotic streets of Calcutta, trying to tame my stress on my way to an important meeting. I slip on my earphones and ten minutes of guided meditation delivers much needed calm.

Try it.

Ego Is the Enemy

Beware founders syndrome. This occurs when the leader's power and influence prevents anyone else from developing in the organization. Everything must cross your desk, and all meetings are little more than rallying exercises; there's no collective responsibility, no strategic input from anyone else. Nepotism is rife, and there is no real succession plan.

If this is you, and if this is your organization, it's time to stop and make an honest assessment of your capacity to scale. Do you struggle to ask for help? Or lack the curiosity to learn from those who have been there and done it already? If you continue to try to do everything, if you must have the last word, if you always have to be the most intelligent person in the room, then your chances of scaling successfully are slim to none. Get out of your own way for the sake of this beautiful organization you have created. Nothing will kill off the scaling capacity of an organization more quickly than an unchecked ego.

You must think of yourself as a custodian rather than an owner of the business. Don't make decisions because you own it. Make decisions because it's the right thing to do for the company. One of the recurring themes in this book is this: What got you this far will not get you the rest of the way. To scale, you need to share power, and you need to take people with you.

And your Why must stand up to scrutiny.

I've said it before and I'll say it again. Scaling requires a huge commitment. You won't sustain that commitment if your motivation is wrong. Don't scale because you imagine people will think better of you. Don't scale simply because you want to be rich. The greater your clarity on why you are embarking on this journey, the greater your adhesion to the goal and the greater your capacity to break through the obstacles that will begin to pile up. We'll be talking about the great why in a little more detail in the next principle, P2 Purpose and Vision. For now, suffice to say that leading is no solitary pursuit. It's a contract between you and those you lead. It's a service agreement. You have the privilege of serving the people you lead. It's not about me; it's about we. You will not succeed if you don't have a great team around you who feel inspired, motivated, and engaged by what you do.

1.4 PRACTICE POSITIVITY

"Not too bad!" is the standard Northern Ireland response to "How are you?" It's a paradigm that we are simply brought up with. We banned "Not too bad" from our office. Why? Because it clearly implies that although things could be worse, they are not good.

Instead, we encouraged people to respond with a smile and to say either "I'm good" or "I'm great!" It's not that we were trying to dismiss or suppress anyone's feelings. The truth is that "Not too bad" has never implied unhappiness or ill-health; it has simply become a default response.

We set out to change that default. An "I'm great" acts as a natural positivity boost. Your body language changes, and your facial expression changes. You stand taller, and you're inclined to smile more.

And knowing my own team members as I did, I could quickly see if the "I'm good" didn't have much conviction behind it. That was my prompt to probe a little more deeply and find out what was going on.

We are drawn to people who are positive. Life's radiators, I like to call them. And we all know life's drains: those who sap our energy.

As you scale, you will need to attract and build the right team to enable your vision. It is so important that you hire positive people. Positivity was something we enshrined in one of our values: "Do it with a smile." We encouraged the team to engage with one another in a positive way simply because, aside from the other health benefits, science has shown that a mere smile can lift your mood.[6]

I have a friend, a CEO who successfully scaled and sold his business. When clearing out his office prior to the handover, he found his father's old journal. He opened it up and found that his father had written the words "Be Positive" at the top of each page. The business was known for its positive growth culture (which we'll discuss in the final chapter). Clearly, this was no accident.

It was often said to me growing up that attitude (the coming together of our thoughts, feelings, and actions) was everything, and I've come to learn that's especially true in business. Bringing positivity into your workplace is a must; diffusing it through your team inspires people to band together to solve problems. "Your vibe attracts your tribe," so be mindful of the vibe you're sending out. The following are seven great ways to cultivate a positive mind.

1. Plan for the Best-Case Scenario

Yes, it's important to assess risks. You do need to consider the consequences if things don't work out; you cannot be reckless. But it's equally important to plan for success and to consider "What if it *does* work out?" Don't underestimate the impact of how you think and what you visualize on the eventual outcome. Choose faith over fear and believe that your vision will come to pass.

2. Stay Focused on the Outcome

On my first, big, cycle club training camp in Nice, France, it took one and a half hours to get to the top of the mountain. The climb may have been tough, but the descent was terrifying. As the road whizzed by below me, I approached each switchback barely able to lift my head to see what was coming next. Once I reached the bottom and stopped shaking, I talked to those who had navigated the corners expertly. It turned out that they were focused, not on the corner itself, but on the road beyond the bend. Why? Because you go where your eyes are focused. The same is true in business. Channel your energy into solutions instead of problems, into positive outcomes, into where you want to go.

3. Ask What You Can Learn

Every testing situation is an opportunity for further growth. Ask yourself, "What's the test in this challenging situation? What can I possibly learn?" Pose those questions to keep yourself grounded in positivity.

4. Invite Solutions from the Team

I've always made myself available to my team…with one condition. In all discussions that center on a challenge (a word I prefer to "problem"), I always ask that prior to the conversation, they think about two potential solutions. Not only is this empowering, but it also prevents the mindless vomit of problems.

5. Ignite Positivity with Affirmations

I know, I know, this all sounds a bit new age, but once again, studies have shown that positive affirmations lead to positive thinking, priming your brain for change.[7] Affirmations act on the subconscious mind, which is where all action begins. When the going gets tough, repeating positive affirmations is a quick and easy way to change your negative thought patterns. Repeated mantras can have a powerful impact on how you think. They can ultimately change your perceived reality and direct your actions. It can be as simple as "I can and I will!"

6. Notice the Good in Every Situation

No one can stay positive all the time. Criticism and negative feedback are essential to learning. What you need to avoid is relentless negativity. I try to look for the good first and preface any negative feedback with positivity. I attended a mindfulness seminar a few years ago, which advocated consciously acknowledging four positive outcomes in every situation before you comment. This is always worth remembering before you open your front door in the evenings!

7. Daily Gratitude

Again, not a new-age fad. The research shows that the practice of gratitude changes your brain, reduces stress, and ultimately increases your optimism.[8] It can be as simple as mentally listing five things you're grateful for first thing in the morning.

1.5 LEAD WITH A GROWTH MINDSET

"Sure I am that this day we are masters of our fate, that the task which has been set before us is not above our strengths; that its pangs and toils are not beyond my endurance. As long as we have faith in our own cause and an unconquerable will to win, victory will not be denied us."
—Winston Churchill

It's human nature to be uncomfortable in new, challenging situations, and scaling will deliver those in great abundance. Learn to recognize that feeling of discomfort and chase after it. Why? Because discomfort always precedes growth. Most often, the challenges that make you feel most uncomfortable are also those that turn out to be the most rewarding. I always make the point to CEOs that there is only one certainty in business and that is the fact that you will consistently face uncertainty. You must embrace it and see through the ambiguity to discover the opportunities beyond.

It's not enough for you to do this by yourself. It is imperative that leaders bring their people with them, to help them cultivate the same appreciation of ambiguity. As Kevin Roberts points out in his book *64 Shots: Leadership in a Crazy World*, we need to move away from thinking about the world as Volatile, Uncertain, Complex, and Ambiguous and move with a growth mindset to perceive a super-VUCA world—that is, Vibrant, Unreal, Crazy, and Astounding![9]

In the same vein, champion the stars in your business and their success will ultimately be your success. In business, leading as a star maker encourages a culture that celebrates individual, team, and organizational success. Do this well and you'll find that you have created meaningful relationships that enable deeper trust and greater performance. This is an important point. The better the relationships within your business, the better the flow of information through it, and consequently, the better the decision making will be.

Many companies base their company culture around performance: who makes the most sales, lands the biggest deal, opens the most client accounts, or makes the most calls. It's great to recognize success, yes, but if you want to cultivate a growth mindset in yourself and your team, it is also important to reward effort, learning experiences, and innovation. Seek to understand the thought processes that underpin the results. You need to create an environment in which your people challenge themselves to try out new ideas and learn from failures. To cultivate a growth mindset in your company, you must create a culture in which employees do not fear failure. In my own tenure as CEO in a successful scaling business, I always treated a mistake which resulted in a measurable financial loss as an investment in training. You just have to ensure that the investment results in identifiable lessons learned.

Encourage your team members to be the best they can be in their chosen disciplines. Nudge them to take on that additional professional qualification or training course. As Richard Branson succinctly puts it, *"Train people well enough so they can leave. Treat them well enough so they don't want to."* You also have a responsibility to grow with your people. Eliminate hierarchy and rank and create environments of greater intimacy in which everyone can grow and evolve together.

DON'T LET GROWTH PULL YOU APART

There's nothing like the energy and buzz of a startup, but as teams grow and processes take root, mediocrity and complacency often creep in. This is poison. Always know what you stand for. Drive the same culture and attitude through your teams and organization, and when inertia or inappropriate processes threaten to derail performance, change them. Fast.

In the last company I led, growth came so rapidly that we outgrew our premises again and again to the point where the car park became a sprawl of disconnected modular office spaces. In a culture where openness and transparency were actively encouraged, it was incredible how quickly these physical constructs precipitated the emergence of silos. So when we designed our most recent HQ, we specified large open-plan workspaces, with private working booths that our team could use as they wished.

Disconnected thinking and gossip are clear signs that silos are getting in the way. I know that not every company can accommodate everyone under one roof; moreover, the need to be close to the customer often requires building regional teams. But it is still possible to create a culture of inclusivity, one that fosters an *intrapreneurial* attitude, a strong cohesion among the team and does away with hierarchies and unnecessary structures. Keep your teams small and ruthlessly focused on the customer, not the corner office.

INCLUSION AND INDIVIDUALITY

A strong set of values—*lived* values—ensures that those who join the team fit with the organization's ethos. But don't misread that. The last thing you want is unthinking clones. Encourage individuality and diversity within the bounds of those values. Remember that it's often in creative friction that the magic happens. Inclusion is about finding like-mindedness in our differences and embracing individuals' unique ideas and ideals. We will be talking values later in P10 Positive Growth Culture.

Judging someone as too young, too old, too inexperienced, or not educated enough for any job is a huge mistake. An individual you deem as "too anything" to get a job done right just might have the fresh perspective necessary to get the job done better. Provide all of your employees with educational tools and training resources to continue learning and challenging themselves. Be open-minded when it comes to the way you do business. Just because your method has proved viable for years does not make it the best, the fastest, or indeed the only method.

We invited our leaders to participate in a 360-degree feedback process, whereby employees invite and receive confidential, anonymous feedback from the people who work with them. This typically includes their managers, direct reports, and peers, though it can be opened up to other stakeholders including customers and suppliers. To use Claire's term, this is "feedback gold." Don't underestimate the value of these self-development nuggets from those who care. Feedback is not about changing who you are. It's not about creating an inauthentic version of yourself. Rather, it is a golden opportunity to understand how you are perceived by those who work most closely with you. This self-awareness, if taken in the right spirit, will pay dividends. Be open-minded when hearing criticism and make good use of it. If negative feedback rattles you, give yourself a night or two to sleep on the comments before you take action. Remember to widen the gap between the stimulus and your response and always respond with a level head.

1.6 ENJOY GREAT ENERGY EVERY DAY

"The best asset we have for making a contribution to the world is ourselves. If we underinvest in ourselves, and by that I mean our minds, our bodies and our spirits, we damage the very tool we need to make our highest contribution."
—Greg McKeown

In a study conducted by *Harvard Business Review* in 2019, managing energy was identified as one of the three critical reasons why 50 percent of CEOs in the S&P 500 vacated their positions less than five years after taking up their post.

"Being time-constrained is a given, but the key is managing your energy. I'm very conscious of where I divert and direct my energy, where I get my energy, and what saps it," said Stuart Fletcher, former CEO of Bupa.[10]

Like Fletcher, older and more seasoned CEOs understand the critical importance of energy management. Leading a scaling organization is one thing. Leading it in a sustainable way is quite another. You must protect the asset. You must protect you. When you think CEO, think "Chief Energy Officer." Bottom line, you cannot and will not inspire, motivate, and energize an organization if you fail to manage your own energy levels.

Your first entries in next week's diary MUST relate to boosting your energy.

I know firsthand the pressure the scaling life places on you. There are times when you are utterly exhausted to the point where you find it difficult to engage fully with family in the evenings, where you tell yourself you'll just do one more email, where you feel both guilty and ineffective at the same time. The fact is that too many of us are sleeping poorly and make no time for exercise. Too many of us grab a bite on the run instead of eating healthily.

Throughout my tenure as a CEO, I never considered our objectives reached unless team energy levels remained high. Why? Because we can only be the best version of ourselves when we are fully energized. And I've also seen that high energy is infectious. When those around you are focused, energized, and driven by a purpose, you can't help but be drawn into that dynamic.

Growth-minded leadership transforms people cognitively and emotionally. In an energized environment, we tap into hidden strengths. We see more, do more, learn more.

Prioritize energy management. Make it a nonnegotiable.

PILLARS OF ENERGY MANAGEMENT

Performance expert Enda McNulty—whom we talk to in more detail in P6 Performance—has worked not only with the Irish rugby team but also with a who's who of multinational corporations. He lays out five pillars of energy management.

1. Move More!

As Enda puts it, "Movement is medicine." You don't have to cycle 50k (31 miles) at lunchtime or run marathons on the weekend. Taking the time for thirty minutes of exercise every day pays back quickly, giving you enough energy to more than compensate for the time taken out of your business. I don't buy the "not enough time" excuse. If you don't make time to be well, then be prepared to make time to be unwell. Make some form of movement or exercise a daily habit, and it will pay dividends in terms of your own energy and that of the team you lead. As Jim Rohn put it, success is a few simple disciplines, practiced every day. Failure is simply a few errors in judgment, repeated every day.[11] Over the past ten years, exercise has transformed my own energy levels, and I've also seen the value of movement on the wider team.

2. Prioritize Rest and Recovery

This is another one that CEOs find very difficult to swallow. The assumption is that once you've decided to scale, you've got to work harder and longer than anyone else, including the competition. Not so. You've got to think of yourself as an elite athlete. Taking the time to recover between sessions is absolutely critical to performance.

And it's not just your body. A 2019 study by the National Institute of Neurological Disorders and Stroke found that our brains may solidify the memories of new skills we just practiced a few seconds earlier by taking a short rest.[12] The results highlight the critical role rest plays in learning.

Take proper breaks often. Completely clear your mind and begin again. Your success depends on it.

In his book *The 4 Pillar Plan*, Dr. Rangan Chattergee says that effective rest and recovery means scheduling at least fifteen minutes of "me time" every day.

"Stop everything and be utterly selfish. Stop treating 'relaxation' as something that you do—or, more likely, don't do—when everything else has been dealt with. Choose to relax. Make it a triple underlined part of your schedule."[13]

Sit in your favorite coffee shop with a book, go lie in a dark room and listen to music, pick up your guitar, go play with the dog, or just sit quietly and do nothing—whatever you want—as long as it doesn't involve your smartphone.

3. Watch What You Eat and Drink

There has been so much said and written on this topic that I am simply going to gently remind you of what your mother has been telling you for years. Eat your five-a-day. We got rid of the sugary treats in our canteen and replaced them with fruit. We brought in nutrition experts to talk to the team and introduced "Free Fruit" days on Tuesdays and Thursdays. This not only helped me to meet my five-a-day, but it also clearly signaled that we were prioritizing our team's health, and that does not go unnoticed.

4. Drink More...Water!

On one of my regular work trips to India, I joined an early morning yoga class, where we were guided through a series of breathing and stretching exercises. Our instructor was not young, and yet he radiated health and happiness. Refreshed and energized at the end of the class, I asked him about his morning routine. His advice? Before we do anything, we should hydrate our bodies with at least two glasses of room temperature water. To this day, I leave a bottle beside my bed at night to drink first thing.

It turns out this yogi's advice is steeped in good science. Some years later, I attended a talk by neuroscientist and leadership coach Dr. Tara Swart. Regular hydration was a key part of her recommendations for boosting performance. Swart recommends drinking half a liter of water per 15 kg (33 pounds) of body weight per day. Hydrating regularly lubricates our joints and eyes, keeps our skin healthy, facilitates good digestion, eliminates toxins, and optimizes the energy produced through our cells. Failing to hydrate properly can create an imbalance of salts and sugars in the body, and that can quickly lead to other health problems. In other words, if you feel a headache coming on or become slightly weak, don't reach for a mid-morning snack. Grab that glass of water first.

5. Sleep Better

If you're like me, then getting a good night's sleep has never been easy. Whether it's the agitation caused by a challenging day or a difficult conversation, or even the excitement of a new scaling idea, whatever it is, I have always found the process of getting to sleep and staying asleep really difficult. And yet, the science is unambiguous. Sleep is a critical component of a high-energy life, boosting everything from concentration to life expectancy. Sleep deprivation, on the other hand, undermines high performance. And conversely, research suggests that just one lost night of sleep reduces a person's IQ by one standard deviation—the equivalent of being impaired by a learning disability.[14]

Here are some practical actions to induce a good night's sleep:

- Create an environment of absolute darkness.

- Avoid stimulation before bedtime—read, watch, or listen to something relaxing.

- Avoid caffeine and alcohol from the afternoon on.

- No gadgets in the bedroom.

- Have a regular bedtime.

- Try tracking your sleep and daily "readiness" with an Oura ring.

WIN THE MORNING

Both Claire and I have always shared a love of early mornings. Getting a dog when I was ten might have had something to do with my love of those early hours. I took the responsibility very seriously and always rose early every morning to take Boomer for a long walk before school. There was something quite magical about being up and about in the silence before the world began to stir. As a CEO, it was when I read Tim Ferriss's *Tribe of Mentors* that the importance of a morning routine really struck home.

The Wim Hof Method in particular has become an integral part of both my life and the programs we run for scaling entrepreneurs. This is based on three pillars: breathing techniques, cold therapy, and willpower (or commitment). In addition to delivering a range of health benefits, cold therapy is an excellent means of becoming comfortable with discomfort—a skill all scaling entrepreneurs need to cultivate.

I absolutely treasure my morning routine. Waking up at 5:00 a.m. before the world gets into gear allows me time to myself. I follow a morning ritual of Wim Hof breathing, which I find always clears the mind wonderfully, followed by meditation, reading, journaling (with gratitude), and exercising, and always finishing off with a cold shower.

I think of the two hours in the evening between ten and twelve as "junk hours" because it's then that we slip back onto our phones, open the laptop, or scroll aimlessly through the TV channels. I realized some years ago that there was an opportunity in that. Today, I can get seven or more hours of sleep by replacing those empty, directionless hours with rest and recovery, giving me two extra hours in the morning. During those two sacred hours, I could not feel more alive. Targeting a successful day begins the evening before. Now I follow what I call My Evening 3-3-3. Taking fifteen minutes before bed, I write down three things I'm grateful for, three wins from the day, and three priorities (aligned to my goals) for the following day.

Having coached and mentored many CEOs in their scaling journey, I've found time and again that those who reinvent their mornings achieve the most profound changes in their lives and generate huge leaps in performance.

If there's only one thing to take from this chapter, it's this: "Win the morning, win the day!"

TAKE ACTION—IT'S SIMPLE!

Scale with a Bruce Lee Mindset! Adopt a "can do, will do" attitude. Use mistakes as an opportunity for self-improvement and adaptation. Be flexible like water and foster an insatiable appetite for learning as the sustenance of personal growth.

Ignite the Power of "Yet." Embrace a "win or learn" culture and face every challenge in your scaling journey with a growth mindset. Focus on solutions, not problems.

Manage Your Mind. In a fast-moving, always-on, stress-packed world, meditation is your way to boost productivity without sacrificing your mental health. Take the time to focus on your breath every day and don't let ego get in the way of performance.

Practice Positivity. Meeting the challenges you face with a positive mind will make all the difference.

Lead with a Growth Mindset. It's not enough to develop a growth mindset of your own. You've also got to cultivate the same attitude in your team and your organization.

Enjoy Great Energy Every Day. Don't be one of the also-ran CEOs who failed to manage their energy resources and had to quit the race early.

Principle in Action—The Happy Pear

Walking into The Happy Pear HQ in the village of Greystones in County Wicklow, Ireland is the plant-based foodie's equivalent of walking into Mr. Magorium's Wonder Emporium. There's an energy and a vibe that you just don't expect in a vegetable shop. But of course this is no ordinary vegetable shop. It's also a café, a restaurant, a crèche, a community center, and a yoga studio. You are hit by a blaze of color and a mix of delicious smells from the kitchen.

Twins Stephen and David Flynn are the living embodiment of a positive psyche. I first met them at 6:00 a.m. on a wintry morning in January. Like so many of the successful people we've interviewed for this book, they're early risers. I'm greeted by the smiling Steve. Even at this hour, he's brimming with life. He leads me up to the top floor to help clear the tables and chairs and make space for the morning workout, which concludes with some Wim Hof deep diaphragmatic breath work—known to reduce stress and bolster the immune system.

Daily pre-8:00 a.m. posts on Instagram showcase the Flynns' regular workout. The morning routine regularly gathers more than 10,000 likes from a following, which is helping the guys spread the Happy Pear message—health, community, and happiness—across the globe.

We finish our workout at 7:00 a.m. Then Steve prepares healthy snacks and a flask of tea in preparation for the morning swim; a ritual that sees the guys bathe in the Irish Sea at sunrise every single day of the year. As we reach the small inlet about five minutes' walk from the shop, a crowd has already begun to gather. You could meet anyone here. Russell Brand and Joe Wicks have numbered among the celebrities who braved the open water with the Flynns.

The water temperature is barely over 6°C (around 42°F) on this windy morning. After some tea and a chat with the locals, the guys take their shots for social media and make their way back to the shop.

Steve makes a point of walking his kids to school before he reappears for breakfast, and it's not yet nine o'clock.

Free porridge is available for all swimmers—a nod to the strong sense of charity and community that underpins the boys' purpose. There are moments when you could be forgiven for thinking that this is some sort of cultish, hippie commune, but I add a few toppings to create what they call fancy porridge, and €5 (US$5.75) later, I get a sense of their commercial acumen.

This is a serious business. Sales across eleven different revenue streams topped €10 million (US$11.5 million) in 2019. These include retail, cafés, education, publishing, and the production and distribution of thirty-eight products through thousands of stores in Ireland, the UK, Europe, the Middle East, and Africa. It is what Steve describes as "a complex web of a business." It is also a purpose-driven business, rooted in a shared journey of personal transformation. When they left college after pursuing business degrees, both traveled separately, and unbeknownst to each other, actually became vegetarian on the same day, despite being on opposite sides of the globe. On his travels, Steve experimented with a wide variety of healthy living options. He became fascinated with community, health, happiness, and in particular, social change. He was in Corsica—fasting—when he called Dave and asked him if he wanted to start a food revolution.

"Let's change the world," he said. "Let's start a fruit and veg shop!"

"How do we start a revolution with a fruit and veg shop?" Dave asked, not unreasonably.

Steve's revelation was simple. Food connects everyone irrespective of religion, politics, or ethnicity. Think of the symbolism of breaking bread together. From this came a conviction that healthy food could create a better world. Despite their success, The Happy Pear isn't about becoming the most profitable health food business globally. It's about making a difference. It's about encouraging social change. It's about using food to connect everything that's wonderful in society. Their first vision centered on building a charity. Ultimately, however, a business proved the more effective vehicle for what they had in mind.

Steve is the first to admit that they took a lot of wrong turns.

In the early days, the Flynns secured financing and successfully opened five new cafés on top of the three they already ran. Soon afterward, however, Steve confided in Dave that he wasn't happy. He was spending too much time in the car and not enough time with his family. He began asking himself what it was all for. A chance encounter with management guru Charles Handy helped to catalyze the solution.

Dave and Steve realized that if they were to scale the business *and* maintain that alignment with community, health, and happiness, it would make more sense to focus on products and digital services (online courses, etc.) rather than a network of cafés. In Steve's words, "You can't have one hundred holy mountains." Products and the internet then became their point of concentration. Instead of getting bigger, they strove to become better. In making this switch, they reaffirmed the commitment that every single person involved in the business—employees, customers, and suppliers—should benefit from it. This would ensure that the company's net impact on society would be positive.

In recent years, acknowledging how difficult it is to measure progress toward so expansive a vision (making the world a healthier, happier place), they refined it to, "To transform our home village into a blue zone."

Blue zones are locations around the world where a particular lifestyle has led to exceptional health and longevity among those who live there. You can read about blue zones here.[15]

When I ask how they're measuring progress toward this goal, Steve laughs. "We're dreamers. It's more important that I love what I do and that I love the people I work with." He says that if he feels out of balance, stressed, or fractious, he'll know that this is not success, that something is missing. When asked how he's feeling about the business right now, he doesn't hesitate. "I love it!"

They might give the impression they're carefree, but Dave and Steve are incredibly disciplined, and their time is carefully structured. Steve puts it like this: "It's only when you use every skill in your whole book you get that wonderful sense of fulfillment."

Here's Steve's daily routine:

- Up at 5:30 a.m.
- Read through the focus for the year.
- Open up the café at 6:00 a.m. for the few regulars who will train with them.
- Train for one hour. It could be yoga, calisthenics, hand-stands, gymnastics, animal movements, running. They deliberately keep it varied so they can become multidisciplinary.
- Meditation.
- Swim at sunrise every day. In summer in Ireland, this is at 4:50 a.m., moving to 8:40 a.m. in winter. The training regime depends on the season.
- Breakfast with the family.
- Social media work.
- Then the day's work, which could be anything from writing a book, filming for YouTube, doing a talk, participating in a board meeting, or taste tests. When I visited, they were in the middle of creating an online vegan baking course.
- Home by 6:00 p.m., ensuring dinner with family every evening.
- Bed at 9:30 p.m.

Dave acknowledges the strength they get from each other. If either one is overly stressed, the other provides comfort and support. They keep each other in balance. They tell me that they feel so psychologically strong that if the business blew up tomorrow, they would be happy selling orange juice down at the train station. There is an infectious optimism at the heart of what they do and zero fear of making mistakes or failure. There's a clear understanding here that failure is not failure; it's simply a prompt to change direction.

Even though the vision is strong, ego is not. Neither wanted to run the company. When they initially borrowed money to fund the rollout of the cafés, they asked their dad to step in as interim CEO. And despite the growing success and celebrity patronage, Dave and Steve stay grounded. Steve acknowledges the importance of keeping ego in check. "I think swimming in the sea helps and just standing behind the counter in the shop, serving people. Anything you can do to understand your own mortality and your own insignificance is really important. The reality is that we are going to die someday, so it's important to remember simply how fortunate we are today."

P1 ACTIONS TO TAKE:

_____

_____

_____

_____

_____

_____

_____

_____

_____

_____

_____

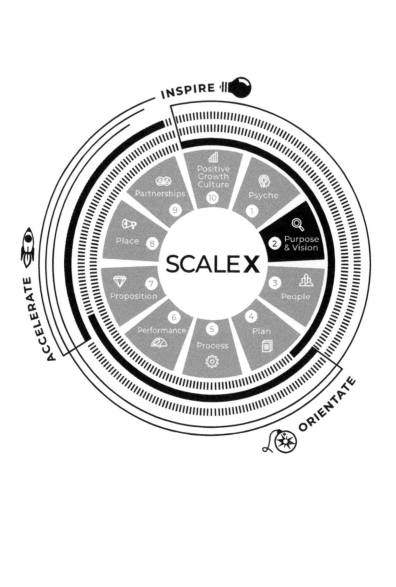

P2

PURPOSE AND VISION

"Definitiveness of purpose is the starting point of all achievement."
—W. Clement Stone

GROWING UP IN BELFAST, NORTHERN IRELAND IN THE SIXTIES and seventies, James Leckey would scavenge the local dumps and junkyards for the materials to build go-karts. That creative drive stayed with him, and he grew up to become an engineer. In 1983, he and a couple of his friends planned to run a marathon. To boost their motivation levels and make the challenge a little more worthwhile, they decided to run on behalf of a charity. The problem was, they didn't know which one.

"Somebody suggested the Segal House Special School in Belfast," says James. "When I visited it and looked at some of the chairs the children were sitting in, I thought to myself, *I could make much better chairs than these.* One of the mothers there told me how uncomfortable her child was and that she hadn't managed to find the right chair for her."

"It was a very powerful experience, a very strong intuition. I connected with these children almost instantly. I knew I could make a difference and I knew too that this was something I wanted to do for the rest of my working life."

Within three months of that visit, James built his first chair for a child with special needs. From that moment, the orders began to flow in, and in 1986, he rented floor space in Kilwee Business Park in Belfast.

It was a big step. Suddenly, I had to pay rent, rates, and staff. I had no money, I was working 24/7, and I had no social life. My friends would complain about me never coming out on a Friday night. But I was doing what I loved. In 1987, I took a stand at the Naidex exhibition at Alexandra Palace. This was and is one of the biggest events in the world for the independent living community. At the time, I had built three seats and three standing frames. That was really the beginning of strong and steady growth.

By 1990, Leckey was the market leader in the UK. Within three years, he had opened an office in Boston, USA and was selling hundreds of products, including postural care seats and standing and bathing products.

One of his simplest but most ingenious products, the UPSEE, has transformed the lives of countless disabled children. Designed by Debbie Elnatan, it's a support harness that enables children with conditions like cerebral palsy (CP) to stand upright. The device grabbed worldwide headlines when a local paper published an unforgettable photograph of a flower girl with CP using the UPSEE to walk up the aisle at a family wedding.

Today, the company James founded—Leckey—employs 220 full-time staff, including researchers, engineers, customer service experts, physiotherapists, and factory workers. With just over £20 million ($30 million) in revenue, the company distributes to more than thirty countries worldwide and continues to grow faster than the competition. In August 2020, James sold Leckey to Sunrise Medical, a world leader in the rehabilitation equipment market.

2.1 START WITH WHY

"The two most important days in your life are the day you are born and the day you find out why."
—**Mark Twain**

Almost 98 percent of SMEs fail to scale,[16] and that's regardless of what sector they're in.

What made Leckey different? What fueled his company's growth? Could it have something to do with the fact that James Leckey struck purpose gold right at the beginning of his career? He knew exactly why he was doing what he was doing, right from the start.

Here's the company's stated purpose: To improve the quality of life of children with special needs. And the vision that flows from that? To create a world where each child is included and they can access their full potential.

Walking the factory floor with James one Tuesday morning, I had an overwhelming sense of someone who was deeply passionate about his work, his customers, and his team.

He said, "It's wonderful to think that such a simple concept and product can make a profound difference. It's enabled disabled kids to play football with their friends for the first time ever and to walk down the road with their mum or dad and wave to neighbors."

A Crisis of Purpose

"Purpose is the new currency; it's one of the greatest untapped forces in the for-profit world. Without purpose, your business model is incomplete."

—Holly Branson

Okay, a company that operates in the wellness space has a clear commercial imperative for adopting a well-meaning purpose, but does that really apply to the rest of us? If I'm in IT, real estate, financial services, engineering, retail, or manufacturing, do I really need to create a purpose and an accompanying vision?

The answer, it would appear, is an overwhelming yes.

A recent PwC study set out to learn how people feel at work and how to better engage and motivate them. The researchers found that only one in five employees feels "at least somewhat positive" in relation to their work. In what PwC describes as a "crisis of purpose," they highlight that only 28 percent of employees feel fully connected to their company's purpose.[17]

Does that matter? Again, the answer, it would appear, is yes. The research finds that defining your purpose inspires your team and invariably leads to greater performance. A November 2020 report from McKinsey found that employees at purpose-driven companies are four times more engaged at work.[18]

In his book *Essentialism: The Disciplined Pursuit of Less*, Greg McKeown cites data gathered from more than 500 individuals about their experience on more than 1,000 teams. The results are startling:

"When there was a high level of clarity of purpose, the team and the people in it overwhelmingly thrived…With clarity of purpose, [the leader] is able to apply 'less but better' to everything from talent selection, to direction, to roles, to communication, to accountability. As a result, [the] team becomes unified and breaks through to the next level."[19]

It's instructive to look at the experience of Discovery Ltd., South Africa's leading health insurance provider, as detailed in a recent *Harvard Business Review* (HBR) article "Marketing Meets Mission" by author and academic Myriam Sidibe.[20]

First of all, here are the nice words from Discovery's website: "Discovery is a shared value insurance company whose purpose and ambition are achieved through a pioneering business model that incentivizes people to be healthier, and enhances and protects their lives."

Is this real? Do they really do this?

Five years ago, the company began rewarding customers for adopting healthy behaviors, screening them through a program called Vitality Healthcheck.

"From 2015 to 2018 the percentage of program members who regularly exercised increased by 34 percent, members' vegetable purchases increased by 29 percent, and their sugar and salt purchases fell by 33 percent and 31 percent, respectively."[21]

Healthier customers means fewer claims, and that in turn generates big savings. The company estimates that the Vitality program saved the company the equivalent of £800 million ($1.2 billion) in the ten years between 2008 and 2018. Put simply, your future growth and the future of your organization is going to depend on the extent and pull of your purpose.

Feeling like a Number

"A purpose gives your company soul."
—Brendan McGurgan

Purpose stops your work becoming just another job. By aligning the thing that gives your life meaning with what you do every day, you begin to operate on a whole new level. And the same goes for your team. If you want them to climb the mountain with you, you'd better be able to tell them why.

Let me give you a number: 374679.

Does this mean anything to you? Are you inspired or motivated by this number? I remember it so well because it was the personnel number I was given on the day I started my first job almost twenty-five years ago. The fact that this number loomed so large probably goes a long way toward explaining why I'm not there anymore. It's the standard line from people who feel no connection with their work: *I feel like a number.*

This is the death zone for your people and for your company. There's no scaling here. If you get to this point, you've cultivated a zombie business. You've cashed in all of your team's goodwill. They're completely disengaged. They're more concerned about getting out at five on the dot, they know the Ts & Cs in their contract intimately, and they can tell you exactly how many holidays and paid sick days they have left.

Critically, they back away from the challenges required to achieve your business goals. In my view, the discretionary effort that motivated people are willing to give is the most important asset in your business. And this, in a nutshell, is why purpose is so critical. Everyone wants to work for organizations whose purpose and business philosophy resonate with them intellectually and emotionally.

In conducting the many interviews for this book, purpose is the touchstone to which almost all of our contributors returned, regardless of the principle under discussion.

It should be clear at this point that when I talk about purpose and vision, I'm not talking about corporate social responsibility. I'm not talking about woolly nice-to-haves or heart-warming stories you can tell on your website. Purpose and vision are critical to every scaling story. I was CEO of an engineering company in the construction sector, probably the least fluffy industry you can think of. And yet, our purpose and the compelling vision we built upon it were crucial in fueling our scaling success.

Let's look at it from the point of view of funding. At some point in your scaling journey, you may require a third-party cash infusion either from a business angel, a venture capitalist, a private equity institution, or perhaps via a listing on the stock exchange.

BlackRock, one of the world's largest investment companies, announced in 2020 that it would exit investments that "present a high sustainability-related risk" and vote against managements and boards insufficiently attentive to these risks.[22] During the COVID-19 crisis, although all stock markets suffered, sustainable funds suffered less. Figures published by Funds Europe indicate that European sustainable funds dropped by 10.6 percent compared with the "overall European fund universe," which fell by 16.2 percent.[23]

2.2 IMPACT THE WORLD

I joined a small engineering company as financial controller in 2003 and was invited onto the board a year later. At the time, we employed twenty people and had revenues of approximately £3.5 million (US$4.75 million). Eighty-five percent of that revenue was earned within Ireland. The company's founder, then CEO, was typical of startup entrepreneurs: colorful, effervescent, and brimming with "can-do" energy. He thrived on product development and the thrill of the sale. I loved the culture of the place. I loved working there. Led by the founder, we bounced from sale to sale and from opportunity to opportunity. Exciting? Yes. But there were consequences.

On the operational front, it's no exaggeration to say that we lurched from crisis to crisis. Because we were in constant firefighting mode, we would often assign someone in a leading ops role as the "CFO" for the quarter. That stood not for chief financial officer but for chief fire officer. We never actually sat down to establish where we wanted to go or map out a route to get there.

In 2007, our founder decided that the CEO role didn't play to his strengths, so he invited me to take up the challenge. I was only thirty-two at the time. I was humbled, flattered, and delighted all at once. As I said, I loved the energy of the place. But I wasn't an engineer and I wasn't an entrepreneur. So what exactly could I bring to the table?

For some time prior to this, the lack of direction and the endless crises had given me a sense of unease that I couldn't shake off. Constantly pounded by the reactive demands of the short term, I craved something less chaotic. So I began a deep dive into vision, planning, and strategy—areas I'd always been passionate about—and I organized our first strategic workshop. Myself, the founder, and the third member of our leadership team, together with our just-appointed head of marketing, spent half a day in a small country hotel close to our office, trying to figure out where on earth we would take this company.

The firefighting and the hopping from project to project was great in the early days, when you feel like a band of pirates out to conquer the seven seas. But that just won't work if you're serious about growth. That session allowed each of us to open up about what we would like to see in three years' time. How many employees would we have? What would our facilities be like? How many countries would we operate in? What would our revenue be? What technology might we have innovated by then? If we were going to grow, *how* were we going to grow? Through acquisition? Organically? Which countries were we going to concentrate on? How were we going to push into those countries? With partners? Distributors? Dealers? Agents? Which parts of the industry would we concentrate on?

It was important to flush out any fundamental differences among the key stakeholders. We needed to make sure that everyone wanted to be in the boat and that we were all in agreement about which way to row.

Over the course of those few hours, we confirmed our vision. Our dream was that we would become a £100 million (US$150 million) revenue company. To put that ambition in context, our revenue at the time stood at around £15 million (US$22.5 million). But crucially, we now had a lighthouse to aim for. This also meant that we couldn't pounce on every shiny new thing that bobbed to the surface. We would only do those things that brought us closer to the vision.

Did we have a clearly articulated purpose at this stage? No, not yet.

Purpose through Crisis

Bang! The global financial crisis hit within a few months of that first strategy session. The construction industry lay directly in the path of the hurricane. Our pipeline went dry overnight. The light in the lighthouse, the one we'd agreed to steer toward? That winked out. Suddenly, it was about staying afloat and nothing else. I saw my friends in "safe" professions like accountancy and law lose their jobs. And purpose? Purpose became survival.

Hubert Joly, former chairman and CEO of Best Buy, is one of the greatest advocates for noble purpose you'll find. But when he took the helm at the ailing electronics retailer in 2012, he understood that this was the wrong time to redefine purpose. In a wide-ranging interview published in the *McKinsey Quarterly* in June 2020, he explained that the key imperative was to address operational performance drivers and simply to save a ship that was sinking.[24]

Once they hit clear water again, Joly was able to begin molding his company's vision and purpose.

He says, "How do you define that noble purpose? I believe you find it at the intersection of four circles: what the world needs, what you are good at, how you believe you can make a positive difference in the world, and how you can make money."[25]

At about the same time that Hubert Joly was beginning to focus on articulating a purpose for the company that he had rescued, I was approaching a turning point of my own.

When you're young and ambitious, work alone can be enough to energize and excite, but a time comes when that's just not enough anymore. You have kids, and you look around and think more deeply about the world and your impact on it.

There were two events that catalyzed a radical change in my thinking.

The first was hearing Kiran Pereira speak. She is the founder and chief storyteller of a website called Sandstories.org and author of a book of the same name. In both, she details the multiple issues associated with illegal sand mining in her country—India—and further afield.

Sand. It's one of the most overlooked and underrated commodities on the planet. And yet, it's everywhere—not just in the buildings we live in and the roads we drive on, but in your toothpaste (in the form of silica), in the ceramic sink you wash your hands in, in the quartz silicon chip in your computer…the list goes on. But it's the construction industry that consumes more sand than any other activity. Here's one startling statistic. China used more concrete between 2011 and 2013 than the United States used in the entire twentieth century.[26] Sand is of course the critical ingredient in concrete.

The global challenge is that we are consuming sand at twice the sustainable rate, and that's causing huge problems.

In parts of the developing world, construction-grade sand is routinely and illegally mined from riverbeds, causing a range of environmental catastrophes. Dredging destroys livelihoods and biodiversity, water drains from lakes and rivers, shorelines are denuded, and coastal erosion intensifies. Moreover, illegal mining is controlled by organized criminals dubbed the sand mafia. *Nature* reported in 2019 that illegal sand mining is happening in about seventy countries and that hundreds of people have been killed in battles over sand in the past decade.[27] Incredibly, in 2017, a ranking of the top global crimes published by *Global Financial Integrity* cited illegal sand extraction as the third most prolific global crime.[28] I had been in the sand and aggregate industry for years before I had any real awareness of this issue. We hosted a seminar a few years ago where Kiran Pereira spoke very eloquently on the issues surrounding illegal sand mining. She talked about lying in bed in her village in India and hearing heavy machinery, working under the cover of darkness, stealing the sand and destroying the local river, putting the inhabitants at risk of catastrophic flooding.

The SDGs

"The best evidence suggests that strong corporate sustainability performance drives better financial returns in the long run."
—**Grayson, Coulter, and Lee**

Around the same time, I read a compelling piece in an in-flight magazine by Marga Hoek, author of *The Trillion Dollar Shift*. Her thesis is this: In the future, the only businesses that will thrive are those with a purpose built on the United Nations' Sustainable Development Goals (SDGs). If you think of all the things the world disagrees on, yet no fewer than 193 countries have signed up to the UN's seventeen SDGs. These include "no poverty," "zero hunger," "good health and well-being," and "affordable and clean energy."

Hoek's book is full of case studies that demonstrate in clear, unsentimental terms how companies that embrace a purpose centered on one or more of these goals goes from strength to strength. Companies like Unilever, for example, are switched on to the potential of leveraging a strong why and simultaneously working for the good of the planet. Hoek's point is that this isn't about setting up a nongovernmental organization or charitable business. This is the route to significant profit.

The more I read, the more it seemed to me that Marga Hoek was appealing directly to me. Just as James Leckey was hit by what he called a powerful intuition, I now could see exactly what Hoek was talking about. I could begin to see how it would change my life and the life of our business.

The truth is that there can be no business without a planet, and fewer opportunities in a world of increasing poverty, climate crisis, and resource scarcity. Her analysis suggests that business leaders who navigate toward the SDGs will unlock market opportunities worth up to £8 trillion (US$12 trillion) by 2030.[29] "Business for good," she asserts, "is good for business."

Our Place in the World

The thing was, as a company, we were perfectly positioned to embrace this ethos. Fifteen years earlier, we had been approached by a customer who had a stockpile of construction demolition waste. At the time, our technology was focused exclusively on the processing of virgin natural materials. Construction waste typically went to a landfill. This was hugely expensive, which is why our client came to us. The huge mound of "waste" he showed us was little better than rubbish to the naked eye—claybound and full of all kinds of contaminants, from polystyrene and plastic to organic material and timber. We took the challenge, however, and went on to innovate processing technologies, which could separate all of these components and rescue the valuable sand and aggregate within. This marked the beginning of a journey that would ultimately allow us to revolutionize the process of recycling construction waste all around the world.

We were playing right at the heart of the sustainability revolution. The problem? As an engineering company, we tended to focus on the technical features and benefits of the technology. This, I began to realize, was a distraction. Our purpose was staring us in the face. We had just never asked ourselves the right questions. We failed to ask, what is it about what we do that really matters? Why is this important for our customers, their customers, our staff, and our community?

It was only when we began to see the work we were doing through a more powerful lens that our true purpose began to crystallize. I would arrive on some sites in the United States, and the technology in use was so antiquated that the levels of waste being generated were frightening.

This was something we could do something about.

2.3 MOLD YOUR PURPOSE

"To get to peak performance, personal purpose and organizational purpose must align."
—**Kevin Roberts**

I want to zone in now on the vision we set in 2015. We called it 2020 Vision; it would be our first five-year plan. In advance of the launch, we held a series of workshops, inviting everyone to apply their own brushstroke to the vision that we would create. First time around, when it was just three of us, getting engagement and consensus wasn't difficult, but as the company grew, I came to the conclusion that if the new vision was to mean anything, it would have to mean something to everyone. I was aiming for an emotional attachment to what we were planning. I had a strong sense of our direction of travel, but this couldn't solely be my vision. It had to be our vision.

This was our approach, but it's not the only one. Cameron Herold, profiled in the Principle in Action section at the end of this chapter, believes the articulation of vision is solely the province of the CEO. You make up your own mind.

The launch event itself could hardly have been more different than the afternoon in the small country hotel eight years earlier. We hired out the IMAX Cinema in Belfast. We created cinema drop stands, branded popcorn, and a movie depicting the future we wanted, with our team members as the stars. It was an unforgettable evening and a great way to unveil our refined vision: *To become the number one solutions provider of wet processing equipment in every country in the world.*

Soon after that, we were able to articulate our purpose: *Championing sustainability to create a new world resource.* We were essentially saying that demolition and construction waste is a great resource. We had been blind to its potential. Now that we saw it, we were going to make it our job to realize that potential.

I'm going to talk more about how we made that dream a reality in P4 Planning. Suffice to say that at that moment, back in 2015, that vision was there to inspire, to stir passion, to excite. After all, who wants to strive to be number two in their industry?

Revealing the Diamond

Cut to three years later. I was attending a meeting in the Kuwait Towers, three striking structures overlooking the Persian Gulf, with His Excellency Sheikh Abdullah Al Sabah, director general of Kuwait Environment Public Authority. We were talking about his plans for urban rejuvenation. I was there to explain how the construction and demolition waste stockpiled throughout the city might be used in those plans. We spent the morning talking about the city's future infrastructure needs, about Kuwait's contribution to achieving the UN SDGs, and about how our company's purposeful direction and innovative product set aligned to his own goals.

He didn't care about the features and benefits of our equipment. He was focused on how we could help preserve the finite resources at his disposal.

In the intervening time, we had traveled light years. Before we refined our purpose, a customer sales meeting would invariably center on the minutiae of the product, which invariably led to a direct comparison with our competitor, which invariably led to the usual arm wrestle on price.

If it had not been for our purpose, which galvanized everything we had done to date, including our product offering, our culture, our vision, and brand, there is no way that I would have been invited to that meeting, let alone been given the opportunity to contribute to such a wide-ranging and worthwhile project. It was one of those wonderful moments where all ten principles of the framework coalesced to deliver something altogether greater than the sum of their parts.

Defining a noble purpose changed our direction and drove conversations that previously we had been too afraid to have. It shaped our culture, our marketing, and brand identity. Try recruiting a star for one of your teams by telling them that you use galvanized paint or that you sell the cheapest widgets in the business. But tell them about your purpose, about the positive impact you intend to have on the world, and that becomes a different conversation.

When everybody, from factory floor through to boardroom, knows why they're there, you get so much more energy and engagement.

We're social animals and we seek to belong. We're constantly searching for our tribe—in the clubs we belong to, the communities in which we live, and the companies we work with. The stronger our purpose, the greater the talent we attract and the stronger our tribe becomes. The industries Claire and I have operated within are not glamorous. Who really dreams of one day working for a company that makes equipment to wash stones and dirt? But when we began those challenging discussions around purpose, we found that we could peel back the layers to reveal the diamond.

Now we had our why and our band of eager followers.

Determining Purpose

"We don't want to come to work to build a wall; we want to come to work to build a cathedral."
—Simon Sinek

Academics argue that a leader's role is to be the custodian of the organization's purpose. Business experts make the case that purpose is a key to exceptional performance and therefore successful scaling. Psychologists talk about purpose as the gateway to greater well-being, a connection to the soul. But how do you go about determining your company's purpose? Where do you start trying to understand it and mold it into something that will resonate authentically with all stakeholders?

Use PURPOSE to kick-start the process of molding your own.

- **P**ose the big questions. Why do you exist? What are you passionate about? What motivates you? What are you really trying to do here?

- **U**nderstand your cause. Use the UN SDGs to guide how your purpose can positively impact one or more of the world's greatest challenges.

- **R**eview your past. Why was this organization established? It will likely have come from a desire to effect change. Look at your own values. What is it you truly stand for and believe in? Do your beliefs chime with what you do in your organization?

- **P**ositive change catalyst. How does what you do affect your team? Your customers? Your community? Your planet?

- **O**riginality. Make your purpose stand out from the crowd. And keep it short.

- **S**trong sense of service. Set out to maximize the number of lives that can be positively impacted by your purpose and stay true to your why as scaling gathers momentum.

- **E**motionally engaging. How does your purpose make you feel when you hear it? Is there a sense of calling? It should energize and challenge in equal measure.

At its core, a company's purpose is a bold, emotion-infused affirmation of your reasons for being in business. It will strongly convey what the organization stands for. It leaves no one in doubt about what you believe in and whom you serve. No matter how it's communicated to your team and to your customers, a company's purpose is the driving force that enables you to define your true brand and create the desired culture.

Purpose in Action

Greg Ellis, former CEO and managing director of REA Group, said his company's purpose was "to make the property process simple, efficient and stress free for people buying and selling a property."[30]
There are many examples of companies wakening up to the role of purpose in organizational success. For example, Ernst & Young is one of the biggest accounting practices globally. They say, "At EY, we put our Purpose—Building a Better Working World—at the heart of everything we do." They go on to say that their research shows that purpose-driven businesses are better at attracting and retaining talent, sparking innovation, navigating disruption, and yes, making a profit.[31]

Virgin Money was one of the first Virgin companies to embrace purpose and run with it: *Everyone Better Off.* In this case, everyone consists of their 5 Cs: Community, Colleagues, Corporate Partners, Customers, and Company. The company pledges to take no action that does not benefit all five.[32]

Two more to ponder:

The Kellogg food company: *Nourishing families so they can flourish and thrive.*

Insurance company IAG: *To help people manage risk and recover from the hardship of unexpected loss.*

George Hatzimanolis is CEO of a company called Repurpose It, based in Melbourne, Australia. The first thing you see on their site: "Creating value from waste." And below that: "At Repurpose It, we hold the fundamental belief that landfills are a thing of the past, and that all waste can be converted to valuable resources."

The company, set up in 2017, demonstrates that being sustainable and being profitable are not mutually exclusive. Repurpose It is highly profitable, with revenues in 2020 of AUD 32 million (US$22 million).

One of the big advantages of running a purpose-driven business, George reports, is that you find it easier to attract talent.

"There are a lot bigger companies paying more money than us, but the talent that we've been able to attract is exceptional. Good people want to work for a company that is leaving something positive behind. The other thing is morale. We've got a very high performing team that believe in what they're doing. When you have a team around you that believe in what they're doing, that's when you get results."

2.4 PROJECT A MOONSHOT VISION

"There is no greater experience than to live your life working to achieve a Vision so bold that it scares you. Any Vision you commit to should be so inspiring that you stay up at night as it pulls you and flirts with you."
—**Vishen Lakhiani**

In this section, you will learn how to craft your moonshot vision. Visit simplescaling.com for more resources.

In May 1961, President John F. Kennedy famously declared his vision to put a man on the moon by the end of the decade. The moon landing—the culmination of eight years of unprecedented imaginative endeavor—was watched by more than 600 million people across the world in 1969. This was the inspiration behind Google's X—The Moonshot Factory, set up to create radical new technologies to solve some of the world's biggest problems. Everything about this company is audacious and groundbreaking. They aim, not for a 10 percent improvement but a 10x improvement. They look for quantum leaps, not incremental steps. To date, X has overseen the development of bold projects like self-driving cars, Google Glass, aerial wind turbines, and Project Loon, which promises internet access to remote regions using helium balloons. Not all of these projects have been successful (yet!) but all prompt the same double-take: Are they really aiming for that?

That was the genius of Kennedy's original moonshot. It asked the question, Can we really do this? It inspired and motivated in a way that a more modest, more attainable goal could never do.

Moonshot goals draw people toward them. When Kennedy visited the NASA space center during the development phase, he introduced himself to a janitor and asked him what he did there. The janitor responded, "Mr. President, I'm helping put a man on the moon."

Lack of Ambition

"Logic will get you from A to Z. Imagination will get you EVERYWHERE."
—Albert Einstein

Earlier, we quoted the 2016 Scale Up report which highlighted the exceptionally low numbers of SMEs that choose to scale. The problem, the authors of that report maintain, is simply a lack of ambition. And the antidote? Projecting a moonshot vision.

There are several reasons why you might balk at a big, bold vision. Foremost among them is your in-built psychological safety system. The brain which evolved over hundreds of thousands of years doesn't want us to set moonshot visions. Ambitious, courageous, groundbreaking hunter-gatherers tended to get eaten, or poisoned, or lost, or kicked out of the tribe. These risks have disappeared, but the brain's primitive fight, flight, or freeze response has not. We're conditioned NOT to dream big. This is why it takes a deliberate, determined effort to step out of our comfort zone and aim for the moon. There are so many attainable goals out there that it's easy to convince ourselves to aim for those instead. Robert Brault put it really well when he said, "We're kept from our goal, NOT by obstacles but by a clear path to lesser goals."

Don't fall into that trap. Allow yourself to dream big.

It can feel like quite a stretch, as an SME, to wrap your head around the sheer scale of Google and X, but the truth is that their philosophy is as applicable to the $1 million revenue scaler as it is to the larger corporate. First, you've got to understand the mindset of the moonshot makers. They lay out ten principles for crafting a moonshot.[33]

AIM FOR 10X, NOT 10 PERCENT

You can't get excited about low-hanging fruit. Aiming high allows you to return to first principles and thinking more expansively about the problem you will solve.

FALL IN LOVE WITH THE PROBLEM

We explore this in detail in P7 Proposition. Don't fall into the trap of focusing too much on your shiny new product or service. Instead, zero in on how you can solve the customer's pain.

MAKE CONTACT WITH THE REAL WORLD EARLY

Spend time with your customers. Get to understand their needs, wants, hopes, and pains. Test your proposition in the market as frequently as you can.

FUEL CREATIVITY WITH DIVERSE TEAMS

Innovation happens at the intersection of diverse cultures, diverse communities, and diverse disciplines. Nothing breaks the mold and catalyzes fresh thinking like diverse teams.

TACKLE THE MONKEY FIRST

This is the Google version of eating the frog. Zero in on the hardest part of the challenge before you think about anything else.

EMBRACE FAILURE LEARNING
Provide sufficient psychological safety so that the team is not afraid to fail. In our last company, we established a "win or learn" culture, which reframed the cost of failure as an investment in training.

BECOME A CHAOS PILOT
Get comfortable with being uncomfortable. It's going to be a bumpy ride, full of wrong turns and sudden diversions. Uncertainty is the name of the game.

LEARN TO LOVE "V0 CRAP"
You won't get it right the first time, so there's no point in perfecting that first iteration. Get the early version out there. Use it to garner feedback that you can use to create the next version.

SHIFT YOUR PERSPECTIVE
The solution doesn't have to be complex. Sometimes a simple answer can emerge from an altered perspective. Unpick fundamental assumptions and try to look at the problem from a new standpoint. Keep your mind open.

TAKE THE LONG VIEW
You're not going to solve the problem this year or next year. Moonshots take time and patience and cannot be subservient to quarterly targets.

Landing the Eagle

In their book *Built to Last: Successful Habits of Visionary Companies*, Jim Collins and Jerry Porras assert that a moonshot, or a BHAG (big hairy audacious goal) as they characterize it, is a long-term goal that everyone in a company can understand and rally behind.[34] As you frame your own, ask these questions:

- Does it stimulate forward progress?

- Does it create momentum?

- Do people find it stimulating, adventurous?

- Are they willing to throw their creative talents and human energies into it?

In 2007, we emerged from that very first strategy workshop with a moonshot goal of creating a £100 million ($150 million) revenue company within three years. This was an *almost* 10x goal, which was instantly derailed by the financial crisis. And yet, even as we fought to keep the company from going under during those turbulent years, that vision remained. When the dust settled, we realized that actually, a monetary target wasn't enough. We revised our moonshot and set out to become number one in our industry. And when we achieved that, we revised our moonshot again to become number one in every country in the world.

Remember, one of the moonshot's big jobs is to jolt people out of short-term linear thinking and to allow them to dream. I'm often asked about the time frame you should set. The short answer is between seven and ten years. Creating the inspiring vision that will guide you for years shouldn't have anything to do with either the now *or* the how. Don't get caught up in questions like, "If we're only doing these numbers now, how can we ever reach that?" Instead, you dream—without limitation—about where this magical organization you're leading could go. Seven to ten years is far enough ahead to allow your imagination to work unencumbered by the present day.

The moonshot should also be action-oriented and exciting. It should galvanize your team, upgrade its desire and capabilities, and positively energize it to achieve something that wouldn't have been possible without the shared commitment.

For a scaling SME, there are three approaches to crafting your moonshot. This typology draws on Jim Collins and Jerry Porras's work.

ROLE MODEL

This is about emulating the success of another company and will be suited to SMEs who aspire to become *like* a well-known company that is not a direct competitor. Examples of role model moonshots include that of Giro Sport Design, which, as a young company in the early 1990s, sought "to be to the cycling industry what Nike is to athletic shoes and Apple is to computers." In the 1940s, Stanford University aimed to "become the Harvard of the West."

COMMON ENEMY

These moonshots focus on overtaking your biggest competitors. Collins and Porras cite the examples of Nike's 1960s mission to "Crush Adidas" and Honda's "*Yamaha wo tsubusu!*" (We will crush, squash, slaughter Yamaha!). In P7 Proposition, we profile BioTector and its former CEO, David Horan. BioTector began as a tiny family-run water analysis company and scaled rapidly to become the market leader in their sector in the United States. Part of their moonshot zeroed in on their biggest competitor in the marketplace, which was called Astro. BioTector set out to "Kill Astro."

TARGETING

Targeting moonshots refer to definitive milestones, such as becoming a $100-million company, as we did, or seeking a top ranking, as we also did. Microsoft's famous early moonshot vision was "a personal computer in every home running Microsoft software." This vision morphed in later years to "empowering every person and organization on the planet to achieve more."

For moonshots to work, they need imagination, courage, and unwavering belief. SpaceX's goal to "enable human exploration and settlement of Mars" caught international attention when it was first presented to the world. From just over one hundred employees in 2005, SpaceX now employs over 8,000 people, all of whom are energized by this astounding moonshot. Google wants "to organize the world's information and make it universally accessible and useful."

These highly successful companies embrace moonshots because they work.

I was always a little uncomfortable with our first big, bold vision, our first moonshot. Maybe this was fear of failure or fear of ridicule from the cynics on the sidelines. Maybe it was the fact that I had been conditioned to target small improvements on last year's results. Maybe it was the need to keep the goal realistic.

But nothing succeeds like success. Becoming number one in our industry (by revenue) made us more courageous, which is why we set out to become number one in every country in the world. This vision was empowered by a strategic plan, which would eventually see us establish offices in six continents and export to more than one hundred countries globally, all from a little town in Ireland.

Vivid Vision

Once you've got your moonshot, the next thing to think about is your vivid vision. This is a concept developed by Cameron Herold, which he discusses in the Principle in Action section of this chapter. The moonshot, with its ten-year time horizon, allows you to break out of linear, analytical thinking and aim higher than pure reason would ever allow. A vivid vision provides the link back to the here and now. It answers the question, "Where will we be in three years' time?" For that reason, it allows you to plan; we'll be diving into that in P4 Plan.

Creating a vivid vision is all about engaging the emotions to craft a four- or five-page document that is fully aligned to your moonshot vision, but it details what you want to achieve in a shorter time frame. Remember, what we think about in our conscious mind trickles through to the subconscious mind, the *emotional* mind, and this determines how we feel, thereby how we act, and ultimately the results we achieve. This is why engaging the emotions to create a vivid vision is so important.

2.5 LEAD WITH VISION

"Where there is no vision, the people perish."
—Proverbs 29:18

In his seminal book, *Start with Why*, Simon Sinek draws a distinction between leaders and those who lead.

"Leaders hold a position of power and influence. Those who lead inspire us. Whether individuals or organizations, we follow those who lead not because we have to but because we want to. We follow those who lead not for them but for ourselves."[35]

Vision is a recurring and powerful theme in the literature on leadership. Blanchard and Stoner, in *Full Steam Ahead*, reaffirm that vision begins with a sense of "significant purpose." Leadership is effective, they assert, when it is grounded in a compelling vision that is inspiring and that "touches the hearts and spirits of everyone."[36] Notice that last word: everyone. The vision, the energized sense of what can be, becomes an organizational glue.

The authors maintain that if we are clear about our vision and honest about our present realities, we actually don't have to figure everything out. Once we can see the gap between our current situation and the ideal one, we don't need to push ourselves to take the right steps. Rather, we find ourselves *drawn* toward that compelling vision of the future. Lean into it. You will inspire people toward your vision. They become the who that brings the how.

Lead to Scale

I've spoken to so many CEOs, who through guts and will, have managed to get their companies to $15 million, $30 million, $40 million in revenues. Breaking beyond this point is always a huge challenge. In fact, the day-to-day battle simply to maintain this level of income can be daunting in itself. Keeping staff fired up and ready to deliver that golden discretionary work in particular is difficult.

Crafting your vision is the key to ending this daily paralysis for yourself, your team, and your business.

When you have made it as brilliant and exciting and breathtaking as it can be, the next step is to get it out of your head and into the hearts and minds of those you lead. I have seen firsthand the power of this process, not only in my previous role but with the CEOs whom I now mentor.

Think about it. How do you know if you've been successful if you don't have a clear view of what success looks like? How do you know you've arrived at your destination if you haven't taken the time to decide where you want to go? And how can you inspire and motivate an intelligent group of followers if they don't know where you're leading them?

It's only fair to you and the team around you that you provide clarity in direction; that's unless yours is a "lifestyle business" only there to provide you and your employees with a certain standard of living, a nine-to-five, and nothing more. But if you are genuine in your desire and commitment to scale the business, a clearly communicated vision, rooted in a strong purpose is vital. If your plan is to exit in five or ten years or not at all, at least be clear about that. You can then work back with the end in mind.

I spoke recently with a young CEO, the daughter of the founder and chairman of a very substantial business. She was keen to create a vision and support it with a plan. But in doing so, she had to withstand the resistance and cynicism of her more traditional father.

"All that soft shit is just a distraction," he told her.

So I asked her what her father would do in advance of going on holiday.

"Well, he'd decide where he wanted to go. He'd share his thoughts with Mum. They'd agree on the destination and when they would go. He'd book flights, arrange car hire, and make sure the passports were in date. If they were going somewhere exotic, he'd make sure they had the right inoculations and medication."

"Exactly," I said. "By that rationale, is the decision about where you should take your business any less important? Consider how few people are affected by how you take your holidays compared to the hundreds or even thousands who will be impacted by where you decide, or fail to decide, to take your business. It's not just your employees and their families but also those whose jobs are indirectly dependent on your business, not to mention your customers, your investors, and so on. There is an entire stakeholder ecosystem dependent on your direction of travel."

The fact is that it's simply reckless not to paint a picture of the future.

Backing It Up

Vision and purpose aren't worth much on their own. You need strong leadership to endorse them and keep them vibrant, to keep reminding everyone why they're here and that what they're doing matters. In a 2018 *Forbes* article "Cultivating the Essential Ingredient in Leadership: Energy," Brett Steenbarger argues that effective leadership plugs people into evermore powerful energy sockets.

"Emotionally energized, we transcend mere functioning. We go from burnout to burning flame. The mission statement of any organization is only a piece of paper unless and until it is felt and experienced on a daily basis, drawing us to our strengths. In providing team members with new, powerful experiences of themselves, effective leaders achieve what Peters observed: the ability to tap into hidden strengths and capacities."[37]

Steenbarger argues that effective leadership transforms people emotionally and cognitively. The leader creates the environment in which the team is energized and empowered to become the best versions of themselves and ultimately deliver on the promise of the vision.

2.6 ENDURE

"When you are inspired by some great purpose, some extraordinary project, all your thoughts break their bonds, your mind transcends limitations, your consciousness expands in every direction and you find yourself in every direction and you find yourself in a new and a great and a wonderful world. Dormant forces, faculties and talents come alive and you discover yourself to be a greater person by far than you ever dreamed yourself to be."
—**Patanjali, Hindu Philosopher, ca. 250 BC**

It may have taken our company a few decades to arrive at our great Why, but that purpose has proved remarkably powerful. For one thing, it has been pivotal in driving us toward the goal we set in that small country hotel all those years ago. In 2015, we came within 0.2 percent of achieving $100 million revenue, and today, the company is the global leader in their sector. Moreover, the fact that the company is a purpose-driven organization is widely understood both within our industry and beyond.

Between June 2018 and June 2019, I participated in a series of investor roadshows across Asia as we prepared to list our Indian-based company. Typically, a manufacturing company in our sector is valued at a multiple of six to eight times earnings before interest, tax, depreciation, and amortization (EBITDA). Clarity in our purpose, alignment to the UN SDGs, and the huge positive impact we were having in India in particular was a significant driver for a valuation multiple in excess of fifteen.

As a business, it's incumbent on you to be profitable, to grow your business, look after your employees, and as appropriate, to invest in R&D. There is no conflict between that drive and the drive to maintain the planet in which you make those profits. We don't just manufacture big, blue, engineering equipment; we are doing something purposeful to preserve a finite resource.

The other point I'd like to make here is that purpose is a living thing. It develops and evolves over time. In July 2019, we had the most profound three days that we've ever had in all of the strategic pit stops we've hosted over the years. We invited Marga Hoek to come in to speak to us, and this time around, the debate centered on whether it was time to wind down our involvement in the processing of virgin sand and aggregate and concentrate exclusively on recycling.

Arriving at your noble purpose takes time. It's like when you get your eyes tested, and as the optician drops down each successive lens, the focus becomes clearer and clearer. Purpose resolves itself from the haze. And sometimes—as with us—that focus can take years to become sharp and lucid. But the earlier you have those discussions, the earlier you arrive at that clarity, the greater the power to ignite your performance.

And once again, this is such a powerful motivator for your team. By involving everyone in the articulation of noble purpose, you're inviting them to participate in a revolution. You're making their work meaningful. You can say to them, yes, you'll be using the latest software and virtual reality tools, but the crux of it is that what you'll be doing on a day-to-day basis will be really, really meaningful. This creates a repository of that discretionary effort that is like magic dust scattered over your company.

I've been privileged to lead a business that scaled successfully. But it's only when you take the time to step out and reflect that you fully appreciate the difference you have made. This positive impact is felt within your team as well as your community, your supplier base, and of course, your customers.

We saw our moon, aimed for it, and got there. The rest of this book shows you how to reach yours.

TAKE ACTION—IT'S SIMPLE!

Start with Why. Businesses with a clearly defined purpose and a vision aligned with that purpose gain competitive advantage, ignite passion within their stakeholders, successfully motivate their teams, and are more attractive to investors than those who lack these attributes.

Impact the World. Explore your company's wider position in the world and seek out a corporate purpose that resonates and aims for something higher than shareholder value.

Mold Your Purpose. A great purpose draws your tribe toward you. Use the PURPOSE questions to explore your own passions and values to arrive at a clearly articulated purpose.

Project a Moonshot Vision. Dare to dream big and shoot for the moon. To assist the planning process, create a more pixilated vivid vision.

Lead with Vision. Purpose and vision without committed, authentic leadership are empty promises. The leader must continually remind the team where their combined effort is leading.

Endure. Purpose is a living thing. To make it last, you must keep it in your sights and revisit it periodically to ensure that it's as relevant and well defined as it can be.

Note: Where is "mission" in all of this, you may ask. We find ourselves in agreement with an increasing number of CEOs who find the term outmoded and woolly. Vision is where you want to go. Purpose tells you why you want to get there.

Principle in Action—
Cameron Herold, Vivid Vision

Cameron Herold has been preaching the vivid vision gospel for nearly fifteen years now. It was a concept that emerged from his work with Brian Scudamore of 1-800-GOT-JUNK? a company that scaled rapidly following the emergence of a clear picture of where Brian wanted to take it. What Cameron realized was that the conventional vision statement that we're all familiar with just wasn't good enough anymore.

In his own words:

> A vision statement is one sentence that mashes up a bunch of your favorite words and is supposed to inspire people. But that doesn't explain your marketing; it doesn't explain your operations; it doesn't explain your leadership team, or your company culture, or what people are saying about you. One sentence just isn't enough to get you there. But a four- or five-page document that describes every aspect of your business, that tells everyone exactly what your company is about? That works. That aligns people. That's your vivid vision.
>
> There's so much more in the mind of the entrepreneur than a seven- or eight-word sentence. The vivid vision, by contrast, clarifies what the business will look like, will act like, and will feel like in three years' time. Employees can't read the entrepreneur's mind. Get it out of your mind and get it down on paper. If you're the only one who can see the vision, you have no support network.
>
> You can't sit in your office and write it. You've got to get out of the box. Go out into nature. Climb a mountain or go sit by the ocean. Somewhere you'll feel inspired. I used to sit in a hammock in my backyard, put my headphones on and start to dream.

Write it in the present tense. It's three years in the future. Sketch out what marketing looks like, what operations looks like, IT, engineering, and so on. What are customers saying about you? Suppliers? What about the media? Get it all down, and don't worry about the how just yet.

These rough notes become the first draft of that vivid vision.

I work on this with CEOs. We go back and forth, and we nail something that perfectly captures their vivid vision. Then we get a great copywriter, and they make it jump off the page.

I don't see the CEO and the leadership team collaborating on the vivid vision. The leader figures out where. The leadership team works out how. It's true what they say: "Vision without execution is hallucination." You can't just present a vivid vision and expect it to happen. You need to get buy-in at the leadership team level. You need them excited about it. You need to get them to start putting plans in place to make it come true. Once you have buy-in there, you can start to roll it out to all the employees.

Some people read the vivid vision and say, "I don't want to be part of that organization. It's not for me." Other people read it and go, "Wow! That sounds amazing! That's exactly what I want." That's one of the great things about vivid vision. We push the wrong people away, and we attract the right people in. And in this way, it becomes a retention tool. It will say, "Here's what we're building. Here's what's going to come true in the first year, but you will need to be here in the second and third years to really see it in action." People get excited about staying with your company for three years because they want to be part of making this thing come true. It becomes a big, aligning force for the organization.

I wrote the first vivid vision for the COO Alliance, which is a COO training and support network I founded in 2017. It described how the company would be in 2020. I said that we would have both an online and an off-line presence. We launched the online model in September 2020 with huge success. This will, I imagine, end up being the core of the model. I said I would have that done by 2020 and there it was—locked and loaded four months ahead of schedule. The look and the feel, the brand, and the associated podcast, all of these things were specified three years ago, and now all have started coming true. Why? Because my employees know what we're building. Our members know what we're building. Everybody who joins the COO Alliance has the same vision that I have, so they start helping to make it come true—sometimes without me even knowing.

I taught Sebastien Tondeur of MCI Group in Geneva, Switzerland the vivid vision concept back in 2009. He was at £80 million ($120 million) revenue and wanted to get to half a billion dollars. He got to £373 million ($560 million) within three years, and his subsequent three-year vivid vision targeted $1 billion in revenue. He got to £573 million ($860 million). So over six years, he went from £80 million to £573 million ($100 million to $860 million).

Bobby Harris is CEO of Bluegrace Logistics. They ranked as the number one company to work for in Florida several years in a row and was one of the fastest growing companies in America in 2012. Another? Viva Naturals in Toronto has gone from £2 million to £34.7 million ($3 million to $52 million) with vivid vision.

I have a BHAG for my overall business. It's to replace vision statements with vivid vision worldwide. I'll be driving toward that for the next twenty or thirty years. People from outside the company might think it's crazy, but inside our company, we see it as possible. So I have a three-year vivid vision for what my company looks like. I have a three-year vision for what the COO Alliance looks like. I have a three-year vision for what Cameron Herold looks like. I drive toward all of these every single day.

P2 ACTIONS TO TAKE:

_____

_____

_____

_____

_____

_____

_____

_____

_____

_____

_____

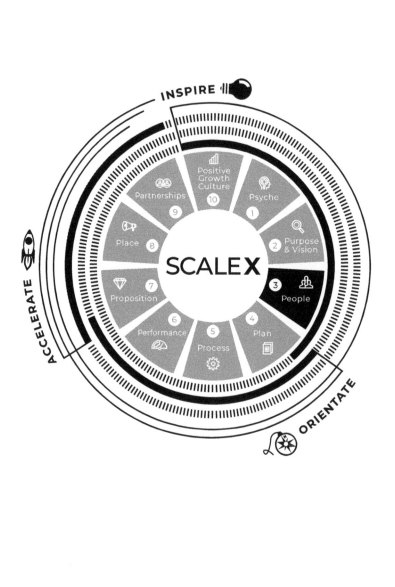

P3

PEOPLE

"You don't build a business. You build people, and people build the business."

—Zig Ziglar

IF YOU WANT TO KNOW WHICH PART OF YOUR BUSINESS IS THE most important in your scaling journey, look no further. It's your people. It's the talent function. Talent is essentially what your people need to do to stay ahead of the competition. Understanding what that means to your business as it scales is critical. Your people are your company's heartbeat.

3.1 SEEK A GREAT TALENT LEADER

"The one who understands their role as both 'pastor' (in terms of keeping secrets) and 'parent' (in terms of telling it straight) and loves to see people grow, will allow you to play your winning game. If you relegate them to processing forms and benefits, you've got the wrong game going on."
—Jack Welch

There has been a tendency to think of the HR function as operational and administrative. It deals with the uninspiring everyday stuff—salary, benefits, policy changes, sickness, absences, and so on. Failure to discharge these basic functions fairly and consistently will certainly cause trouble, but the entire concept of talent management means so much more than this.

So what is talent management?

Talent management recognizes the innate talent within each person and each team. It is all about challenging them to grow and develop, to become as good as they can be.

In his 2005 book, *Winning*, legendary GE CEO, Jack Welch, argues that HR is the driving force behind every winning team. I was at a Jack Welch Institute of Directors talk at the Royal Albert Hall in London when that penny dropped for me.

Jack asked the audience of 2,000 people, "What's the most important asset in your business? Is it people?"

Two thousand hands went up.

"Well, okay, that's great, that's encouraging. Now, how many people have an HR function in their business?"

About half the hands stayed up.

"Okay, of those, how many people have those HR people represented at the boardroom?" I looked around and estimated that about one hundred hands remained in the air.

"How many people have a head of talent? Or a talent director who sits on the board?"

Two hands out of 2,000 stayed up.

"Right, everybody has told me that people are the most important asset in your business, but it turns out that in the vast majority of cases, the most important asset in your business is not represented in the boardroom."

This made so much sense! I had never even heard the term "talent director" before. Jack was right. We talk about talent all the time, and yet this most important asset is not represented at the most important discussions in the company. I realized that I didn't need an HR compliance person; those duties could be contracted out. I needed somebody who would champion people in the business.

To attract that great talent leader to your business, you will need to think about how you describe the role. Be warned: If you lean toward the compliance aspect of the role—which goes hand and hand with the old-fashioned command-and-control style of leadership—you will not deliver the great benefits that come from developing the people within your team. When you champion compliance, you get mediocrity.

3.2 INVEST IN WHAT YOU ALREADY HAVE

Great talent is so often right there in the company, but we simply fail to recognize it. Every business has people who have already proven their capability, their loyalty, their teamwork, and their values:

- Those who deliver strong results year on year.

- Those who are exemplars of your company's culture and values.

- Those with in-depth functional knowledge, perhaps even those who have demonstrated a capacity to master new types of expertise within their field.

- Those who track advances that are being made in other companies.

- Those who have an enterprising spirit and are always searching for productive ways to create new avenues for growth.

- Those who have a drive to excel, who leave their comfort zones, and raise the bar for everyone else.

Scaling breakthroughs come from individuals like these who demonstrate passion and potential—those who are not trying to simply satisfy your customer needs, but who are thinking of ways to exceed them. Talent exists everywhere. We just need to open our eyes to find it. The better we become at doing this, the better we will become at improving performance and scaling successfully.

Of course, there are many cynics (I know them well) who deem any activity that cannot be proven to drive straight toward the company's bottom line as suspect. It is difficult to measure the impact of learning. It is change that takes place on the inside, while performance takes place on the outside. But the truth is that you can't have performance without learning. What is learning except an increased capability to perform, while performance is the evidence that a capability exists. An exclusive focus on performance at the expense of learning is dangerous. It produces a kind of tunnel vision that prevents us from being fully aware and focused. When we sacrifice learning and personal growth for the delivery of short-term results, long-term performance suffers.

How many of us establish a training budget without really thinking about what we are trying to achieve or how this investment will impact the company's core capabilities? Too often, we don't have an accurate picture of what those capabilities are and what we need our people to do differently to achieve greater results. This in turn leads to decision making based on personality rather than on agreed facts or principles.

Create a Learning Culture

The better you become at identifying and building key capabilities, the better you will become at improving your performance and scaling successfully. Part of that process involves creating a learning environment in the organization. This doesn't need to be formalized. Some of the best learning I have observed happens when it simply becomes part and parcel of the day job, when it is linked to real-life challenges. Better still, it's when it's aligned to a pressing business need. Look for opportunities to develop team members by pushing them out of their comfort zones. When is the last time you took one of your team to an important customer meeting simply to observe, learn, and later ask you questions? Look for opportunities to delegate. Always ask yourself, "Can this activity be performed by someone else?" Delegating is a win-win. It's a wonderful way of creating the additional capacity you will need if you wish to scale. More importantly, it requires the person to whom the task has been delegated to also step up.

- Invite the person who lacks confidence to present to the board.

- Invite an emerging leader who struggles with shyness to chair a management meeting.

- Invite the person with managerial ambitions to tackle an underperformance issue.

They may not thank you for it at the time, but by identifying the right opportunities, positively challenging your team, encouraging deliberate practice, and providing them with a safe space to make mistakes, you are building valuable capability and at very little cost. Growth always comes after discomfort. Your team must be appropriately challenged to achieve your scaling success.

Delegate to elevate; elevate to grow.

Make sure your people are playing to their strengths. Every business has subject matter experts who have developed technical mastery. But these skills are very different to those needed to manage or indeed to lead. We often made the mistake of promoting these experts into management positions when they have neither the desire nor the capability to manage. Don't fall into the trap of promoting to management if management is not where their unique ability lies. It's important to place people according to their strengths. So explore ways to help them to progress in their careers, but don't attempt to fit square shapes into round holes.

FastCap founder and CEO Paul Akers is our Principle in Action exemplar in P5 Process. He's also got a fascinating approach to people development.

He says:

> We don't send our people to Harvard; we don't go to conferences. We have a morning meeting that lasts a half hour, and that's where we develop our people. We are teaching and training each other to think differently every single day. Not when we have time, not if we're not too busy. When we're in the heat of the battle, we have that half-hour meeting. We study everything, from the Constitution of the United States to Deming's principles. We review our mistakes; we look at all our key performance indicators for all departments. We've been having learning experiences and robust discussions every day for the last fifteen years.

Encourage Ideas, Creativity, and Learning

In P5 Process, we'll be talking about building systems to facilitate growth. When creating your people systems, don't kill your team's creativity with excess instruction. You don't need a policy for every single thing. An obsessive need for codifying everything usually indicates a fear of making a decision. Challenge it. Is it really necessary? Providing your team with the psychological safety to work, explore, and make mistakes is crucial to growing trust and confidence. Don't allow policy and procedure to inhibit that creative urge and the freedom to experiment. And where you do put a policy in place, write it in plain, everyday, conversational language.

A great way to encourage this is to build your performance management system around great quality conversations with your team. Enable managers to really get to know your team. Only by knowing them can they inspire exceptional performance. Forget lengthy, convoluted, paper-based systems that no one ever uses. Focus on the quality of the conversation. Teach managers to deliver feedback masterfully, and teach all employees how to receive feedback properly.

David Marquet is a former submarine captain with the US Navy who has written extensively on intent-based leadership.

Here's his insight into encouraging innovation among the team:

The product team comes in and says, "Hey, we have a new idea for a product."

Let's say you are a fintech company and they say, "It's a feature where you type in your net worth, your salary and your savings and how you want to live and it tells you whether you are saving enough money."

Now, this strikes you as not a very good idea because it is overly invasive. You're reluctant to believe that people are actually going to type all that information in and trust that some algorithm is going to tell them anything useful. You're sort of thinking that it's a waste of time. So, you say, "Okay yeah, but why don't you change it this way…"

By saying that, you've just denigrated something really good the team did. One, they were thinking; two: they took initiative; three, they came up with a plan; four, they pitched it to you. You crushed all that by zeroing in on changing the product. What do you do instead? You invite them to tell a story. You say, "Wow, tell me about that. How did you come up with it? What were your inspirations? What books did you read? What TED Talks did you watch? What were the key decisions you guys had to make? What was really hard about this? What were some alternatives you considered and rejected?"

Let them tell the story and two things happen. One, they're going to feel listened to and respected. Even if you end up saying, "Yeah, we're not going to do that," they will at least know they were listened to. The second thing is that you're going to learn their thinking. You are going to learn how they think, and if the thinking is truly messed up, now at least you know what to fix.

We say, "Pride, not praise." Praise is, "Oh, you did a good job." It comes from a position of judgment. You want to be standing side by side with a person, walking together in the same direction. Then be very specific. Don't say, "It's well designed." Anyone could say that. Instead, say, "I noticed you put that icon in the top right-hand corner. That was great; that was clear." That's showing interest; that shows you actually paid attention.

So here's the key point: Show interest in the process. The superficial part that you see is the outcome, but you need to understand how they got here. Cherish the process because the process makes it repeatable.

3.3 MASTERMIND THE TALENT PIPELINE

In the same way you work constantly at building your sales pipeline, you also need to think about your talent and leadership pipeline.

How are you engaging with your future talent pool? Those in local schools, colleges, and universities? Do they know you exist? Do you open your doors and provide opportunities for them to experience your business at a time when they are making significant career choices? Is your team evangelizing among their friends about the company and the opportunity we represent?

In our early stages, traditional work experience placements were, frankly, painful. Every week, an unassuming teenager would turn up at reception, triggering the same argument over who was going to look after them. Nothing was organized and nobody learned anything.

The truth, however, is that any intervention that attracts early talent into your business is a golden opportunity that must be taken seriously. So I resolved to do something about it. I came up with the idea of a talent camp. We consolidated the endless requests for work placement into one intense week of learning and fun. Twenty students, aged fifteen to seventeen, from fourteen different high schools, came together to participate in that first event.

The experiment was such a success that five of those twenty talent campers went on to secure a place on our apprenticeship program. The fact that multiple members of our board had joined the company as apprentices twenty years earlier gives some idea of the value of these apprenticeships to the business. And critically, it was also a big win for the schools that fed into the camp.

The Leadership Pipeline

It is equally important to identify and develop your potential leaders. Our Emerging Leader Program saw fifteen carefully selected participants, all of whom put themselves forward for a rigorous application process, embark on a two-year development program. This brought them together regularly to work on a live project in which they were supported by mentors within the business.

I had seen firsthand just how powerful a great mentor can be. I was in my mid-twenties and had spent the first four years of my

HR career in the hospitality industry before making the move to the world of technology. In my new role, I was responsible for setting up the HR function. I'd been there for about a year when the managing director, David Mawhinney OBE, invited me to sit with him in his office. We always got on well and I enjoyed our chats, but this meeting was different. He asked me to tell him what I had observed about the business, what I believed our core capabilities to be, what our strengths were, and what areas needed development.

Nervously, I shared my thoughts and observations—and I had plenty of them. I've always been naturally curious about both business and people, but on this occasion, I was able to show David that I understood the *impact* that people could have on our business.

From that moment on, things changed.

David invested his time and energy in developing me, both personally and professionally. He helped me to think outside of my narrow perspective and saw, I think, potential in me that I hadn't yet identified in myself.

He needed assurance that I was focused on the needs of the business and was working to enable us to move forward. My first year had been well spent, and I had a strong understanding of where we were. I was solutions focused and relished tackling each new obstacle to growth. David encouraged me to be generous with my time and to use it to get to know people so I could fully support them on their personal journeys, while at the same time stretching and challenging them to achieve what I knew they were capable of.

And we were scaling. We were an indigenous company with annual revenue growth in excess of 30 percent, operating in a highly competitive industry.

I'm delighted to say that David and I have remained friends. I have a huge amount of respect for him and his capability. I'll be forever grateful for the time and attention he gave me in my early career.

The world needs more mentors and more people who will invest their time in raw talent.

Get Recruitment Right

Talent pools are shrinking and natural skillsets are changing, so you need to be creative. You need to be willing to experiment. Most of all, you need to be crystal clear about what you're looking for.

One of the first things I discovered when I became a talent leader in a rapidly growing engineering company was that the company was finding it difficult to attract great talent. Line managers could not keep up with the company's growth because they didn't have the capacity to deliver an ever-increasing workload. What was causing the problem? Why was it so difficult to attract and appoint great people? If you are failing to attract great talent, it's nearly always down to one of three things:

- Your culture is wrong.

- Your recruitment processes aren't working.

- Your employer value proposition (EVP) is not impactful.

I knew it wasn't the culture. It was the wonderful culture that drew me to the company in the first place (and we'll talk about creating a positive growth culture in P10). That's why I began exploring our recruitment processes and our employment brand.

What I found was a reactive process being managed by someone who was already overstretched.

This is not an uncommon scenario. Most SMEs don't have a dedicated recruitment team. Typically, recruitment falls within the remit of HR, which tries to fit it in as a sort of secondary function. This is a big mistake. Recruitment is one of the most important functions in a scaling business. You need to get it right. The greatest gift you can give your team is the appointment of a wonderful new talent to support their goals.

At this point in our scaling journey, we could not justify employing a full-time, dedicated recruiter, so I engaged with a local recruiter in what's called an RPO, or recruitment process outsourcing arrangement. It works like this: The agency employs the resource, but they are based in your business. It's a service many of the larger recruitment agencies offer. We interviewed and appointed the recruiter, then, over the course of the following year, we got to know him really well. He turned out to be excellent—one of the best recruiters I've ever met. In the second year of the arrangement, we took him on permanently.

Now we set about creating a simple resource plan for the future. Despite my best efforts to forecast resource needs three years ahead, the rapidly changing environment in which we worked meant that invariably, I had to scrap the projections. Twelve to eighteen months was the best we could do.

There's no magic formula for figuring out how many people you should take on. The important thing is to be realistic about how long it will take to both find the right person *and* to develop them into a valuable contributor. Remember, too, that the repercussions of hiring too many people or hiring the wrong people can be extremely harmful to your team, their families, and your business. Plus, there are a few more difficult conversations than those when you have to let someone go.

When it came to trying to peer into the future to establish our needs, we factored in things like upcoming projects, the introduction of a new ERP system, and the digitalization of our business. We also looked at our plans for expansion into new sectors and new regions, as well as predicted changes in those sectors.

If you're beginning to achieve high growth and profitability, consider adopting a revenue-per-employee or profit-per-employee target. There will be a sweet spot for where this is in the business. Too many people and it becomes too low. Too few and you risk team burnout.

Think Different

We also did a lot of brainstorming about how we were going to find all the people we would need. In fact, at one point, my office window was almost blacked out by yellow post-it notes covered with suggestions for what we might do. We challenged our assumptions around recruitment and asked some searching questions:

- Do they really need previous experience?

- Can we retrain people?

- Can we recruit people fresh from universities and colleges?

- What qualifications do they need?

- Do they really need that specific degree?

- Should they be located in our regions or at HQ?

- How should we differentiate ourselves? (The development of our purpose helped significantly here.)

- Could partnerships help here?

- How do we build a compelling employer brand?

I was able to bring some of my earlier experience working in the software industry to bear on this process.

At one point, there were an estimated 2,000 unfilled technology roles in Northern Ireland alone, and yet, despite the shortage of resources, it was unheard of to appoint a software engineer without at least a software degree. We interviewed so many disengaged software grads who were under no illusions about just how valuable they were. They were so laidback that they all but had their feet up on the table during the interview.

So I sent out a blanket email to all of the colleges of further education in the area, asking them about their Higher National Diploma qualifications and apprenticeships. This kick-started what turned out to be a wonderful new relationship with what is now Northern Regional College in Newtownabbey. One of their key objectives at the time was to establish stronger links with industry, while ours, obviously, was to widen our talent pool. Together, we identified the cohort of students most likely to fit our needs and created an online psychometric test, which we offered to all sixty course participants. The highest scorers were invited to a daylong interview and assessment, after which the top five were offered work placements. For the next five consecutive years, we had 100 percent employability from that internship program. Every candidate who emerged was really polished, really impressive, and really eager to be part of the team.

The key point here is that it's very easy to respond to the tsunami of requests for experienced people to go out to talk to local universities and colleges of further education without thinking about the value it can bring to your business. With clear goals and a bit of creativity, we were able to partner with the education sector to develop something more systematic that added significant value to our talent magnetism.

3.4 PROMOTE YOUR EMPLOYER VALUE PROPOSITION

You need to draw in people who are tuned to the same frequency as you, people who share your excitement, your positivity, your ambition, and your purpose. We often hear frustrated CEOs protest that they simply can't get the right people. Every time I hear this, I ask them to take some time that evening to explore the company website. Once they've done that, I ask them, "Are you inspired by what you see? Would you want to join that company?"

Long before any applicant comes in direct contact with your business, they will be gathering information about you from the news, social media, job boards, internet searches, acquaintances, and many other touchpoints. How you present yourself as an employer will differentiate you from the rest and draw the focus of the best talent in the market.

Before you create and promote your employer brand, you need to understand why people would want to join your company in the first place.

Your employee value proposition or EVP isn't just about reiterating the purpose and values of your business. It's about identifying the different elements that come together to make your business an awesome place to work, and then going on to translate that into real, lived experience. In other words, it's all about telling your story.

When I set out to do this, I cast a wide net. I interviewed the team and the agencies that recruited for us, as well as a range of our customers and suppliers. The recruitment agencies in particular were able to help me understand how we compared to other employers in our industry and, in particular, how we stood out.

Here's what I learned:

- **Autonomy.** Many of our team were given a significant amount of responsibility early in their careers. Some, with the right training, were managing projects worth up to £1 million ($1.5 million). The learning that they were exposed to was intense. As a result, we had a number of people in their late twenties who held senior roles. The team was given autonomy to make the right decision on behalf of the company and the customer.

- **Diversity.** Being a global company, we fully embraced different cultures and welcomed people from far and wide into the company. (We even had a customer in Outer Mongolia!) We encouraged our team to travel, and many of our people spent time in our regional centers. It was both personally and professionally enriching for them, and in virtually every aspect, it helped them to raise their game and enhance their own and the company's capability.

- **Challenge.** The team was highly competitive. They loved a challenge and had a habit of making things work. Nothing got in their way.

- **Togetherness.** We held a lot of social and well-being events. In fact, we embraced any opportunity to bring the team together to have fun, and set aside a significant budget for that purpose. The events were fantastic and attended by almost everyone from the founder and board through to the newest recruits.

- **Win or learn.** As a boundary-pushing organization, there was an understanding and acceptance of the fact that we wouldn't always get it right. Company leaders actually built in financial capacity for this, and that mindset gave the team the psychological safety to innovate new products and services.

These key characteristics formed the basis of our EVP, which we brought to life in a people brochure that went to every recruitment event. I made sure the brochure was seen by candidates at an early stage of the selection process. Written in inspirational language, it was covered top to bottom in photographs of our team. I have to say, it made me very proud just to look at it.

It allowed potential team members to visualize themselves wearing the blue company jacket, which was modeled by those in the brochure and which was given to every new recruit. I worked closely with the marketing team to help make sure the brochure was well promoted and always reached the right audience.

Sixty percent of CDE's employees were under thirty years of age, and each year, we hired approximately a quarter of our new recruits straight out of university or college. Many of our teams were connected on Facebook along with other social media platforms, and all followed the company page. We often joked that they found out more about the company on social media than by reading any of our internal communications. And when a message was sent out by the marketing or talent team on these channels, it received a huge number of likes and shares by our team, who in turn promoted our message on their own networks.

The fact is that we're all looking for a great place to work. Moreover, there is still huge competition out there for the best talent. A well-defined employer brand can set you apart from the rest and make your business famous for the experiences it gives its people.

3.5 LET THE RIGHT ONES IN

For me, it's very much about behavior. Great behavior is, without a doubt, the most significant driver of great results. The best bit is, it's something that we can all learn. In a 2016 *Harvard Business*

Review article, "Talent Matters Even More than People Think," Tomas Chamorro-Premuzic argues that great performers share three key personality and behavioral attributes: ability, likability, and drive.[38]

- **Ability.** Primarily the technical expertise and knowledge that we have acquired in our field can be identified from a traditional CV or LinkedIn profile. The second component of ability, however, is "learnability," defined as "the person's capacity to learn new things"—a trait that is commonly found in someone with a growth mindset.

- **Likability.** Mainly associated with levels of emotional intelligence and people skills, both of which are pivotal to success no matter what field we're in. To grow your business, you will need collaborations and synergies. A team of individual high-ability superheroes with low likability will struggle to contribute to a collaborative working environment.

- **Drive.** This is "a person's general desire to compete and the ability to remain dissatisfied with one's achievements."[4] I've always found that drive and curiosity are great indicators of higher performance, and these are things that are so easily discerned during a good, quality interview. A session with plenty of interaction, questions, and general curiosity from the potential candidate always leaves me buzzing!

Design questions to assess each of these attributes. Then weave them into your recruitment process and create a consistent language that reaffirms the behavior that you want to see in your business. This approach enabled me to access a much greater pool of talent and to bring in great people, both from within and outside our industry.

Make Your Team Diverse

The term "diversity" is often misunderstood. We tend to think of it in terms of political correctness, in terms of gender balance, racial equality, religious denominations, age spectrum, and so on. Diversity is important not as an arbitrary concept or compliance exercise. When we open our minds and have our dominant assumptions challenged, we are much more likely to find the best solutions, the best ideas, the best new products, and the best value for our customers. When we bring in different people—who are aligned with the business and share our values—we are much more likely to avoid blind spots. We're much more likely to hear different ideas, to trigger new and divergent thinking, and ultimately, we'll have a more complete picture of the task at hand.

British journalist and author Matthew Syed argues that a lack of diversity in the CIA was a significant factor in the failure to prevent the 9/11 attacks. Syed contends that the CIA missed a potential threat and obvious warning signs before the event, despite being staffed with outstanding people. This was because these individually brilliant people all thought in the same way—there was no challenge and therefore no uplift.

He says, "If you bring a group of people who share similar perspectives and backgrounds, they are liable to share the same blind spots. And this means that far from challenging and addressing these blind spots, they are likely to be reinforced."[39]

To help our leadership team better understand their dominant-thinking preferences, we used a simple but powerful tool called the Herrmann Brain Dominance Instrument (HBDI), a system developed by William (Ned) Herrmann while leading management education at GE. It's based on left-right brain lateralization, indicating how individuals think and learn. Although the tool has been criticized for being overly simplistic, it nonetheless helped us to build diverse teams and encouraged a healthy level of curiosity within those teams. In fact, it worked so well in the teams in which we piloted the assessment that we decided to roll it out through the organization. The assessment taught us a great deal about how we thought, how we perceived those around us, and how we might improve internal and external communications.

Many people reported that it helped them to build self-confidence and to become more compassionate to those who thought differently to them.

Recruitment Rules of Thumb

There are two key rules that I will never compromise on:

1. Make sure that you have your best people working on recruitment; great people recruit great people. Your best recruitment people are those who create the right energy and can build an authentic connection between how your company presents itself as an employer and how it really feels inside.

2. If you can't find the right person, be patient. Recruitment is time consuming. Getting the right person into the role can be difficult. Don't get panicked by the mounting workload and end up bringing in anyone just to help out. In my experience, a 50-50 call never works out. The truth is that bringing in the wrong person can be really harmful to your team and to your business. Don't rush it.

Here's Paul Aker's recruitment process:

If you want to work for FastCap, you don't send in a résumé; you send in a one- to two-minute video about yourself. If Paul likes what he sees, he'll invite you in for an interview. If that goes well, he'll offer you one day's paid work.

Throughout that day, as you move from department to department, everyone is watching and evaluating you. At the end of the day, we bring in all the people who worked with you. If approval is not 100 percent unanimous, we do not take it to the next level. If it is, you're offered a test week. Again, you're paid, and at the end of that week, everyone gets together to talk about how you worked out.

If it's not 100 percent unanimous, we don't hire you. If it is, you're hired.

3.6 ELEVATE LEADERSHIP AND TRUST

"Don't wish it were easier; wish you were better."
—Jim Rohn

In a 2018 *Harvard Business Review* article, "What Happens to a Startup When Venture Capitalists Replace the Founder," Michael Ewens and Matt Marx cite a range of studies that assert that venture capitalists commonly replace 20–40 percent of their founders with more seasoned leaders at critical transition points in a scaling business.[40]

This is why building the right leadership capability needs to be an ongoing priority for any ambitious SME. Instilling continuous development for this group in particular is critical to your scaling success.

In an intense scaling environment, where everyone is emotionally and often financially invested in the success of the firm, it's not always easy for the business leaders to acknowledge the possibility that their skills are no longer sufficient for the next phase of the journey. For this reason, the leadership team needs to work together to identify their collective development needs and make the necessary shifts.

When I joined that same engineering firm in 2016, developing the leadership team was a priority. There were a lot of questions to answer:

- Did we have the right people in the right roles to take the company to the next level?

- Were we aligned with the most pressing business opportunities?

- Was our way of working right for the next stage of the business?

- If not, what shifts did we need to make?

We put in place a leadership program, kicking it off with a 360-degree assessment to inform our decisions about the group's development. The program highlighted individual strengths, revealed blind spots, and encouraged everyone to become painfully self-aware. We talked candidly about what was working and what was not. We provided deep coaching for some of the team, and most importantly, we brought the team together to build trust and solidarity.

Entrepreneur, CEO, and author Margaret Heffernan is one of the UK's most highly regarded thought leaders, and she has greatly influenced my own thinking. In her book *A Bigger Prize*, Heffernan takes an eye-opening look at what high levels of competition in the workplace are actually costing us.

She says, "We depend on competition and expect it to identify the best, make complicated decisions easy and to motivate the lazy and inspire the dreamers. But competition regularly produces just what we don't want: rising levels of fraud, cheating, stress, inequality and political stalemate."[41]

Heffernan points out that winners seem to take all, while the desire to win consumes all, inciting panic and despair. She contends that competition often doesn't work out, that the best do not always rise to the top, and that competition, far from creating efficiency, actually generates a great deal of waste.

Talking to scientists, musicians, athletes, entrepreneurs, and executives, she discovered that individuals and organizations are finding creative, cooperative ways to work that don't pit people against each other but support them in their desire to work together.

"While the rest of the world remains mired in pitiless sniping, racing to the bottom, the future belongs to the people and companies who have learned that they are greater working together than against one another."[42] These, she suggests, are the real winners, sharing a bigger prize.

And this is why I felt that it was vital that every member of our leadership team sign up to this process so that we could move forward collaboratively, as one team.

By examining and developing the team's capability at regular intervals, we gave ourselves the tools to make our vision real. What's more, we also gave ourselves the opportunity to learn and develop while building sustainable leadership within the business.

Create a Co-movement

"The way a team plays as a whole determines its success. You may have the greatest bunch of individual stars in the world, but if they don't play together, the club won't be worth a dime."
—**Babe Ruth**

The most successful scaling businesses are powered by great relationships. Trust and not rigid, reporting relationships take a central role here. Taking action to promote trust in the workplace not only generates happiness and engagement, but it also boosts the sharing of ideas and makes it easier to challenge each other's thinking. Boundaries get pushed back and businesses thrive. When we care about our work and our coworkers, when our team is energized around a purpose, and our team members trust one another, when we can turn up and simply be ourselves, everyone wins. We channel our energy toward the vision; it doesn't get drained by office gossip or boardroom politics. Goals become attainable. Work becomes fulfilling and fun. Days don't drag.

Shareholders, too, get a much better bang for their buck. A recent Gallup survey found that teams who score in the top 20 percent in engagement realize a 41 percent reduction in absenteeism and 59 percent less staff turnover.[43]

Much of the theory around building trust in the workplace centers on giving praise when praise is due, discouraging gossip, and being fair and consistent. Even though all of these are valid, in my view the two key things that need to be in place to build trust in the first place are time and transparency.

To get to know somebody, you have to give each other sufficient time. By being transparent and open in all of your dealings, you create the right environment for trust to grow. If we believe that someone has the right intention, then we begin to trust them, regardless of the impact of the decisions they make.

Being visible and available is the critical first step. This isn't just about walking through the office and showing the team that you're happy to get your hands dirty. It's about talking to people, asking them questions, and showing an authentic interest not only in their role but in them as human beings. It's about sharing company information with the team and trusting that they will treat it professionally.

When people are intrinsically and emotionally invested in you and your company, they will bring their brains, bodies, and their hearts to work. They create a co-movement.

After listening to a talk by Matt Porter, CEO of Equiniti Intelligent Solutions, one of the greatest "commovers" that I have ever known, my colleague leaned toward me and said, "I don't know if I want to marry him or if I want my son to grow up like him." Matt had the ability to connect easily with others. He touched people's hearts and their minds, bringing people along on his journey. When times were tough, he let others know that he was in the trenches with them. When times were good, he recognized and celebrated others. This was key to inspiring exceptional performance.

Recognize that until you start thinking about others more than you think about yourself, you will struggle to make that human connection. And making that connection will take you to places you've never dreamed of.

Cultivating a "co-movement" within your business will prepare you for many of the challenges you will face as your business scales.

If you can create a team that shares a common vision, one that collaborates well, that both challenges and supports you, that is relentless about improving, and that holds each other accountable, you are cultivating something very special. A co-movement will not only transform your business, but it will also transform your life.

How Novosco Created a Co-movement and Scaled

Patrick McAliskey spent six years in the Royal Air Force before founding an IT company called Real Time Systems, which he went on to run for thirteen years. By 2007, it employed twenty-five staff and was taking in revenue of between £2 million and £3 million ($3 million and $4.5 million) annually. At this point, Patrick decided it was time to take things to the next level. Together with a new business partner, John Lennon, he established Novosco. Within twelve years, the business had grown by more than 10x and employed 300 people. In 2019, Novosco was bought by Cancom for £70 million ($105 million).

So much of their success stemmed from the fact that Patrick and his leadership team created a co-movement at Novosco.

"We had an open-door policy for the team," he explains. "We never said we were too busy to talk or asked them to book in a meeting. We allowed people to walk through the door more or less at any point in time. We wanted them to have the freedom to ask questions whenever they wanted."

The company developed an app, We Are Novosco, that was full of company-related content and resources, from news to training to prompts for new ideas. The team could also use it to nominate people who had gone out of their way to demonstrate company values, which were teamwork, excellence, respect, and fun.

"If you have a happy staff," says Patrick, "the happy customers come. It's that idea: 'If you do this first, the rest falls into place.'"

He would schedule two-hour offsite lunches for each of the fifteen key individuals in the company every six weeks. During these meetings, the talk would range far outside work to home life and family, hobbies, and education. He made it his business to know what was going on with everyone and to help out in any way the company could. "I always asked, 'What thing can I do to help you?'"

The company also invested heavily in education and either funded or part-funded postgraduate courses for their people. The training budget varied between £50,000 and £100,000 per quarter ($75,000 and $150,000).

"I used to say to people, 'I want you to put something new on your CV [résumé] every year, because if you're not, something's wrong.'"

Here's the Novosco purpose statement: Be the Fearless Champions of Better. This was not set by the leadership team. It emerged from an eighteen-month company-wide consultation process.

"We asked, 'Does this resonate with you? Are you happy that this is what we're saying?'"

It resonated so well that at one point, a band started up among staff and they called themselves The Fearless Champions of Better.

When it came to planning, inclusivity was the name of the game.

"We were good at making sure that we got as many people as possible involved in our planning sessions. The magic was that they felt like they were a part of it. We asked them to tell us what we were overspending or underspending on, what we weren't doing enough of, and what we were doing badly. The worst thing, I feel, is when people say, 'I didn't hear that' or 'I didn't know that' or 'When did that happen?'

"It might have seemed at times like overcommunication, but having an open-door policy, having regular company meetings, celebrating success—when you do all that together, people then feel part of it, there's buy-in."

When someone complained that Patrick was treating the team like children, that he needed to toughen up, he would simply point out that changing the approach didn't make financial sense.

"I used to say, 'Look at the numbers; look at how we've grown. This formula works!'"

Reward

Build a recognition system that allows you to say "thank you" a lot. Consistently acknowledge when someone behaves in a way that helps to move you forward. At our last company—as in Patrick McAliskey's Novosco—we encouraged our team to log comments, thanking their team members, and publicly calling out their great work. At the end of each quarter, we pulled out examples that most clearly demonstrated our values in action, and the employees involved were presented with a gift by the board. This small initiative proved highly effective. A little thanks and recognition boosted engagement and energy levels across the organization.

Create a system that allows you to stay competitive. Consider how you reward people in the context of the value they add, as well as the potential pain of losing them. Bear in mind that even though there has always been a positive correlation between pay and motivation, applying it unfairly and inconsistently will have a huge adverse impact on motivation and engagement. Externally benchmarking your salaries will allow you to stay on top of this. To keep costs and the level of disruption in your business in check, implement changes once per year only.

Don't stress about perks. Free coffee or gym passes don't make a big difference. In one company that did offer perks, I was asked every single day about additional benefits. In another—one that didn't go in for perks—I wasn't asked the question once in three years. Guess which company had the higher engagement, better retention, and lower absence levels? What really matters is basic inclusion, strong leadership, a compelling purpose, an inspiring vision, and an empowered team.

TAKE ACTION—IT'S SIMPLE!

Seek a Great Talent Leader. Your HR/talent function is the most important role in a scaling business. If the HR person is relegated to transactional processing of forms, who is advocating for your most important strategic investment?

Invest in What You Already Have. Your existing team is often the best source of scaling talent. Create a learning culture and nurture creativity.

Mastermind the Talent Pipeline. When it comes to sourcing the people you will need to enable your scaling vision, you have to get creative and come up with the very best ways of channeling talent into the organization.

Promote Your Employer Value Proposition. Find out from stakeholders what makes yours a great place to work, and then get that message out there. Draw in people who are tuned into the same frequency as yours—your excitement, your positivity, your ambition, and your purpose.

Let the Right Ones In. Always interview for ability, likability, and drive. Ensure your team is diverse. Put your best people on recruitment and be patient with the process.

Elevate Leadership and Trust. Building the right leadership capabilities as you scale is crucial, as is creating a workplace based on trust. When the team is emotionally invested in the company, they will bring their brains, hearts, and minds to work.

Principle in Action—Kainos

Kainos Group plc (commonly referred to simply as Kainos) is a software company headquartered in Belfast, Northern Ireland. They develop IT solutions for businesses and organizations in the public, healthcare, and financial services sectors. Founded in January 1987, Kainos's scaling success has been remarkable in terms of revenue and profit growth, and cash generation. It is one of the first Northern Irish-listed companies to breach the £1 billion ($1.5 billion) market capitalization mark, and in the twenty-four months to December 2020, the share price rose almost 300 percent.

Brendan Mooney joined Kainos as a graduate software engineer in 1989. At the time, there were twenty-eight people in the company. After taking on several technical and commercial roles in Dublin, London, and the USA, he was appointed CEO in 2001 at age thirty-four. At the time, the company was generating revenues of just under £10 million ($15 million) revenue. In addition to his role at Kainos, Brendan has been a non-executive director at several technology startups and is on the board of the Probation Service of Northern Ireland. He has also served as a lay magistrate. In recognition of the contribution Kainos has made to the local economy, Brendan has been awarded honorary doctorates in both economics and science.

What strikes you in the first five minutes of meeting Brendan is his humility, his modesty, and his passion for people. A self-confessed introvert, he is quick to play down his role and elevate that of his team. When I asked him about the numbers employed by Kainos, he came back straight away with the *exact* figure—2,204, based in twelve locations across Europe and America.

Four of his six personal objectives for the year are focused on the well-being of the Kainos community—as he terms them. At the time of writing, forty members of that community have more than twenty years' service. The company went on a recruitment drive in 2021, receiving over 34,000 applications for

425 positions. To whittle that number down, they conducted more than 5,000 interviews. Moreover, during this rapid growth, they maintained a 93 percent retention rate.

Brendan believes fundamentally that a happy, settled, and engaged team makes a much better business model. Here are the three principles he lives by in Kainos:

1. **Hire great people, but do it carefully.** Brendan is cautious with hiring, and there are extensive measures in place to ensure that the company gets it right. With 82 percent of new recruits hired directly by a recruitment team of twenty-two people, he encourages the team to decline any application where there are *any* question marks. He believes that the disruption caused by hiring badly is significant—for both the individual and for the company.

2. **Trust people to get on with the job.** Brendan sets three team objectives for the year but does not spell out these goals in minute detail. Having set expectations, he then reviews progress toward the target. He describes how he has learned to surround himself with people who are better people than himself. "If you're not seeking to improve yourself," he says, "it's time to look for a new job." He continually asks himself, "How can I be better at my job?"

3. **Create the right investment capacity.** Brendan describes how profitability gives a company options and allows them to take risks without endangering the business. He takes a long-term view and does his best to provide people with a secure and enjoyable employment experience. Out of the 450 new recruits who joined Kainos in 2019, one hundred came straight from college and twelve were hired directly from secondary school (high school). The company can afford to offer these opportunities to people because they have built capacity for it.

Just as importantly, Brendan describes the three things that he has learned to *stop* doing as a leader:

1. **Not everyone is destined to make the same journey.** Allow those who wish to leave leave; don't take it personally. Today, he takes a more balanced view about someone's departure, in no small measure because he is confident that someone else can pick up the baton in their absence.

2. **You may have to allow some parts of the business to decline.** He discusses the fine balance between the need to "pivot or persevere" and explains that he has no magic answer for where to draw that line. Once the decision is taken that growth in a certain area has stopped, align your costs, ensure you can deliver customer satisfaction, and redeploy some of the team.

3. **Stop doing stupid stuff as a habit.** He describes how things that work when you are a smaller organization do not always scale, and yet you still perform them as a habit: *We have always done it this way.* Look for ways to identify these harmful habits and design a better solution.

Since employee engagement underpins the successful growth of the business, asking for feedback is vital. There are multiple opportunities for the people in Kainos to provide this feedback. The company runs an annual engagement survey, which uncovers what's going well and what needs improvement.

P3 ACTIONS TO TAKE:

_____

_____

_____

_____

_____

_____

_____

_____

_____

_____

_____

_____

THEME 2
ORIENTATE

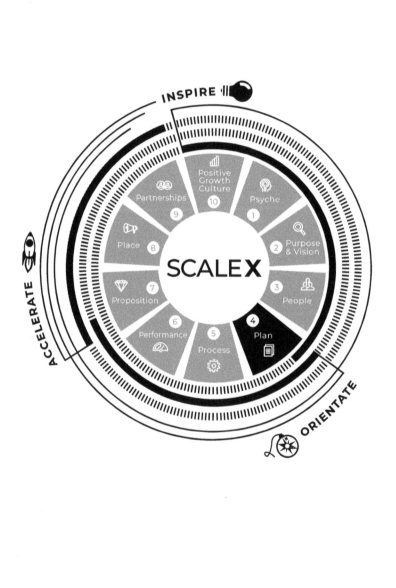

P4

PLANNING

"Vision without action is merely a dream. Action without vision just passes the time. Vision with action can change the world."

—Joel A. Barker

STOP READING FOR A MOMENT AND ASK YOURSELF, "WERE THE tasks I busied myself with today the best use of my time? How important were they? Could I have delegated more?"

Broaden the question: "Are the activities that I've chosen to focus on (and remember it is a choice) today, this week, this month, this quarter aligned to my vision and purpose? Have I conducted myself as CEO and focused only on the *essential*, delegating everything else?"

Don't be fooled. The capacity to react to the next call, email, or message does not improve the trajectory of your business. We're all guilty of getting caught up in the tyranny of the now, of failing to lift our heads, and question where our time is best focused. Our results are a direct reflection of where we focus our thoughts and attention.

This is why you need a plan.

Let's take the holiday analogy again. Imagine simply jumping into a car and taking off without any notion of where you're going to end up. At first, the journey may seem exciting, filled with endless possibility, but very quickly, the lack of any clear direction will leave you drained and confused. Your passengers will become anxious, enthusiasm turns to doubt and frustration, the mood sours. Startups often have the feel of a road trip. That sense of possibility. You feel that you can take on anything and win. But to continue the analogy, the scaling company is more like a coach full of people who have signed up for an organized excursion. Planning is critical. A Japanese proverb nails it: "Vision without action is daydream. Action without vision is nightmare."

An ambition to scale must be underpinned by a plan.

This is the point where many entrepreneurs begin to zone out. The mere mention of the phrase "strategic planning" will cause eyes to glaze over and attention to wander. There is tremendous excitement in dreaming up a vision. Figuring out how to bring it to life? Not so much. And this is probably why the majority of SMEs overlook this vital principle. Whereas dreaming up a vision requires creativity, planning requires patience and clear sight.

Then, of course, there are the volumes of material written on planning and strategy. Trying to establish the best way to bring your organization forward risks getting lost in a fog of jargon, overly intellectualized theories, and academic literature. Plug "strategic planning" into Google and you get 583 million hits in half a second. Amazon doesn't narrow things down for you either. You've got everything from *The Strategic Planning Kit for Dummies* to Sun Tzu's *Art of War*. It's no wonder founders and leadership teams try to dodge this stuff. It's far easier to tend to the next sales call, the next product development meeting, and the great new marketing initiative.

We can tell ourselves, I'm busy, therefore I'm productive. Unfortunately, it's not that simple. Being busy doesn't matter if it *doesn't matter* what you're busy for.

So let's demystify all this strategy stuff. What we're talking about is simply a plan, and a short one at that. It will seek to close the gap between the present and your vision. It will outline the components of the vision. It will direct how we allocate resources (your time, money, people, and assets) and guide our actions to reach the stated future outcome. Each activity to which you allocate your time should always be preceded with the question, "Does this serve my vision?" If not, stop. You shouldn't be doing it.

One of the great benefits of having a plan is that not only will it guide you to where you want to go, but it will also keep you from going where you shouldn't. As you scale, you will invariably encounter a myriad of opportunities. One of the biggest challenges you will face as a CEO is sticking with the agreed strategy and not being distracted by every shiny new thing that appears before you.

If we had lacked the discipline of keeping on plan in my last business, we would, without a doubt have drifted away from our vision. When conversations got heated about which opportunities to chase, someone would always ask, "Is this aligned to where we're trying to go?" "Does it resonate with our purpose?" We don't need to bring sterling if our holiday is in France, no matter how attractive the exchange rate. It's a decision we simply don't need to make.

Without Purpose and Vision (P2), supported by the right People (P3) underpinned by a Plan (P4), companies will drift aimlessly from one deal to the next, one customer issue to the next. New hires will fail because we don't really know what skillset is needed, nor what needs to be done. A plan puts an end to "How about we do this? How about we do that?" A plan dulls the other noise and lets your vision sparkle. A plan gives your team a pathway—that is, clear steps to take toward the target destination.

One other point: Planning requires true leadership. In this world of instant gratification, it's not easy to accept the truth, which is that you may not even reap the full rewards of a well-executed plan. Understand that it can take years to truly manifest the real, long-lasting results. These are the results that will lead to a legacy, *your* legacy.

Okay, so where do we start?

4.1 START WITH THE END IN MIND

"It's incredibly easy to get caught up in an activity trap, in the busyness of life, to work harder and harder at climbing the ladder of success only to discover that it's leaning against the wrong wall."
—**Stephen Covey**

At this stage, you will know the broad direction in which you wish to travel. You can see the lighthouse flashing in the distance. In addition to your view of the future, you also need to understand where the organization is today, right this moment.

Creating a plan does not require hundreds of pages of notes or years of research until you're certain you've got the right one. Yes, other stakeholders will likely require a more detailed business plan, but that's not for now. Business plans can only be built out once this part of the process is complete.

As a novice runner, I've always loved the analogy of running a marathon to help explain purpose, vision, and the importance of a plan. During a night out ten years ago, I took a friendly bet to run a 10K for charity, even though I hadn't done any running before. My *purpose* was simply to get fitter. My *vision* was crossing the line, preferably before the friend with whom I had made the bet. My plan was to run three times a week to achieve that.

I started with the end in mind: the race in just eight weeks' time. I talked to friends who were runners and they reckoned that I'd need to train three days a week, starting at two miles and building to five. This is exactly what I did, and I achieved my goal.

The following year, spurred by this success and loving how good I felt from all of this activity, I decided to run the Dublin City Marathon. Where did I start? First, by determining my *purpose*, to increase my fitness still further and to inspire my kids to get into sport. My *vision* was to complete the course in under four and a half hours. I sought advice from marathon-running friends and found Hal Higdon's marathon training website. Starting with the end in mind, I pictured myself crossing the line and being presented with my medal. I also needed a clear view of where I was—my existing levels of fitness. The *plan* set out the series of runs I would need to do to bring me to the point where I could run forty-two kilometers (twenty-six miles) without stopping.

Here's a key point: The plan needed to be flexible. One challenge was that I was traveling a lot with work, so at the start of each week, I would have to explore what was practically achievable over the coming days. Which country was I going to? Could I get my run there? Would the hotel have a treadmill? Would late nights with customers upset the plan? Of course, I always made sure to pack my running shoes. My *purpose* informed the *vision*, which drove the *plan*. And the plan dictated my SMART (Specific, Measurable, Attainable, Relevant, and Time-bound) actions and tasks.

Even though I was motivated by the achievement of completing a marathon, I was careful not to let the thought of forty-two kilometers overwhelm me. And this is the power of the plan. It takes a bold, ambitious vision and deconstructs to put it into achievable chunks. In this case, my plan was simple. A five-mile run today, a four-mile run in two days' time, a seven-mile run at the weekend, and so forth. Every run, though a stretch, was both achievable *and* aligned to the vision. I printed it off, and it became incredibly cathartic to tick off each run one after the other. By week eighteen, the forty-two-kilometer run, which could have looked impossibly intimidating at the beginning, simply fell out of the plan.

Our approach within the business was exactly the same.

One of our early visions was to become number one in our sector in the world (the metric we used was revenue versus our competitors'). When we achieved this through our strength in three key markets, we realized that we needed to raise our ambition levels and take the success to the wider world. We would become number one *in every country*. That was the moonshot vision. Big, bold, and inspiring.

Okay, now we break that down.

There are over 200 countries out there; targeting them all was a daunting challenge, and figuring out how to do it gave rise to a lot of robust, healthy debate. We agreed to group those 200 countries into eight strategic regions and created business units that would assume responsibility for revenue growth within each one. These regions were further broken down into what we called hot zones—areas within each region where we would focus our initial effort and resources. Additionally, each strategic region would command a certain level of resource: people—a regional manager, a business development resource, and a service team; infrastructure—offices and spare parts warehousing; and dedicated support from HQ.

Let's look at how this worked in practice.

North America was one of our strategic regions, one that we believed had the best revenue growth potential in the business. And within that region, our assessments suggested Texas—where we already had customers—was the best place to start. We had also established that being perceived as local offered a significant marketing advantage and undergirded our proposition, so it was critical to have boots on the ground. Within a short time, we secured a fantastic office just outside Dallas-Fort Worth, and a regional manager was appointed to support the setup and build out of the team. Internally, we launched a secondment initiative in which people at HQ were encouraged to regional centers for a period. All of these actions were guided by a plan aligned to our overall vision and direction, and it all started by taking the vision and working backward.

Vivid Vision

As discussed in P2 Purpose and Vision, where moonshot is the big, bold, long-term conception of the future, a vivid vision is nearer term—typically, three years out. It is vivid in its construction and brings a little more pixilation, a little more detail, and is a great way of offering a near-term goal that represents substantial progress toward the moonshot. Importantly, it is written with real feeling. It is personal (not corporate), oozing emotions about how this wonderful organization will look, feel, and act in three years' time. Once the moonshot vision is understood and the vivid vision has been crafted, the next step is to consider the strategic pillars.

4.2 IDENTIFY THE STRATEGIC PILLARS TO SUPPORT THE PLAN

Over the last decade, I've spoken with and mentored many CEOs who are overwhelmed by day-to-day tasks and struggle to identify the areas that need consistent focus to deliver the best results. My recommendation is always the same. Group the high-level aims of your business—the aims that, if met, will mean that the vision is realized—into key areas of focus, or what I call strategic pillars. They provide structure, support, and critically, boundaries—delineating what you focus on, to the exclusion of all else. These pillars will touch every part of the organization, such that progress in each will move you toward the achievement of your vision.

A strategic pillar therefore is an area of the organization at which you must excel in order to achieve the overall vision. The good news is, these are broadly the same from business to business. Examples include:

- Business/Revenue Growth—Typically, this will focus on increasing customer numbers or overall export sales revenue

- Operational Excellence—Reducing costs, reducing lead times, or improving quality

- Customer Service Excellence—Improved net promoter score or customer retention

- Technology and Innovation—Percentage of revenue derived from new product development

- World-Class Team Development—Increased revenue and/or profit per employee alongside increased employee satisfaction and improving team retention rates

The strategic differentiator for your organization will be the goals and objectives that are intrinsic to progressing each theme. More about these later in this chapter.

Identifying Strategic Pillars

I took a panicked call one morning from our then-operations director. He had just discovered that our backup disc drive had not been running correctly. There had been a storm during which power at the office had failed. The upshot? Seven months of design material was gone. Just like that.

This was a huge blow.

The root problem was that our IT function, which we had always outsourced, had not grown at the same pace as the rest of the company. IT was still handled by the same three-person firm we had signed up when our total headcount stood at thirty people. Now our team had grown to 300, and that put very significant pressure on an IT infrastructure that could not cope. Now, following the data loss, we began interrogating the extent of the damage across the business. It quickly emerged that our IT was in a complete mess. Not only did we require a huge hardware upgrade, but the software systems in operation across the business, from CRM to accounts, were more or less independent of one another. They were outdated and wholly incapable of scaling. Simply put, if we had serious aspirations to grow rapidly, technology would play a critical role in enabling that. Updating technology then became one of our strategic pillars, a vital component of our scaling strategy.

4.3 MOVE FORWARD WITH CLEAR GOALS, OBJECTIVES, AND KEY RESULTS

"Planning is bringing the future into the present so you can do something about it now."
—Alan Lakein

Let's recap.

We have our moonshot vision (seven- to ten-years time horizon), which captures the long-term focus of the company—our desired landing spot. We also have our vivid vision (three years) from which we extract four or five themes that form our strategic pillars. The next step is to identify the goals that underpin these pillars and the objectives that set our desired outcomes and results toward the attainment of our goals. We also need to know the key results that will gauge progress toward the attainment of objectives and goals.

Goals are statements of desire and capture what you want to achieve within twelve months. They are set annually. A goal is broad and general. We recommend one goal per pillar and that each goal be owned by an accountable person. For example, aligned to the revenue growth pillar, our goal for the next twelve months could simply be "Increase export sales from 30 percent to 40 percent of total revenue," while the accountable person would be the sales lead.

Objectives are aligned to goals and are set quarterly and are narrower in scope. They form the first part of a widely used goal-setting methodology, known as objectives and key results (OKRs). Objectives have a ninety-day time frame. Aligned to our one-year goal to "Increase export sales from 30 percent to 40 percent of total revenue," the quarterly/ninety-day objective could be "Identify and agree on export channel partners."

Key results can be measured on a 0–100 percent scale or other appropriate numerical unit. Progress against each key result is progress toward the overall objective. Key results are measurable and should objectively quantify the success or otherwise of your objective. We will discuss them in more detail in P6 Performance.

- **Strategic Pillar #1:** Operational Excellence

  - **Annual Goal:** Reduce costs of manufacturing by 10 percent

    - **Objective (next ninety days):** Decrease factory overhead by 2 percent in the next ninety days

      - **Key Result 1:** Operations Manager to identify and visit Exemplar Co. and present findings to management team in twenty days

      - **Key Result 2:** Begin ten-minute companywide morning meetings starting next week highlighting initiative to reduce waste in our processes

- **Strategic Pillar #2:** Innovation

  - **Annual Goal:** Increase sales revenue from new products by 15 percent per annum

    - **Objective (next ninety days):** Train sales team in new product releases by the end of this quarter

      - **Key Result 1:** Product Manager to visit customer X and collate five points of feedback on product changes

      - **Key Result 2:** Product Development Manager to record a video highlighting features and benefits of the new product and value to the end customer by end of this month to aid sales training

- **Strategic Pillar #3:** Business Revenue Growth

  - **Annual Goal:** Increase revenue in export sales to South America by 10 percent within the next twelve months

    - **Objective (next ninety days):** Set up the new legal entity in South America

      - **Key Result 1:** Finance Director to appoint advisors to enable the new legal entity to set up (by the end of next month)

      - **Key Result 2:** Factory Manager to shortlist three new potential sites for final selection

To return to our experience after that major data loss, we determined that "World-class business IT" was a strategic pillar for growth. The goal that flowed from this was, "Develop a world-class IT infrastructure." In the early stages, we had only one objective attached to that goal: "To recruit a world-class head of IT who will develop a best-in-class IT strategy." That triggered a successful recruitment, and our new head of IT developed a technology strategy that required significant investment over the following two years. We set a series of new objectives: overhauling our IT infrastructure, enhancing security, and implementing both Microsoft 365 and an integrated ERP system across the business.

Objectives in Action

Our vision, as I said, was to become number one in every country in the world. One of our strategic pillars to support that was revenue growth for the business. This generated an annual goal: grow revenue across all eight strategic regions. Then, within each region, we had clear objectives for revenue attainment.

We used the IDEA criteria to write those objectives:

- **Inspiring.** The objectives should be motivational and aspirational. We liked to ensure our own objectives were unique, bold, and original.

- **Difficult.** Aim high to grow more! The objectives should be "stretchy" and challenging. They should spark healthy discomfort.

- **Explicit.** Be clear in what you're aiming to achieve. This is where the language becomes important.

- **Achievable.** Although "stretchy," you should only confirm objectives that can be accomplished. If they're simply unattainable, then your team will be demotivated from the outset.

When set effectively, your ninety-day company objectives will cascade down through divisions, functions, departments, business units, and individuals. They will be unambiguously aligned with the attainment of your one-year goals, three-year vivid vision, and ten-year moonshot.

I have seen the power of having clear objectives firsthand many times. Well-constructed objectives give a great sense of direction. As Ryan Panchadsaram, founder of whatmatters.com, puts it, when properly designed and deployed, they're a vaccine against fuzzy thinking and fuzzy execution. You do of course have to measure that progress very carefully. We'll talk about that in detail in P6 Performance.

Ultimately, if you can state the purpose of your organization and if you have a clear vision of the future and a strategic plan to get you there, you will have a compelling competitive advantage over all your other competitors. In my last role, we led our industry, and although some competitors copied our products, they couldn't replicate our purpose or our values. They could not clone the culture we built on those values, nor indeed the vision that served as a beacon for our success.

Who's Involved?

Involve key people early in the planning stage in order to get their full engagement. Exactly who the key people are is a matter of judgment; once you get beyond the senior team, there's a little bit of art involved in making the choice. Use your intuition: it's about getting the right mix of support and healthy challenge. As a minimum, the group must include those who will own the plan, those responsible for the delivery of goals. These are the people who will bring the how. Remember, *how* the plan is executed is not your sole responsibility. Nor do you need all the answers at this stage.

Take care not to bring in so many people that some voices are not heard. The last thing you want is a sea of nodding heads—people simply agreeing without fully understanding what they are agreeing to. Be wary, too, of those who struggle with matters of the future and those who don't see what you see. The future is always uncertain; team members who crave certainty in all things will find it hard to sign up to that vision. The room should contain those who are willing to think from the future back and explore the best way to connect that future with the present.

Consider using an external consultant to facilitate the session. I always took the team off-site for a few days, away from the distractions of the office.

You need to emerge from the planning process with a group of company leaders who are passionate about *our* plan and who will champion it and will be cheerleaders for the vision. If it's *your* plan simply delegated downward, it has a much lower chance of succeeding.

4.4 PUT THE RIGHT JOCKEYS ON THE RIGHT HORSES IN THE RIGHT RACE

One of the most profound and rewarding advantages of having a plan is the alignment and clarity it gives the team. In P3 People, we talked about the importance of getting the right people in the right roles. This is critical when it comes to identifying accountable individuals who will successfully execute the plan.

I love cars! When recruiting, I always knew the person was right because of the butterflies-in-the-stomach feeling. I would get as excited at the prospect of working with that person as I would when buying a new car.

As a CEO, one of my favorite events was an annual get-together with another director and shareholder, Enda, and coauthor (then-talent director), Claire. This was our "Horses and Jockeys" meeting. Enda is a passionate horse-racing fan and a highly competitive amateur show jumper, and he always characterized strategy implementation like this: The *right jockeys* are those aligned to company values who are passionate about our vision. They fit the culture and are motivated by the scaling challenge. They face the jumps eagerly and are unafraid of the possibility of falling. The *right horses* are simply the roles that have to be filled to execute the plan. The *right race* is the appropriate market. With the right jockeys on the right horses, you can be confident that they will skillfully navigate the jumps and make it around the course.

So you need to know your team extremely well. You need to know their strengths, their blind spots, how they operate, and the scale of the role most appropriate to them. In practice, this often meant acknowledging that the growth of the business had outstripped their capacity to execute. Or that their skillset lent itself to a technical role rather than a managerial one. This would trigger conversations around either learning and development or a move into another role. And in this process, we always recognized the skill and experience that the person had developed, and we always did our best to redeploy them into a role where they could really shine.

Sometimes, too, it would trigger a compassionate conversation about whether the company was right for the person and the possibility of considering their future elsewhere. This is fine. You must accept that as you scale. There will be long-established team members who will have to acknowledge that this particular race is no longer for them.

The annual "Horses and Jockeys" debate would always see us create new opportunities for existing team members, and our plan was always at the center of conversations with those team members. We discussed opportunities to travel, to learn new skills, and to take on additional responsibilities aligned to the vision. We explored opportunities to create "intrapreneurs" within the business—that is, those with entrepreneurial flair who required a little more freedom from the core business to develop a new region or sector.

This process saw some wonderful synergies as we scaled. One person relocated to South America and within six months had become near fluent in Portuguese. Others moved their families to North America and Australia to embark on new opportunities. One of the great benefits of scaling is undoubtedly the wonderful experiences you can give your team as they execute the plan.

4.5 LEARN THROUGH REGULAR CHECK-INS

"Vision and strategy development is never a 'one-and-done'; leaders must revisit and reshape it continually as their assumptions are tested against reality."
—Mark Johnson and Josh Suskewicz

Back to the family holiday analogy.

Let's assume that our plan is to visit Italy in three months' time. As I write this, in the early days of the COVID-19 pandemic, anyone with this intention would be keeping a watchful eye on the daily news. They would be seeking government advice, talking to their doctor, and checking their travel insurance. And as the situation becomes more serious, alternatives to the original plan would have to be investigated: travel to a less-infected region perhaps or holidaying closer to home.

Planning becomes an iterative process, where we refine and adapt as the situation unfolds. We monitor closely and base those adaptations on the external situation as well as changes in our assumptions, risks, scope, budget, or schedule. In the context of an organization's strategic plan, this process will consider changes in the market conditions, the entrance of a new competitor, a substitute product, or indeed changes in legislation.

In prior roles, I have led the creation and execution of both three- and five-year strategic plans. In all cases, regular six-month reviews of those plans formed a critical part of our overall execution process.

We called these reviews "pit stops," the phraseology inspired by a benchmarking visit to the Mercedes/McLaren factory in Stuttgart, Germany. These pit stops were a way of auditing the plan, an opportunity to check the assumptions, review market conditions, determine the success, or otherwise of various elements of the plan and adapt where necessary.

This often meant stopping some things that weren't working, starting some that we hadn't initially included, and refining those that we agreed were still critical to the business. We asked if we needed to make changes to the crew. We reviewed their skills and resilience. We looked forensically at what was and was not working.

These three-day events followed a WIN format:

- **Willingness** to engage

- **Investigate** options for improvement

- **Navigating** next steps

Day 1 was typically assigned to team development, allowing us to strengthen the bond between team members, checking in on our mindset and general well-being, and assessing everyone's willingness to engage. On day 2, we interrogated the plan, assessed the impact of macro events, and investigated options for improvement. On day 3, we focused on navigating next steps and ensuring we were all aligned and on course.

The six, monthly pit stop process gave us the opportunity to step away from the day-to-day and work *on* the business rather than *in* the business. To put it another way, you will never get a clear picture of the label on the jar if you are always inside it. Always take the time to climb out and take a look. If you're not doing it, no one else is.

A VUCA World

In his book *Creative Destruction*, Richard Foster asserts that the rate at which companies disappear from the S&P 500 is increasing. In 1958, the average life span of a company on the index was sixty-one years. Today, it's eighteen.[44] Given the fast-moving, uncertain world in which we operate, businesses must have the capability to change course quickly. We saw this vividly during the COVID-19 pandemic, when some companies pivoted successfully and thrived, while others were slower to react and paid the price. This is why regular reviews are critical.

During one of our strategic planning pit stops, we concluded that our export strategy was failing. We had thought that the best way to break into new markets was via a distributor network. All of our goals and objectives were built on this strategy. It became clear, however, as we evaluated the evidence, that this was simply not working. Our overall direction and ambition hadn't changed, nor had our vision, but we realized that if we were to achieve that vision, we would have to change our approach. The plan and its goals and objectives were adapted based on the feedback the pit stop forensically analyzed. Without it, without that process of stopping and taking stock, we would have continued as we were. We would have tried to work through the pain of attempting to sell through these failing distributor channels. This, ultimately, would have fatally damaged our capacity to make our vision real.

Changing the plan had serious ramifications for the business. Investment requirements for each of the targeted strategic regions increased as we installed local business development, project management, and service teams. Even though this took longer than we had planned, building our own teams locally and investing in the infrastructure to support both customers and teams within these strategic regions ultimately proved much more successful than the earlier distributor approach.

Vishen Lakhiani is co-founder of educational technology company Mindvalley and author of two bestselling books, *The Code of the Extraordinary Mind* and *The Buddha and the Badass*. He explains that audio content used to form a large part of the 1,000-odd courses that Mindvalley offered. When Amazon bought Audible in 2016, however, the leadership team realized that the existing business model and its associated plan would have to change.

"Audible became super cheap," he explains. "They were going to kill us if we didn't innovate, so we started expanding to video courses. But here's the thing: There's a ridiculously low completion rate in video courses. The industry average is 8 percent. If people aren't completing your program, you're not getting a repeat customer, so we had to innovate on completion rate."

Mindvalley created a new model called Quest, which gamifies the learning process. The result? Dramatically improved course completion rates. Had the company stuck rigidly to its original plan, it's almost certain that it would not be the success it is today.

Regular check-ins on progress allow you to discuss what's going well, what's not going so well, and what best practices are out there to lean on. There is also a significant benefit in bringing the leadership team together regularly to discuss these issues, because it engenders much greater buy-in and ideas. To repeat: *Our* plan is inherently stronger than *my* plan.

In a fast-moving world, plans need continuous adaptation and refinement. I always think of the review process as a visit to the optician, where you're invited to read the chart with its rows of letters and numbers arranged in descending order of size. At first, you may be able to read only the top two rows, but as the optician inserts new lenses, the smaller rows are revealed, and the letters become clearer. Just as with the plan, each check-in should give you greater clarity on the line of sight, another lens creating sharper focus.

Keep It Honest

Encourage a healthy learning culture, one that welcomes these check-ins. Invite constructive challenges to the plan. When we first instigated these reviews, I got quite a bit of resistance from some members of the team. They argued that they simply couldn't afford time out of the market to participate in the process. As time went on, however, they witnessed the benefits for themselves. Resistance died away and was soon replaced with full-blown engagement. As Stephen Covey famously commented, "Make time for planning. Wars are won in the general's tent."

In a 2016 Brookings's briefing about Alan Mulally's work with Ford, Elizabeth Haas Edersheim talks about the weekly business plan reviews (or BPRs) that Mulally instigated when he became head of the ailing motor company in 2006.[45] Attendance was compulsory for the senior team. At the first meeting, after hearing nothing but good news from attendees, Mulally pointed out that the company was set to lose billions that year. Why, he asked, was every line green? Wasn't there anything going badly?

It would emerge later that none of the executives had believed Mulally when he'd promised that honesty in these reviews would not be penalized.

A week later, Mark Fields, then-president of Ford Americas, presented a more truthful projection to the new CEO.

"Fields's slide showed red. There was dead silence. 'Dead man walking,' thought one of his peers. 'I wonder who'll get the Americas,' another mused. Suddenly, someone started clapping. It was Mulally. 'Mark, that's great visibility,' he said, beaming. 'Who can help Mark with this?' Thus was born new collaboration at Ford, born of honest communication."[46]

4.6 EXECUTE WITH RUTHLESS VIGOR

"Strategy...is simply finding the big aha and setting a broad direction, putting the right people behind it, and then executing with an unyielding emphasis on continuous improvement. There's no mystery to it!"
—**Jack Welch**

Planning is good for the mind. The Zeigarnik effect, named after a Russian memory researcher, refers to the phenomenon in which unfulfilled goals and tasks are remembered better than those that are completed. It's those things that you needed to do but never got around to that can generate uneasiness and make it difficult to concentrate on anything else. In a 2011 study in the *Journal of Personality and Social Psychology*, students were asked to make a plan to complete certain personal tasks. The researchers found that students who wrote out their plan were better able to focus on reading a novel than students who were asked simply to think about the tasks they needed to complete. Once there was a plan, their brains could let the matter go and turn to other things.[47]

Jack Welch, the revolutionary former CEO of GE, sums up with this: "In real life, strategy is very straightforward. You pick a general direction and implement like hell."[48]

What does that look like? What does implementing like hell really mean?

First, understand that there's no such thing as the perfect plan. Don't spend months tearing your hair out, trying to arrive at perfection. Perfection, if it can be achieved at all, can happen only through the iterative process of regular amendment following check-ins.

Over the last twenty years, I've created "perfect plans" with detailed thirty-six-month projections on sales, operational costs, profit levels, cash, and a wonderfully presented balance sheet. These lengthy documents were typically made to satisfy other stakeholders or aid financial support, but because they lacked flexibility, they always ended up forgotten at the bottom of the filing cabinet.

By emphasizing execution, it is made clear that the plan is a living, breathing, evolving one, which requires regular review and updating based on things that are going on in real time. Committing to a regular meeting cadence that keeps your team connected to the plan without bogging them down with too many meetings is critical to keep the plan alive and to maintain a healthy team dynamic. Getting these into everyone's diaries well in advance will allow them to prepare.

There is no right or wrong meeting cadence, but the one that has always worked for me is a weekly check-in first thing on Monday morning. These meetings are backed up with biweekly one-on-ones, monthly board meetings, and a quarterly review against the plan and OKRs.

This approach allows for greater "bouncebackability." When unforeseen challenges threaten to derail the plan, the built-in review process assesses and navigates those challenges systematically. A plan that is perceived as perfect at the outset but lacks that flexibility will very quickly be revealed as seriously flawed, with devastating consequences for the business.

TAKE ACTION—IT'S SIMPLE!

Start with the End in Mind. A plan is crafted by taking the end result and deconstructing it into a series of doable steps.

Identify the Strategic Pillars to Support the Plan. Group the high-level themes and priorities of your vision—those that, if met, will mean that the vision is realized—into key areas of focus.

Move Forward with Clear Goals, Objectives, and Key Results. Undergird these pillars first with one-year goals and then into ninety-day objectives and key results.

Put the Right Jockeys on the Right Horses into the Right Race. Ensure that the team members charged with executing the differing elements of the plan are carefully matched with their roles.

Learn through Regular Check-ins. The plan should not be set in stone. The CEO and the senior team need to take time out from working in the business to ensure that the plan is still fit for its purpose.

Execute with Ruthless Vigor. Don't get hung up on the perfect plan. In the words of Jack Welch, "Implement like hell."

Principle in Action—
Brian Quinn, Intel Ireland

Brian Quinn spent twenty years in Intel, during which time he developed a unique insight into the corporate planning process. Within the company, he taught strategy up to senior management level. He spent most of his senior leadership time in Intel Labs and participated extensively in the planning processes of Intel Labs Europe. He explains that Intel Labs—which employed circa 1,100 people—has a lot in common with an SME. They are empowered to create their own vision—aligned with the Intel vision—and their own agenda. The plan designed to realize that vision is built around four or five key deliverables under a methodology called MBOs: management by objectives. These were mapped out over a twelve-month period and included measurable quarterly objectives that were assigned to individuals. Brian explains how the planning process was managed.

RUNNING THE MEETING
In these situations, to give a new twist to Simon Sinek's idea, the leader *speaks* last. You stay schtum for forty minutes after you've set the scene. Why? Because you'll be amazed at how restrictive you make a conversation as soon as you start zeroing in on one thing or another. Understand the power of what you say will unleash. Let everyone thrash out the issues before you ride in.

Be aware of team dynamics. The natural competitiveness in your leadership team will come out in the planning stage. You frequently have two people with similar characters, of a similar age, and similar ambition, who see each other as the competition. So in planning sessions, they can tend to out-ambition each other. "Twenty-five percent? We could do fifty!"

If you don't manage it—and I saw it left unmanaged many times—it will crash the team. That team does not have to be composed of bosom buddies; rivalry and competition can be good, but you do have to watch it and make sure that it doesn't turn into a negative dynamic in either your planning or your execution.

Other little tips: Have food available. Take three breaks instead of one. Take everyone off-site. No phones and no laptops. If a team is focused on their expert area for months on end, getting them to switch off the laptops and focus on something very different can be a challenge. To help this, I sometimes brought in SME CEOs to tell their story. That would change the atmosphere and get people onto a different mindset.

There are always those who are assertive and articulate and will dominate the meeting if you let them. It's crucial that those who are more reserved get a chance to speak as well. The process must be inclusive and diverse. You can't leave the meeting until everyone has had their say.

BUY-IN

Suppose our twelve-person leadership team in Labs Europe decides we're going to go after sensor integration, because sensors are important to the internet of things, which in turn is important to sustainability—a key element of the Intel vision. We look at the state of the art in this discipline and take that as our reference point. Just as an SME would, we look at what the competition is doing, and we make sure that we don't try to do what they did last year. Rather, we aim to go beyond state of the art and align to an Intel value.

The twelve-person group includes our sensor team lead, who will be a key figure in helping to determine what's achievable over the coming twelve months. We discuss this in depth, and at the end of that meeting, we have a target—a 25 percent improvement on the best sensor integration model that is out there at the moment. A key point is that ultimately, that objective is down to the judgment of the leader. As soon as that meeting is over, I have that buy-in. The meeting doesn't end without it. That's one of the ground rules. If you're my sensor guy, you don't let me out of that room unless you're happy with 25 percent. You know that I'm going to the chief technology officer immediately after the meeting, so we can't have a situation where I come back to you and say, "We've got acceptance on the 25 percent," only for you to say, "Oh no, what did you say that for?"

One thing I found really helpful in planning, and in all management for that matter, was reflective listening. This is a communication strategy designed to prevent misunderstanding. I mentioned that I know I've got buy-in when I leave the room. But what if the 25 percent improvement in sensor integration means something different to the sensor integration lead who has committed to it? What if they thought it was from a different base? To prevent this, you always check your understanding. So I would ask that person to write it up and send me a precise account of what we've agreed. Alternatively, I would say, "Okay, let me replay that to you so that we both know what's being committed to here."

ACCOUNTABILITY

Two things are fundamental to the success of a planning process: ambition and clarity. You've got to have ambition in what you want to achieve. And everyone must understand completely what's expected of them. This perhaps was the most challenging part of the process. You have some very strong-willed, very intelligent people, with up to twenty years' experience. Sometimes they'll try to game the system a little. They'll sandbag; they'll try to spread their bets. Managing that dynamic was probably the hardest thing. Pinning down highly talented technical people on what they're going to do in twelve months was frequently difficult. They fought for wiggle room. They would say, "Maybe we can do between 5 percent and 20 percent" or "If this turns out to be the wrong approach, we'll do this instead."

Accountability is vital, too, of course. Sometimes you will not get consensus on the plan. It is preferable, but it's not essential. Here's another phrase from my planning days in Intel: disagree and commit. It's a tough one because you're asking intelligent, independent, proud managers—leaders in your team—to override their own views and instincts in order to commit to the plan.

Everyone who was accountable for an objective was in the room and engaged in the planning process. You would never emerge from the meeting and hand an objective to someone and say, "Right, you're accountable for this." To repeat, all accountable people must be in the room.

EXECUTION

It's a cliché, but it's true: As a leader, you communicate, communicate, communicate.

It's absolutely vital to have full clarity and understanding on the objective. I met with my team once every two weeks, at a minimum, to formally review objectives. And within that, we would have plenty of corridor conversations or instant messenger conversations. That's part of the process and part of the management. In addition, you would also have team reviews, where, for example, the sensor team would come in and present. Here are our objectives. We are *here* in relation to them. To facilitate that process, we had a number of different dashboards and mechanisms built in around the objective.

AVOIDING TUNNEL VISION

Intel is a corporation with 110,000 employees and a market capitalization in excess of £133 billion ($200 billion). How can you make sure that it doesn't get so focused on its twelve-month objectives that it ignores a changing world? You need laser focus on your objectives, but if you don't keep tabs on what's happening in the rest of the world, you risk being left behind. This was a pitfall into which the company stumbled more than once. It became so fixated on the agreed goals that it failed to react to underlying movements in the market.

The company developed a number of processes to mitigate that risk. One of those was a brilliant initiative called TSLRP—Technology Strategic Long-Range Plan. It was a very fancy title, but in essence, it worked like this: Anybody in the corporation could write up a proposal at any time, present it for review, and have it progressed up the chain.

So suppose you're an engineer in Stuttgart and you think autonomous driving is going to be huge. Intel isn't in autonomous driving. So you write up your thoughts via an online submission form and specify how it would benefit Intel. That part was critical. These submissions were reviewed by technical leaders. If they saw merit in an idea, it was then taken through a process. Once every six months, the twelve best ideas that emerged from the process were presented to the executive management leadership team. Several times, the company changed direction as a result of something that emerged from it.

Unless something came from the TSLRP process, it was a case of right, we're in these swim lanes, and we're continuing with the objectives to get us further down the pool. This parallel process not only allowed new ideas to emerge, but it also prevented shiny new things from interfering with established trajectories.

One other point: Process isn't everything. Culture is vital, and things are at their best when process and culture overlap. The TSLRP process presented a culture that says, "We're not dumbing you down with the management by objectives. We are listening to what's going on outside these swim lanes. You can start a conversation, your ideas are welcome, and they can be hugely influential."

You're trying to move from a culture of "Keep your head down, get your objectives done this quarter, or else." Yes, you've got to do them, but we have an eye on the bigger picture as well.

P4 ACTIONS TO TAKE:

_____

_____

_____

_____

_____

_____

_____

_____

_____

_____

_____

_____

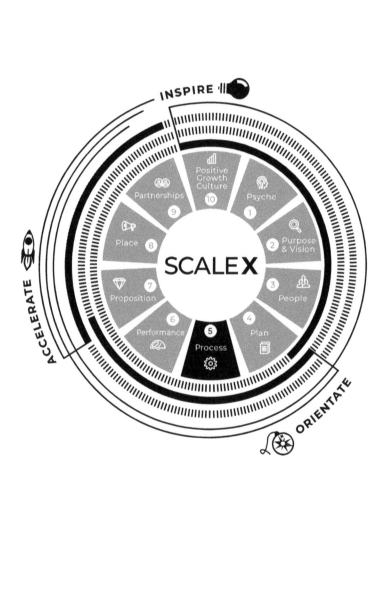

P5
PROCESS

"We don't rise to the level of our goals; we fall to the level of our systems."

—James Clear

RAISE YOUR HAND IF ANY OF THIS SOUNDS FAMILIAR:

The sales lead makes the sale, gets the order signed, then moves on to the next potential customer.

Weeks pass and the customer realizes that nothing has happened. So he calls the sales lead—his only point of contact with the company—and says, "I haven't heard anything from you guys. What's happening with my project?"

The sales lead says, "Oh…okay, don't worry, I'll sort this out."

He calls the technical team, who tell him, "Oh, we've spec'd it and passed it on to design." So he calls the design team, who tell him, "It's finished with us. Try procurement."

So he tries procurement. They say they've sourced the materials and that the orders have gone to the fabricators.

"Try them," he's told.

He's spent the morning being shunted from one person to the next, running an errand he doesn't want to run, and getting zero return on his efforts. So what does he do? He calls the customer and reassures them that things are going fine and that all will be well.

This is probably the high point of the whole project, because from here, things only get worse. The sales lead becomes the de facto project manager but without actually being responsible for delivering the project. Although he's now busy doing a job he doesn't want to do, he's *not* out there doing what he's supposed to be doing, and that implies a substantial cost to the company. And all the while, the lack of internal accountability is a ticking time bomb.

Cut to the delivery date, when all of the expensive heavy engineering is due to arrive at the customer's site. The crane (typically costing in the region of £500 [$750] per day) is in place and the commissioning team is ready to spring into action. But lo and behold, sizes are wrong and holes are drilled in the wrong places. Nothing fits together. The crane driver is sitting there, feet up on the dashboard, reading the paper, delighted with this unexpected holiday.

In that moment, customer confidence disappears and out come the torches and the pitchforks.

Now the sales lead—still the only point of contact—is screaming down the phone to design, or technical, or procurement, or whoever. "Give the customer what he needs—whatever he needs—just to rescue this disaster!" And if the sales lead happens to be the founder, all of the above is amplified. Other projects are relegated to secondary status as everyone tries to shield the boss from the results of weak or nonexistent processes.

That was us, that was our company.

I should say that we always managed to deliver for the customer. We wrapped our arms around them and made sure that everything turned out well in the end. But we unintentionally put them through hell to get there. What's more, we put ourselves through hell. In P2 Purpose and Vision, we wrote that the discretionary effort that motivated people are willing to give is the most important asset in your business. That asset is squandered in this febrile atmosphere, as the team is forced to work long hours to redeem the situation. In the end, there would be so much acrimony and blame that no one would escape without shrapnel wounds. Monies were withheld, expensive equipment sat idle on-site, and too often, it became a case of delivering at all costs. The customer might have ordered a family saloon, but because we frustrated them so much during delivery, the only way to salvage the situation would be to deliver a Rolls Royce. Projects would finish with half of the budgeted project margin.

And because the experience was so fraught, there was no great inclination to follow up post-handover for fear of what might come at you. After-sales was an afterthought, something that could only react to customer requests.

SETTING THE PLATFORM ALIGHT

The global financial crisis—that was what set fire to our platform and forced us to change. We won a project right on the cusp of the meltdown; a project that we had no right to win. Not only that, but at over €2 million ($2.3 million), it was one of the largest European projects we'd ever won.

It was based in Bulgaria. Our regional sales lead had done a fantastic job of nursing the customer toward a close. He introduced me to my opposite number—let's call him Alan—and we quickly established a great rapport. When it came down to the final day, when he was due to sign, it was very clear that something was wrong. He was very agitated and kept standing up and leaving the room for no clear reason. We too were extremely nervous. As the financial crisis took hold, the pipeline completely dried up, and we knew that if we didn't sign that day, we would be in very deep trouble, to put it politely. I was doing my best not to give that impression, of course. As far as Alan was concerned, everything was great, the future was bright, and we were full of confidence.

Eventually, I asked him if he was okay.

He told us that the company had just announced a CapEx freeze. Although his co-directors were against signing the contract with us, they had empowered him to make the call. He shrugged and said, "I don't know what to do."

So I explained that this was a great project, an amazing project, and that he had to sign, and we would not let him down. We eye-balled each other. and eventually he said, "Okay, I'm going to do it. I believe in you guys."

This was just before Christmas in 2008. The last thing Alan said to me before we left was, "Please make this a really successful project." It was quite clear that his career was on the line.

There were shivers running down my spine as I shook hands with him and said, "Don't worry, Alan. We will deliver a world-class project."

I sat bolt upright the whole way home in the plane. *How do we sort our project delivery? How do I ensure we keep the promise I've just made?*

5.1 SIMPLIFY EVERYTHING

We were a sixty-person company at the time. When I got home, I gathered everyone into a room. I explained that the financial crisis had made forecasting future work exceptionally difficult but that we had been gifted a lifeline.

"We now have to do something we've always struggled to do. We have to deliver under budget and on time. And we also have to deliver to the very highest quality standards."

This may not sound contentious, but in the context of what we had been doing, it was fantastical. Up to this point, the accepted wisdom in the company was that if you wanted to deliver quality, you had to go over budget. Now we were saying, "No, not anymore; that's over. This needs to win on all three: quality, cost, and delivery."

There were a couple of catalysts for what happened next. One was something the legal guy had said during the negotiation or rather, a question he had asked.

"Who's going to be the Spock on this project?"

I had looked at him, puzzled. Was this a mispronunciation? Some kind of Star Trek reference? Then he spelled it out for me: SPOC, single point of contact.

Single point of contact.

It was so brilliant and yet so simple that I felt inspired and stupid at the same time. One person responsible for delivery. One person who would stand in the customer's shoes within the company. One person who would keep them posted about what was happening and coordinate everything so that when delivery day came, there were no nasty surprises, no mismatches, and no impromptu holidays for crane drivers.

That was the first thing.

The second was something I read about: the simplicity (there's that word again) of business. Everything—*everything*—comes down to three processes:

- Win the business

- Deliver the business

- Support the customer's success

The critical point here is that everything within the business supports these three functions. HR, finance, marketing, technical, design, procurement—everything.

Win the business. We were good at that, and in any case, I had a horrible sense that there would be no more business to be won until the economic storm passed. So all of our focus went onto the second stage. Deliver the business.

Believe it or not, the next thing I did was simply search the phrase "project management" online. I already knew the points at which the customer would withhold money because they expected one thing and got another. I knew we had to establish a series of incremental sign-offs—at technical stage, at design stage, at procurement. Transparency would have to be built in so that expectations were always in line with reality.

Then and there, I wrote out a process for a project management methodology. We shortened it to pro-man. To be clear, this wasn't gendered; the "man" was an abbreviation of "management."

Rather than waiting for everything to get on-site and have the customer shout at us, we would assign a pro-man (manager), who would represent the customer's interests internally. They would manage the interface between functions within the business that were responsible for the delivery of the project. They would liaise with those functions; they would understand what was happening at all times. They would communicate proactively with the customer on a weekly basis and let the customer know exactly what was going on. They would agree to a timeline of delivery at the outset so that expectations were managed. And they would communicate that timeline internally while coordinating all of the different functions.

This meant that once the sale was made, the salesperson could shake hands with the customer and say, "Thank you very much, Mr. Customer. You are now dealing with Anne here who is going to deliver your project. All communications from here on in will be with Anne." They might drop back for a cup of tea and shake hands at some point, but their involvement with the project would cease. They could now get back to their core role: selling.

The first thing that the project manager would do was take the order acknowledgment form and have a kickoff meeting with the customer. They would say, "Mr. Customer, this is what you've been sold. Is this your understanding?"

That question alone was enough to flush out the hornets' nest of misunderstandings that had plagued projects before this. There was a tendency for salespeople to overpromise at the closing meeting, but again, that would not emerge until late in the project. Now, however, the creation of this new role, accompanied by a simple handover process, meant that any issues could be nipped in the bud.

So here's the key point: Processes don't stifle; they liberate. Process guru David Jenyns, whom we talk to in more detail later, puts it like this: "Systems set you free."

You Can't Scale without Process

Some of the biggest corporations in existence today began as startups, but they didn't reach their current size by working proportionally harder. Instead, their leaders created smart processes with scaling in mind. Smart processes allow you to hire a new employee, provide instructions on how to perform a task, and get consistent results within days rather than months. In short, processes and systems play a fundamental role in the transition from startup to a scale-up.

Look at it like this: The founder/CEO may have the necessary expertise to do everything the business needs at the outset, but soon, it becomes necessary to bring in marketing expertise and perhaps an expert on the sales side. Once sales start to ramp up, you'll need operational and finance expertise. A single product or service may become a range, generating a need for additional production support. Attracting the best people, issuing contracts of employment, inducting a new team, and retaining them may then generate a need for HR. Your customers want to see evidence of your quality systems, health and safety, data protection, and so on, so you need to bring in the resources to meet *these* demands.

All of this creates complexity. Moreover, these myriad demands beget a range of other questions. Is our health and safety good enough? You are accumulating a lot of data and information, but is it secure? Are your suppliers good enough? Do they have the capacity to meet your demands as you scale?

You don't have to look too hard to discover the adverse impact of systems failure or indeed the complete absence of systems. In October 2019, GoPro cut its revenue forecasts following a production delay in its latest cameras. This triggered a 19 percent drop in the share price.[49] Nor does Wall Street view data breaches benignly. According to a ZDNet analysis, when a company discloses a data breach, its average share price falls by 7.27 percent.[50] Supply chain failures, too, can cripple the most robust company. Toy company Mattel took a huge reputational hit in 2007 when the US Consumer Product Safety Commission forced it to withdraw millions of toys because of design faults and concerns over lead paint.[51]

As you scale, your processes must handle significant increases in demand. That means that you need to identify those processes, strip out unnecessary complexity, and automate as much as you can.

5.2 IMPLEMENT CUSTOMER-FOR-LIFE PROCESSES

Process saved our company. The pro-man strategy, which effectively systemized that second step, delivering the business, meant that we completed the Bulgarian project to the very highest standards. The customer was delighted. And crucially, for the first time in our history, we delivered a large project on time and within budget.

The whole experience showed that if we did everything in those three overarching processes right, we would have a customer for life, so that's what we called it: the customer-for-life process. Win the business, deliver the business, look after the customer. If you do these things properly, the customer never needs to leave you.

We would go on to have customers that bought five, six, and seven projects from us. Why? Because they had no reason not to.

When we implemented this system, we stopped losing customers. Well, I can think of one exception. We had a UK customer who said, "Come on, guys. I've given you the last four projects. I need to go to the competitor."

So he tried that, but it was such a negative experience that he came back to us for the next three projects.

We've already discussed "deliver the business," so let's look at "win the business" and then "look after the customer."

Win the Business

It's simple. Without sales, there is no requirement for any other function. In the days before digital marketing, winning customers meant lots of door knocking and a lengthy sales process. Some of the projects that we chased could take anything from six months to six years to actually land. Sales lead information, together with pricing information, was typically captured in the classic black book of contacts. These books were eventually supplanted by spreadsheets held on company servers.

Project pricing was also erratic. For a number of years, we would watch our margin shrink bit by bit as invoiced costs trickled in with dismal familiarity.

This taught us to begin streamlining pricing, creating a centralized system—based around spreadsheets initially—in an attempt to capture all project costs up front before a price was agreed with the customer. Every project presented a learning opportunity to refine our pricing and get more accuracy into our costs. As we grew, we created a separate department for project pricing. Although it was independent of sales, members of the sales team—depending on seniority—would still have visibility on costs and margins.

Eventually, too, we outgrew our spreadsheets and implemented a CRM system. Getting a sense of the sales pipeline allowed us to begin assigning probabilities to winning each sale, and that allowed us to forecast future sales. This was powerful in that it justified the allocation of resources. We could invest in our vision with much greater confidence. Project business is notoriously difficult to forecast, but bringing this level of rigor to the process of capturing and interrogating the data did give some comfort to stakeholders.

The process of creating and sharing design drawings with customers and potential customers also evolved over time. In the early stages, we simply gave the customer what they asked for. Scores of drawings, which took considerable resources to produce, could be handed over without any assessment of whether the customer was likely to purchase.

In the early stages, this approach allowed us to win business over our larger, less agile, and more complacent competitors. But as we grew, we realized we would need to install processes to aid better qualification of sales leads and would guide the level of investment we would make in each lead. Designs also became more streamlined. We invested heavily in software, which would allow the sales team to send indicative design layouts. These didn't require the support of the design team, which meant they could channel their valuable time into high-probability/-value sales leads.

Support the Customer's Success

Because project delivery was often damaging, there was limited desire to have much contact with the customer once we'd finished up and handed over. This meant there was no appetite for customer care, and when a customer called looking for parts or support, we did not make things easy for them.

That stopped.

Under the new dispensation, customers changed their tune completely. "That was a great project! We're delighted with how it's been delivered. Now, how can you guys help us to get the most from it?"

This was the third element to the customer-for-life process. We established a proactive, custom-care function to actively support our customers after handover. We developed it to the point where we would target a certain percentage of revenue every year from after-sales support. And we innovated with great relish. We created an internet of things; customers were given an app that sent them all sorts of data about how the asset was performing: productivity, downtime, and so on.

We created what we called asset-care packages, which were essentially annual maintenance contracts. We could say, "Right, this asset that you've invested in? You'll need to maintain that over its life, and we can help you with that, too." Because projects were delivered more smoothly, the customer had sufficient confidence to sign up further.

One example was the Custom Care Cabin. At a big mining project in southern Australia, we delivered a container fully stocked with parts. This was connected directly with our ERP system. When a spare part was removed on-site, the cost was logged and a new part dispatched to take its place. You can't imagine how useful this was in a location that was six days' drive from anywhere. When anyone asked, "How can you support us from the other side of the world?" we had a compelling response ready to go.

We created different levels of customer care depending on requirements. And this great after-sales experience fed directly into the presale process for the next project.

That's the other thing. The whole customer-for-life process was self-fulfilling. Once you had accountable people in each of these three overarching functions, things worked much more smoothly. It was no more complicated than winning the business and having somebody accountable on the winning-the-business side. Then delivering the business and having someone accountable on the delivering-the-business side. Then maintaining the relationship and supporting the customer (identifying needs rather than reacting to demands) on the aftercare side once you deliver what you said you were going to deliver. Do that world class each and every time and the customer stays with you and tells everyone how great you are.

I can't understate either the simplicity or the success of the customer-for-life process. It was a game changer. We filed a loss of just under £500,000 ($750,000) in 2008. In 2009, our small team, determined to conquer the recession, established pro-man. That same year, we returned a £600,000 ($900,000) profit on just over 40 percent of 2008 revenue.

And in the ten years that followed, our processes supported the delivery of almost £500 million ($750 million) in revenue across literally hundreds of projects.

5.3 MAP YOUR PROCESSES

David Jenyns is *the* process guru. A protégé of Michael Gerber (author of the famous *E-Myth*), David's book *SYSTEMology*[52] sets out in clear and simple terms exactly how to go about imposing order on the chaos that so often characterizes business processes. Each of the seven steps in his methodology has been designed to challenge the misconceptions people have around systems.

He says, "So often, founders and visionary thinkers believe 'I'm not a systems person.' They'll look at a franchise business and think, 'That's what systems-run businesses looks like.'"

The reality of course is very different. Every business has the potential to be a process business. Allowing it to become a process business, far from stifling it, actually unshackles it.

"The biggest trouble that visionary creatives have is transitioning from having a small team around them to removing themselves from the operations, systemizing, and building for scale." So often, we see the visionary "fire starter" become the arsonist simply because of their inability to set the matches down.

David sets out the seven steps in his methodology.

1. Define

This stage is all about identifying the "critical client flow" of the business, which is the series of linear steps from claiming the client's attention through to delivering the business and aftercare. As David points out, you will not create anything new at this stage; you're merely uncovering what you're already doing. "Poor recruiting systems will lead to staffing issues, poor financial systems will lead to cash flow issues, and poor marketing systems will lead to lead flow issues. All problems within business are, ultimately, caused by poorly performing systems. And the first step to improving them is to become aware of their existence. See your business as a collection of interconnected systems."

2. Assign

"If your business can't run without you, if you can't deliver the core product or service or run the critical client flow without the business owner, then the business is broken, because it will always fall back on that person's shoulders." This stage is all about locating the knowledgeable person in each department, finding out where all of the information about key tasks lies.

3. Extract

The third stage sets out to capture the knowledge from your team and to turn it into a shareable system. Critically, this is a two-person job. One person shares their knowledge (the knowledgeable worker) and another documents it (your systems champion). Start with one particular task or function, with a view to using the same approach to document all of the other processes within the business. Use the appropriate tech to capture the info: screen record, audio, video, and so on. If confidentiality makes this difficult, role-play the process. You then document and review.

4. Organize

The fourth stage in *SYSTEMology* is to organize the systems you have captured and implement the right technology to ensure your team actually follows them. As David points out, systems-run businesses are worth more because they run without key-person dependency.

5. Integrate

Now you need to get buy-in. "Positioning the benefits of the new initiative in relation to the individual, rather than the company, is one of the secrets to making this work." People are more likely to support what they help to create.

6. Scale

The next stage is to extract and organize the systems required to scale your business. "The goal is to get your business to a point where there is no single-person dependency and you're well positioned to leverage every opportunity that comes your way."

7. Optimize

This is all about creating a dashboard that gives visibility into your fledgling processes and setting out to make them as good as they can be. The Kaizen ethos of continual improvement—which I'm going to talk about in more detail in the next section—is embedded in David's methodology. "We identify the problems, make system improvements, and then monitor the results. When the team becomes unconsciously competent in this skill, it unlocks the door to complete business reliability."

5.4 PURSUE CONTINUOUS IMPROVEMENT

In the past, because our projects were always fraught with issues, there was no appetite to review and figure out what we did wrong—or what we did right. This led to repeated stupid mistakes. For example, equipment would arrive at a far-flung customer site with a UK electrical spec rather than the local one. If this happened once, you would forgive it, but it happened again and again. We simply weren't capturing all of the information that these experiences were generating.

That stopped.

At the end of each project, the pro-man brought everyone together and talked openly about what went right and what went wrong. We captured the good, the bad, and the ugly and amended processes to ensure we got it right the next time around. You checked a box to say which country the equipment was destined for, and that would trigger the required specification for that country, which we had gathered through experience, customer conversations, and relevant research. For example: Equipment going to Australia? That meant painting handrails yellow.

Again, it was a simple but a highly effective initiative. Now we could say, "We did this really well. Let's continue to nail it. But we didn't do this bit well at all. What do we need to do to nail it the next time?" These reviews helped to create an open and challenging culture aligned to our "Do it right" value. They also generated incremental improvements to our processes that eliminated cost and stress in one fell swoop.

For example: Projects would be delivered and working perfectly for six months, but the customer would retain 10 to 20 percent of the contract value simply because they hadn't received end-user manuals. Now we made sure that handing over the manuals was built in as a check and that the customer got a form in which they were required to confirm that they had received the manuals. We had checks and sign-offs established at every turn to ensure that quality, delivery, and cost were managed simultaneously at each stage of the process. Nasty surprises were eliminated—for us and for the customer.

We built our own factory and brought all of the subcontracted fabrication in-house.

Invariably, when you build big, engineered products from scratch, things go wrong. But now, we could sort those out under our own roof and not under the glare of the customer on delivery day. And now, too, any order that left the factory was accompanied by an assembly engineer, who had supervised the assembly of the equipment in the factory and would now oversee its reassembly on-site. It was great for these guys because it gave them an opportunity for global travel.

Paul Akers of FastCap is unquestionably a process genius. In our Principle in Action section at the end of this chapter, he takes us through his thinking and methodology, of which "continuous improvement" is a key tenet. You never stop refining; you never stop making things better.

The project review process fueled the same imperative in our company. At the beginning—during the recession—we didn't want to let anyone go, so we redeployed our resources. Engineers and facilities people became project managers. But as we grew, project management became a separate function with its own manager. In fact, the process worked so well that it became a USP, to the point where customers would approach us and say, "Sorry, I've been a bit naughty. I didn't buy your product. I bought something a bit cheaper elsewhere. Could you guys do the project management for me?"

Vulnerability at Point of Handover

You implement; you learn. We discovered the vulnerabilities that exist at the junctions between winning and delivering the business and, likewise, between delivering the business and looking after the customer. I mentioned earlier how the temptation to overpromise at closure can lead to mismanaged expectations during delivery. In the bigger projects, we began introducing the project manager *before* the project was won so that they were exposed to the final contract negotiations and so that they could get a deeper understanding of customer requirements. This generated a more seamless handover.

And likewise, depending again on the scale of the project, the pro-man would introduce the customer care person at the right moment. They'd say, "Look, we're going to be up and running in four weeks' time. Let's now have a conversation about how to maximize the uptime and minimize the downtime." In some of these projects, an hour of downtime can cost tens of thousands of dollars. Ensuring adequate maintenance and repair was critical from the get-go.

In time, both project management and customer care functions became so central to our business model that they were brought in at technical presales to present to potential customers as part of our overall value proposition.

Innovate for Continuous Improvement

Within each function, we incentivized innovation. Take finance, for example. First, you've got to ensure everyone understands why they're there. And why are they there? To enable the customer-for-life process. So they're always asking, "How can it be made smoother?" There's a point in the cycle at which nothing can happen until the customer signs off and pays the invoice. Okay, so let's make sure the customer has the invoice early. Let's make sure there's a communication to let them know that the invoice is coming. Let's make sure we don't upset the customer. Let's ensure that the customer is told that if it's not paid by this date, it's going to delay the project. Let's ensure that the administration of letters of credit do not impede the project.

It's the same in HR. They identify the skills requirements that enable the methodology. Then they innovate and recruit in full alignment with that methodology.

5.5 LEAD WITH THE RIGHT ORGANIZATIONAL STRUCTURE

With the customer-for-life process now at the heart of how we worked, the organizational structure had to adapt so that it, like everything else in the business, became an enabler rather than an impediment.

Let's just mention that original vision again: To become the number one company in our sector in every country across the globe. For that to happen, these three overarching functions have to become world class. And within that, everyone has a role to play. If you're the stores guy, you've got to be the world-class stores guy. If you're the person responsible for installing the plant on-site, then be the world-class installation person. For this to work, everyone has to have an understanding of the importance of their role in relation to the overall vision *and* the customer-for-life process. And that role is critical regardless of title, pay grade, or whatever.

No more "I'm just doing what I'm told, boss." Your role begins not with an instruction but with an understanding. The customer-for-life process is how we become number one. This is all about passing the ball through the organization. You receive it, you execute brilliantly, and you pass it on.

The organization becomes flatter simply because everybody's working in a line toward the vision. We're all working for our customer. Everybody's signed up to the same goal: delivering the next project in the best way that it can be delivered. Because there's an understanding that if we do that, it will move us one step closer to becoming number one in that country. With a hierarchical structure, your line of sight is blocked; only the guy at the top can see the vision. But if everything is flat, *everybody* can see the vision; we all know what we're aiming for.

David Jenyns agrees. "In larger organizations, hierarchy might make more sense, but if you're talking about between ten and sixty staff, I don't think it's helpful. You still have a leadership team to direct strategic vision, and then below that you have department teams and department heads.

"Everyone has individual goals and objectives arranged under a common vision. Everybody is responsible for their set of numbers. We know what we're looking to achieve, and everybody has got their bit to play. You want the team member to understand where they operate in the critical client flow. *I* need to understand that if the people before me drop the ball, they make my job harder. And if I drop the ball, that makes the job harder for those who follow me. So you get high levels of transparency about your role in the process."

Leadership

Traditional leadership models have changed beyond recognition. As one Silicon Valley CEO put it, "There is absolutely nothing wrong with command and control leadership, it's simply irrelevant in the twenty-first century."[53]

Hierarchical, authority-based organizational structures just aren't fit for purpose anymore. Today, good leadership is about motivating the team to cooperate and engage to achieve the best end result. Today's strong leader doesn't need to enhance personal power or rely on self-promotion. We follow leaders not because of their authority but because of who they are, what they stand for, and most importantly, the example they provide.

Today's effective leader needs the skills to:

- Build a culture of trust

- Understand the constraints under which their team operates

- Create realistic plans around achieving goals

- Make commitments based on capacity available

- Work across functions regardless of their level on the traditional org chart

Traditional leaders were more concerned with projecting strength, status, and authority. Today's effective leader taps into the power of emotion to create the kind of work-based relationships that facilitate getting stuff done.

And structures need to reflect that. Good structures illustrate how your processes flow, end to end, throughout your business, showing how your product or service is delivered to your customer. A structure that tells your operational story and illustrates how the different functions and processes interact to deliver the end goal will bring you the greatest value.

5.6 EMBED A PROCESS CULTURE

"The myth that systemization destroys creativity stems from the idea that systems turn everyone into robots, incapable of original thought. This is just flat-out wrong. In reality, systems create space, and space opens doors to creativity, inspiration, and opportunity."
—**David Jenyns**

In addition to implementing project reviews, our half-yearly pit stops reaffirmed that the customer-for-life process was how we were delivering on our overall vision. We clarified our understanding of our purpose, our vision, and the processes that would get us there.

More critical than that, however, was the establishment of a culture where process and its value were universally understood. It's about making everyone alive to the possibilities so that if they spot a way in which a process can be improved, they make that change.

Although those half-yearly reviews worked for us, David Jenyns isn't a huge fan. He points out how easy it is for reviews to lose their place in the diary when there's so much else going on.

"Systems need to be simple enough that even if one person owns it, everybody can comment and find ways of making things better. Then, once you get base systems in place, it's all about spotting all of the other problems in the business and thinking about them with a systems mindset, realizing that *this* problem is caused by a lack of a system, or a poorly documented system, or something that remains trapped in someone's head."

Everyone needs to understand the vital role of process in making things work and making things work brilliantly. For that reason, process improvement needs to be adopted as a corporate value. "It can't just rest on the shoulders of one or two team members because if it is, things will be missed, and there will be bottlenecks."

He goes on, "I used to think of values as a bit airy-fairy. The longer I'm in business, however, the more I realize that you've got to get a clear vision for the business that you are building, and as the leader, you have to communicate that. Once that's done, identifying your values is key because that helps you figure out who to hire and fire, and what your nonnegotiables are. Obviously, these values have to be real, they have to be lived. Values are not marketing bumf. Values only work if they are kept front and center."

Founder of Vivid Vision and the COO Alliance Cameron Herold describes an experience shared with him by a past mentor, Greg Johnston. At one time, Greg was in a leadership position in Starbucks and reported directly to then-CEO Howard Schultz.

One evening, Howard called Greg, upset that one of the letters on one of the Starbucks signs wasn't lighting up. He asked why, and Greg replied that he wasn't going to answer that question because it wasn't a leadership question. Howard asked, "So what would the leadership question be?"

"The leadership question would be, what system do we have in place to ensure that every letter on every sign at every location is always working? That's a question I'm willing to dig into."

At that time, Starbucks had 14,300 locations, and Greg wasn't going to spend his time worrying about one letter in one location.

In a scaling SME, we need to step our leadership thinking up a couple of notches. We need to look for the missing or broken systems and put the right systems in place, systems that ensure corrective action is taken as needs be. Once we do this and we assign accountability to the management of these systems, we preserve our time, our energy, and our focus on scaling our business.

Buy-in

Imposing structure on things didn't harm the agility of the business in any way. In fact, I would say that it actually stabilized the business. It created a USP and a stark differentiator between us and the competition. Yes, sometimes there were customers who kicked back and who asked, "Why do I have to sign this?" And yes, some of the old guard might have felt a little stifled, but these issues were nothing besides the compelling need to change. And once these processes were established, new hires knew nothing else, so there were no olden days to hark back to.

In P1 Psyche, we talked to Sebastian Bates about how he scaled his martial arts business, The Warrior Academy. He's ideally positioned to talk about just how liberating great processes can be.

"We were getting married in Lake Garda in Italy in 2019, and just before the wedding, a sales rep left at a very critical point in the year. No one told me because they didn't want to ruin the wedding. When I got back, there was an email sitting in my inbox. 'Hi, Seb, hope you had a great time at the wedding. Just to let you know, I'm the new sales rep in the UK. I'm fully trained up and here's my monthly report.'"

The company's processes were so well documented and embedded that onboarding was painless. "Hands-free," as Sebastian characterizes it.

"A lot of people," he says, "create monsters that absorb all of them and they can't escape their businesses. They become like prisons."

To repeat David Jenyns's aphorism: Systems set you free.

There are two ways to enact change. One is hope of a better future; the other is fear. And of the two, fear is the stronger. The burning platform was critical to getting process into the business in the first instance.

If your platform's not on fire, getting buy-in can be challenging. Downloading information from a key person can leave them feeling vulnerable. *Great, I've got to document everything I do, and then they'll hand my job to some college grad.*

Solving this problem returns once again to purpose and vision. Your clear, inspiring vision, reaffirmed every day, shows the way. If we're going to be number one in the world, then we've got to overcome our dependence on individuals. Process provides the means to that end.

David Jenyns suggests the best way to recruit key people to a systems mindset is to demonstrate that it's in their interest. "Typically, a key person goes on holiday and nothing happens for two weeks, then they spend three months trying to catch up when they get home. Implementing good systems allows people to go on holidays and not have to pay for it for weeks and weeks when they come back."

And by liberating key people from systemized roles, you're telling them that you want them to deploy their creativity elsewhere, that you want them to progress through the organization. Imagination is one of the higher mental faculties; liberating people from the chaos of disorder allows space for them to be creative, to grow, and contribute to the vision. You're telling them that you need to delegate parts of their job down the chain to lower-cost team members. To do that effectively, you need to document and capture.

David puts it like this: "The best-case scenario is establishing a culture of open, transparent, thriving teams that respect and appreciate systems, where they can see the purpose and vision clearly, and know in what direction they're traveling and how they're going to get there."

If there's ongoing resistance from team members, it becomes a performance management issue, and David suggests that you ask if certain team members who got you this far can get you to the next level.

"But let me stress: This is your last resort. We are going to try everything before we get to that, but it is possible to find people that don't fit with the direction in which you're heading and it's okay as the business owner or part of the leadership team to say, 'This is the culture we want.'"

TAKE ACTION—IT'S SIMPLE!

Simplify Everything. The strategy that brought you to this point will not get you where you want to go now. You need to create simple processes that facilitate brilliant execution without compromising creativity.

Implement the Customer-for-Life Process. Win the business, deliver the business, look after the customer, and ensure their success from the investment they have just made. Do these things right and the customer never needs to leave you.

Map Your Processes. Use the *SYSTEMology* method to create the processes necessary to facilitate scaling growth.

Pursue Continuous Improvement. Good processes are under constant development. When multiple, small improvements are added together, they generate substantial change.

Lead with the Right Organizational Structure. Structure your organization from left to right rather than top to bottom; hierarchical structures are irrelevant in the twenty-first century.

Embed a Process Culture. Make systems thinking a value so that everyone sees the role that process plays in the success of the organization, and everybody is signed up to make those processes as good as they can be.

Principle in Action—
Paul Akers, FastCap

Paul Akers had been a cabinetmaker for twenty years when he got the idea for a self-adhesive screw-cap cover, which he called FastCap. Today, the company that bears that name makes a wide array of woodworking products and tools, which are shipped to forty countries around the world. But it's FastCap's processes that I want to talk about here. They are truly extraordinary. There's nothing you can teach Paul about lean culture. The way in which the FastCap HQ in Ferndale, Washington operates has to be seen to be believed. In Paul's own words:

> I struggled like crazy to get through school, but I did get my degree in education as a woodshop teacher. I started my general contracting business building things: homes, cabinets, and so on, and I invented a simple product called the FastCap. I want to emphasize this concept of *simple*. It was a peel-and-stick cap to cover screw holes inside a cabinet.
>
> That product took off. People heard about how an ordinary cabinetmaker developed a product that was now being sold through distribution all around the country. At trade shows, all these cabinetmakers would come up to me and say, "I got an idea." That gave *me* an idea. We now create a vast array of woodworking products, all based on ideas suggested to us by a vast array of ordinary people.
>
> FastCap employs fifty people, and we have revenue in the tens of millions of dollars. We're still a family company, so I'm not going to give specific figures, but here's the important thing. The revenue that each employee generates makes every other company on the planet look like they don't know what they're doing. The number is astronomical.

Here's the thing. I don't care about growth. It's not that I don't want to grow, but our company is not structured to grow. Our company is structured for operational excellence, for us to work in a very fluid and smooth way, devoid of defects. Our customers want the product when they want it, at a really fair price. And they want good quality. That's what they want, not growth.

We have a distribution network in forty countries. We have no sales department. We have no marketing department. We have no HR department. We have no maintenance department. We don't have all the crap, all the layered bureaucracy, and that is why our revenue-per-employee is so high.

You walk in the door and everyone has stand-up desks. There are no walls in our factory; shipping, production, everything happens together in one space. Everything's on wheels so it can be reconfigured if we need to reconfigure. Our conference room has no chairs. We don't spend hours in meetings; we make decisions and get back to the real work.

Everybody is responsible for everything. I'm the president of the company and I clean the bathrooms when it's my turn.

There's a place for everything and everything in its place. No mess anywhere. Floors spotless all day. The way we put it is that we keep the rope so tight that you could bounce a dime to the moon. The highest standards in everything we do.

I didn't go to Harvard, I didn't go to Oxford, I was a C and D student. But that was actually a blessing to me because it forced me to make things simple so that the average person could hear what I'm saying and just grab it and run.

Our processes are based on continuous improvement. There are literally tens of thousands of processes in our facility. If everybody is intent on shaving a few seconds off those all the time, what does that do? The quality goes up. The joy goes up. When things are easier and you're not struggling, you perform at a higher level.

Everyone has autonomy and everyone is focused on process improvement—not just one or two people. Anyone can change anything they want at any time they want. They don't have to get permission; they don't have to suggest it at the morning meeting. Now, the only exception to that would be if you have a person who is new to a process. If they want to change something, they're asked to go get the expert and run it by them. This is to respect the stakeholders in the process. But anybody can stop anytime they want and fix anything they want.

You don't have an issue with one or two people holding key information in their heads. Every single one of our processes is recorded on video, all accessed by QR codes, which are those black-and-white squares which you scan with your smart device in order to access the relevant video.

There are no holders of information. Everything is open and easily understood.

I'm heavily influenced by Japanese culture and *The Toyota Way*. Some manufacturers see people as cost and set out to automate everything. Toyota does just the opposite. Their target is not to eliminate people; their target is to improve quality.

The vast majority of the efficiencies we've introduced don't use IT. With us, it's not *automate, automate, automate*; it's *elegant, elegant, elegant*. We say, "Use your wits, not your wallet." It's not that we can't use our wallet, but we use our wits first.

In fact, the low level of automation in our facility is almost shocking. When we get an order, it gets printed out on colored paper, a different color for each day of the week. Today is Tuesday, so we're using blue today. No scanning, nothing digital. Everyone looks on the board, and if they see a stack of blue orders this thick, we know we've got a *burden*. That means everybody from every department needs to run to the shipping department and start picking and packaging orders. Then there's no *burden*, so everybody from the shipping department runs back to production where we're actually making the products.

The entire company runs on a system which uses small cards called Kanban cards. Each one is four inches tall by three inches wide. We use them everywhere. When you grab the last roll of toilet paper, there's a Kanban card that says "Reorder." If you go to the grocery store, which is what we call the place where we pick all our orders, and there's five parts left, you'll find a Kanban. It's always there at five parts remaining. So you put it in a little tray, which triggers a light that signals the water spider (the person who manages stock replenishment). They come over, grab the Kanban, and order the required stock. There are no computers. No automation. It is so unautomated it just takes your breath away.

Our KPI is simply this: Giving the customer what they want when they want it, defect-free. That's what we're obsessed with.

We ship all of our orders in two hours. So if you order a thousand-dollar Best Fence—which is a stand for chop and miter saws—that order goes to the Best Fence department, and in two hours, it's done and in the truck. Two hours fax to truck. I don't know any other company in the world that can do that.

We have a flat structure. How many people do you think run this company? That does tens of millions of dollars of business all over the world? Six. That is the entire overhead of a company that is doing this kind of volume.

Continuous improvement. What does that mean? Fix what bugs you. Develop a culture where everybody is obsessed with one thing. Continuous improvement; fixing what bugs them. There isn't a process that's both good and stagnant. If it's not improving all the time, it's no good. Change it.

P5 ACTIONS TO TAKE:

_____

_____

_____

_____

_____

_____

_____

_____

_____

_____

_____

_____

_____

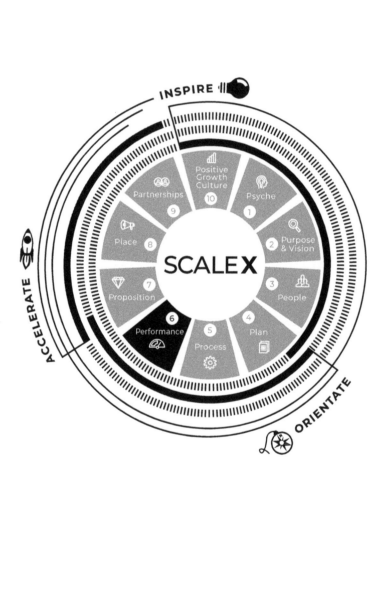

P6

PERFORMANCE

"The price of success is hard work, dedication to the job at hand, and the determination that whether we win or lose, we have applied the best of ourselves to the task at hand."
—Vince Lombardi

WHAT DO WE MEAN BY PERFORMANCE? THE DICTIONARY DEFINITION doesn't cut it: "The action or process of performing a task or function."

For me, performance is a revered sports star holding a trophy aloft, a great actor receiving a standing ovation, a master surgeon working medical miracles, an expert pilot landing smoothly in a storm. I'll never forget Chris Martin from Coldplay on the stage of the Amsterdam Arena, holding 50,000 people in the palm of his hand for over two hours. That's performance.

I think of my friend and colleague Brendan Mooney of software company Kainos, profiled in P3 People. He began as a graduate software engineer and progressed to become the CEO of the company. With a combination of intelligence, empathy, and humility, he built a world-class business, valued at more than £2 billion ($3 billion) and employing over 2,000 people as of November 2021. That's performance.

What does it mean when it comes to a scaling business? Vince Lombardi said that the achievements of an organization are the results of the combined effort of each individual. This starts with you. As the leader, you have to make sure that your own performance is optimized every time you show up. Do that and you will inspire and motivate the team, allowing them to reach their full performance potential and driving your company to do the same.

Let's break it down and look at the components of outstanding performance.

6.1 SPOTLIGHT CASH

"Cashflow is the pulse—the key vital sign of a company."
—Jack Welch

My first job after qualifying as a chartered accountant was with a newly formed tech company during the dot-com adventures of the late nineties. I had a fancy job title, a great salary for someone with my experience, and a pile of share options to go with all that.

It was a crazy time. The markets seemed awash with money. Anyone with a startup venture, a website, and a set of projections had private equity and venture capital firms queuing up to hand out cash. Investment banks, because they stood to profit from IPOs, poured fuel on the fire. And these IPOs often took place before a single customer order had been won. Brand awareness could justify almost any extravagance. I remember our marketing director asking me to approve chartering a jet to Las Vegas with the company logo on the side. The cost? Just over £100,000 ($150,000). "Just think of the publicity!" he exclaimed.

The "get big fast" imperative, the growth-over-profits mentality, and the seeming invincibility of the so-called new economy swept away rules that had guided us for generations. "Cash burn" was a phrase that you heard a lot at that time. The burn rate told investors how many months' cash were left to cover our growing overheads. And yet, our excesses paled in comparison to those of companies like Boo.com, which spent £125 million ($188 million) in just six months.

I vividly remember our first Christmas party. Canapés were served by waiters in black tie while a locally famous band played jazz. Staff who had been flown in from around the world were drinking company champagne, and the atmosphere was celebratory, hedonistic even. The company hadn't turned a profit despite being in existence for two years, and yet there was a huge excitement about the growth prospects that surely lay ahead of us.

It didn't feel right. I'd had a solid grounding in the fundamentals of good business, and operating profitably and cash positively was at the heart of that. But I looked around at all the clever, experienced people—tech entrepreneurs twenty years my senior—who had bought into this brave new world. They knew what they were doing, didn't they? Like so many of my colleagues, I invested a chunk of my savings in the dot-com bubble, only for the investment to end up worthless within a couple of years. I recall colleagues setting up investment clubs and some even quitting their secure day jobs to engage in full-time day trading. Like Boo.com, which filed for bankruptcy in 2000, these experiments all ended badly.

Cash is king. It's a cliché because it's true, especially as you scale. I may have lost savings in the dot-com era, but really, the cost was probably good value for the lesson it taught. In all of the companies I have worked with since then, cash management has always been at the heart of our scaling strategy.

The Lessons Learned

If it doesn't feel right, it probably isn't. Trust the data, but listen to your gut.

Stick to the knitting. Focus on what you're great at. Your unique ability. Don't chase the next big investment fad. I know several companies who sunk years of hard-earned reserves from their primary business in property, only to lose it all in the 2008 crash.

Sales is vanity, profit is sanity, but cash is reality. Make "cash headroom" a key metric. This is a fancy term for how many months' cash is available to cover overheads and other commitments if you win no further orders. This is a critical performance metric for a project-based business, where sales forecasting is particularly complex. Target at least six months' cash headroom. Creating a cash buffer has a wonderful impact on your psychology. Knowing exactly what you hold in reserve makes it much easier to make important decisions.

Ask your bank manager for an umbrella when the sun is shining. After 2008, we always made sure to present the bank with a year's solid performance, complete with sales, profits, and strong cash growth. Then, and only then, we would ask for an extension to our overdraft facilities. This made it much easier for the bank to say yes, and we secured far more attractive rates than would have been possible if the rain had been hammering down and we desperately needed that umbrella. In later years, we converted the overdraft facilities into bank guarantee facilities, which helped secure significant export orders.

Foster good habits in relation to cash management. Taken together, solid payment terms, strong collection habits, and consistent headroom reporting will provide an excellent platform to ensure you have the necessary fuel for growth.

Schedule a meeting with your head of finance to review key metrics at least once a month. Finance should be a key part of your board and management meetings. There is a lot to be learned about the performance of your business from the balance sheet. "Debtor days," for example, will tell you if customers are delaying payments. If this is happening, you need to find out why. Is it as a result of poor quality or late deliveries? Similarly, delayed payments to suppliers may suggest consistent poor performance from them. Ask your finance lead to provide you with four or five key metrics to focus these discussions.

6.2 IMPLEMENT PERFORMANCE METRICS

"People can't connect with what they cannot see; networks cannot blossom in silos. *Objectives and key results* (OKRs) are open and visible to all parts of an organization, to every level and department. As a result, companies that stick with them become more coherent."
—John Doerr

I'm a huge fan of having a direct line of sight toward the vision. Anchor your intentions and activities to a desired future state and work back from there. Drown out everything else—from boardroom to factory floor, through all functions, and across regional business units, no matter where in the world they are. Once everyone has clear sight of the vision, great execution is where the magic is made. Every team member must know how their day-to-day tasks, initiatives, projects, and objective achievements contribute to moving the organization forward. You want everyone on the boat rowing in the same direction, to the same rhythm, toward the same lighthouse.

An open and transparent flow of information through the organization is vital. It kills silos, encourages cross-pollination of ideas, and increases innovation.

The Search for the Right Metrics

After we agreed on our very first company vision, we set about prioritizing several key performance indicators (KPIs). Most of these were financial by their nature. Things like sales growth, gross and net margin performance, costs as a percentage of sales, and so on. The problem was that they failed to represent what was happening across the entire business. They weren't holistic; they didn't reflect the soul of the organization. Moreover, a team member operating away from the office, one responsible for installing equipment on our latest project, would struggle to make the link between his performance on-site and the KPIs we were using to measure our performance.

This is why I went looking for a process of goal-driven performance measurement, which could capture what was going on more comprehensively. One of the first things I tried was the balanced scorecard or BSC, which is a strategic planning and management system that organizations use to communicate what they're trying to do and align day-to-day work with strategy. I struggled to get real engagement with this, not due to any fault in the scorecard methodology, but because I had prepared and launched the initiative without the involvement of the senior team. I really wanted it and assumed everyone else did, too. Collective action, I would learn, is far more valuable.

The next search for the right system hit on a software package developed by a local company. They called it an enterprise goals optimization system. We decided to give it a six-month tryout. Although the principles behind the system were sound, the software itself was clunky and lacked usability. Encouragingly, though, there was a much better level of engagement and a general appreciation of what we were trying to do across the company. At the very least, it created an appetite to keep searching, to find something better. Everyone bought into the principles of effective goal setting aligned to overall vision.

It was at this point that a team member discovered objectives and key results. OKRs were pioneered by Andrew Grove in the seventies while he was working as a manager in Intel. Grove, who would go on to become CEO, was described by John Doerr in his book *Measure What Matters* as the "greatest manager of his or any era."[54] He "ran the best-run company I had ever seen."[55]

Doerr, a highly successful California venture capitalist and current chair of Kleiner Perkins, knows what success looks like. He was bowled over by Grove's system and began to roll it out within his investee firms, most notably Google.

He says, "I have the utmost reverence for entrepreneurs...but I've also watched too many start-ups struggle with growth and scale and getting the right things done so I'd come to a philosophy, my mantra: *Ideas are easy. Execution is everything.*"[56]

He says that OKRs provided the scaffolding for seven of Google's most successful, billion-user initiatives: Search, Chrome, Android, Maps, YouTube, Google Play, and Gmail.

OKRs in Action

Simply put, OKRs provide a collaborative goal-setting protocol for companies, teams, and individuals. They are designed to ensure that the company focuses its efforts on the same issues throughout the organization. They give you a way to eat the elephant!

To achieve a goal, you need to do something every day that will take you closer to it. Knowing where to start can be challenging, particularly when you're talking about the kind of "stretchy" that goal-ambitious scale-ups need to aim for. This is where OKRs come in. They help chunk down the goal into ninety-day objectives (discussed in P4 Plan), while progress toward those objectives is measured through key results.

OBJECTIVE: TO INCREASE PARTS SALES IN NORTH AMERICA

Key Result 1 (i.e., time-bound measurable milestone): Locate a parts storage warehouse in-country to reduce lead time availability by May 31 (two months from now).

Key Result 2: Contact one hundred existing customers by phone and email and inform them of in-country parts availability by June 30 (three months from now).

Key Result 3: Set up warehouse parts management system and parts CRM by June 30 (three months from now).

OBJECTIVE: IMPROVE SEARCH ENGINE OPTIMIZATION (SEO) FOR PRODUCT X CONTENT

KR1: Ten Product X content articles to have five or more backlinks (complete within thirty days).

KR2: Publish ten guest blog posts linking to Product X content on relevant sites (within sixty days).

KR3: Complete three customer case studies with testimonials and links back to Product X (within ninety days).

OBJECTIVE: IMPROVE COMPANY COMMUNICATIONS TO SUPPORT A BETTER COMPANY CULTURE

KR1: Source and shortlist three employee satisfaction tools/survey software by June 30 (within sixty days).

KR2: Issue *Wins of the Week* communication from CEO (by May 15).

KR3: Launch quarterly town hall Q&A meeting on company performance and alignment to our vision and plan (first meeting to be held in July—after Q2 results).

We introduced OKRs to the company in 2016, gradually rolling them out under the strategic pillars that we identified as critically important in the pursuit of our 2020 Vision. We used a technology platform to provide all employees with a clear line of sight through their own objectives, their team's objectives, and overall company objectives. All were interdependent; all were clear and unambiguous. Everyone could see how their day-to-day work contributed directly to our big-picture vision.

Engagement went through the roof.

It's vital that OKRs inform your daily, weekly, and monthly activities. Always ask yourself:

- Are the tasks, initiatives, and projects I am devoting time to directly contributing to the OKRs aligned to the annual goals?

- Can I see a direct line of progress?

- Is that progress visible to everyone else?

You want to get from point A to point B with joy, flow, and ease. Setting daily priorities aligned with OKRs, which in turn are aligned with your goals, allows you to create momentum, witness progress on a daily basis, and critically, to celebrate wins. And that generates a nice dopamine hit!

Vishen Lakhiani credits OKRs with helping to fuel Mindvalley's explosive growth. He says, "We started OKRs in August 2017; the following year was one of our fastest growing years. All in all, we grew 70 percent year on year in terms of revenue."

Managers, armed with the right information, should manage their teams and operations as objectively as possible. OKRs enable this. And team members like to know where they stand. The visibility the system provided on a weekly, monthly, and quarterly basis cuts away all of the subjectivity. Everybody knew exactly what was expected of them.

The research bears out our own experience. A two-year Deloitte study found that no single factor has more impact than "clearly defined goals that are written down and shared freely…Goals create alignment, clarity and job satisfaction."[57]

6.3 MENTOR FOR PERFORMANCE

"Great teachers and schools expect and nurture quality work and quality performance. Great teachers inspire and demand quality, ever urging their students to higher levels of excellence. They shun mere conformity and expect their students to think and perform to their ever-increasing potential."
—Oliver DeMille

I was impressed by Tom from the moment I met him, which was when he interviewed for a position with our sales team. Still in his early twenties, he was mature, emotionally intelligent, and humble. He had done his preparation and was confident in his delivery. No one was surprised when he got the job.

A few years later, at a sales event, Tom asked me about my own career, about how I had progressed to my current position. In the course of that conversation, he asked me if I would consider mentoring him. The question took me by surprise. I had never formally mentored or coached anyone before. He also had a direct reporting line to our business development manager. I didn't want to upset this relationship, so I asked what he thought a mentoring arrangement should look like.

"If you could meet me once a month for one hour, I would really appreciate your insight and perspective on my own development and some of the challenges I face."

I agreed, subject to approval by his manager. And I set one condition. He was also to mentor me in a process that I later learned already existed and had its own term: *reverse mentoring*.

The reason I asked for this reciprocal arrangement was simple. I wanted an honest perspective of our company, our vision, and our strategy from someone who spent his days on the front line. What's more, like so many of our team members, Tom was a millennial. I was keen to understand his experience as a twentysomething in our company.

- What were we doing well?

- Were we communicating effectively?

- Were we deploying technology well in that regard?

- Was our purpose resonating?

- What was our culture like?

- How could we be more relevant to the younger generation?

In seeking to understand Tom and his peer group, I could in turn make whatever changes necessary to encourage better performance.

Over the ensuing twelve months, we met as agreed each month. Twenty years his senior and now CEO of a fast-growing business, a husband, and a parent, I was able to provide an insight not only on the company and our direction of travel but also my experience of life in general. He would bring his latest challenge to each session, and we would discuss it. Sometimes I would act as a mentor, other times a coach, a counselor, an advisor, and in time, a friend.

In turn, I looked for his advice and guidance. This process was hugely beneficial for both of us. Tom went on to become the highest performing salesperson in the company and was promoted to regional manager. To be fair, he was destined for this role, but I believe our conversations helped!

Over the next few years, I mentored and reverse mentored several younger team members. Advice was sought in a range of areas: How do I balance becoming a father with the travel requirements of the latest project I'm managing? How do I discipline the use of my phone at home in the evening? I was asked where I thought the company would be in twenty years. How did I think the latest macroeconomic trend was going to affect us? These were open and trusting sessions, which took place outside of what you might call our "normal" relationship. (In most cases, I would not otherwise have had any contact with my coachees.)

These sessions were really well received, not least because they proved what we claimed, which was that we had a positive growth and learning culture. Here, too, was a clear signal that the CEO cared, that he was approachable, and that he wanted to learn and grow just as much as those twenty years younger.

We talked in P3 People about Patrick McAliskey's highly successful mentoring initiative in Novosco as the company scaled. We also went this route. We identified fifteen mentors within the company and matched them with fifteen emerging leaders. Coaches and coachees met regularly to exchange information and to help improve performance and accelerate progress toward our vision.

Our team understood this absolute truth: For our company to perform, to be world class, we needed every department and function, every business unit, and team member to maximize their potential.

6.4 PRACTICE!

Being a leader means that very frequently, you have to stand in front of your team, your peers, your board, or your investors and convince them of the need to change direction, the need to restructure, the importance of the impending customer visit...The list is endless. There are two times when clear communication is absolutely critical. The first is when you're encouraging your people to climb Everest with you, when you're inspiring them to support the bold vision. The second is in time of crisis. I'm writing this in the throes of the COVID-19 pandemic, and the need to communicate decisively and instill calm has rarely been more important.

Few of us are brilliant communicators. Moreover, standing up to talk to a group generates huge levels of anxiety. As a CEO, nothing quickens the pulse more than the company-wide presentation. Standing up in front of a packed room, exposed and vulnerable as people await the news, your story, the latest position, words of inspiration...It can churn the stomach of the most seasoned leader.

Nor is communication just about public speaking. Dealing with an angry customer, delivering bad news to a supplier who has lost the latest pitch for your work, announcing job losses, or meeting with the bank manager—Claire and I had to deal with all of these.

How do you improve your communication skills?

Practice.

Think about the latest presentation you made. Did you set time aside in advance to physically rehearse with the slide deck? Did you isolate the two or three critical messages that had to be emphasized? Did you ask anyone for feedback in advance, to seek ways in which it could be improved? Did you familiarize yourself with your audience?

Or did you merely glance at the slides ten minutes before you were due to talk?

I attended a public speaking workshop recently, and one of the guest instructors, as part of his own preparation, had created a half-page bio of each participant. He had done his research and could relate directly to our varied experiences and backgrounds. As a result, he endeared himself to all of us immediately. We completely bought into what he was saying. Why? Because his preparation demonstrated that he cared.

Bottom line, we all get nervous before a presentation; it's entirely natural. The difference between letting those nerves paralyze you and a successful performance comes down to three things. Practice, practice, practice!

Born or Made?

The good news is that experts are made, not born. Swedish psychologist K. Anders Ericsson led studies on expertise and performance across a wide range of disciplines: surgery, acting, chess, writing, computer programming, ballet, music, aviation, firefighting, and many others. He concluded that expert leaders are not a natural phenomenon. He asserted that a particular kind of practice—*deliberate practice*—could be used to develop expertise. His research showed that working—with deliberation—at what you can't do, delivers the skill you need. He says, "Deliberate practice is different. It entails considerable, specific, and sustained efforts to do something you *can't* do well—or even at all. Research across domains shows that it is only by working at what you can't do that you turn into the expert you want to become."[58]

It's hardly contentious to suggest that practice does indeed make perfect. You might think, however, that it only holds true in a sporting context, where there is a start line, a finish line, and a timekeeper. We can measure and monitor performance very easily here, but how does practice relate to leading an organization?

Look at the case method now widely used in business schools. Because the outcomes of these cases are known, students can set their solutions alongside these outcomes and see how they compare. In this way, what are they doing but practicing decision making? As

Ericsson points out in the same article, war games serve a similar training function at military academies.

Dan Lowes is a former RAF fighter pilot and executive officer of the world-famous Red Arrows. Only a handful of the many thousands who apply every year to become an RAF fighter pilot are chosen, and of those, a still smaller group become eligible to be considered for the Red Arrows. In our interview, I asked Dan if he believed that experts were born or made. He replied without hesitation. "Made. One hundred percent. Made." He explains that the Red Arrows practice regime was exceptional. "In the Reds, we flew three times a day, five days a week. That's all we did."

Achieving genuine expertise requires struggle, discomfort, sacrifice, and honest, painful, self-assessment. This is the point at which real growth happens.

Self-Assessment

To know where you need to go, you need first to understand where you are. The truth is that we all have blind spots. There is often a significant gap between how we think we are and how we are actually perceived. This is why I began inviting 360-degree feedback from the team, and why I encourage all CEOs to do the same thing. In order to encourage honesty, the HR team can facilitate anonymous responses. I found the process painful at times, but the value of the information far outweighed any discomfort.

If you want to build better relationships with your team, you need to know how you are perceived. You need to know how your actions and behaviors are landing. You need to know if you are inspiring or demotivating, whether you're enabling or obstructing. You may think you know, but until you ask, you're only guessing. If you enter this process with humility and a genuine desire to improve, you will ultimately reap the rewards.

The Red Arrows' motto is simply "*Éclat*," which is a French word meaning "excellence." Yet, Dan Lowes explains that the three qualities looked for in a Red Arrows pilot are humility, approachability, and credibility. At debriefings, which happen after every performance, every aspect of that performance is thoroughly analyzed. "We never, never, never had a private debrief. If there was anyone who wanted to sit in on these sessions, we always invited them. We wouldn't hide anything from anyone."

Although this level of openness probably won't be appropriate for a scale-up implementing a system of review and feedback, the point is clear. You need to have a clear, objective view of where you are in order to get where you need to go.

We talked in the last section about coaching and reverse coaching. I want to reinforce that point here. It's no surprise that a high-performing sports star would have a coach. Why not the CEO of an organization aspiring to outstanding performance? Suppose you have fifty staff, and they each have a partner. That's one hundred people. Suppose they have fifty children; that's 150. Add in your customers, suppliers, and other stakeholders, and you quickly see how your decisions as the CEO of a fifty-person company can have ramifications on hundreds of people. Moreover, being a CEO is a lonely, difficult job. Having someone to confide in, to interrogate your decisions, to counsel, and advise you is essential if you wish to scale successfully.

As far back as the 1930s, Napoleon Hill cited the importance of joining a mastermind group. This is simply a coming together of two or more people who hold similar ambitions to support each other in the decisions that they have to make.

There are of course many ready-made organizations that fill this role: the Young Presidents Organization and the Entrepreneur Organization, to name two. My own mastermind group was a monthly jog and breakfast with two other CEOs who held similar ambitions to grow their companies, people with whom I shared an insatiable appetite for learning and development. We now have our own Elite MasterMind sessions hosted monthly as part of our ScaleX™ Accelerator Program.

When, in 2011, we decided to strengthen our board of directors, I realized that I had no expertise in this area. I set out to find out how I could address this deficiency and discovered the Institute of Directors' Director Development Program.

At a later stage in our development, I invited a board performance expert to sit in on our meetings and rate us on how our meetings were structured, on our agenda, how people spoke, the quality and effectiveness of the information presented, and so on.

Finding a group of people facing similar challenges provides a great platform for seeking inspiration, comfort, insight, benchmarking, and experience.

6.5 LEVERAGE PERFORMANCE THROUGH REGULAR CHECK-INS

I vividly remember, quite early in my career, standing alone in a stuffy, windowless meeting room in front of fifteen gray suits—all hostile. Why? Our performance management system.

"These ratings are disengaging for my team!"

"That guy's far too soft, but the system makes his team look like heroes!"

"We never get an honest performance discussion because my team is always pitching too hard for a pay increase!"

"This takes up far too much of my time! There are too many forms to complete! Why doesn't HR do it?"

These challenges and accusations came like a flurry of jabs from Floyd Mayweather. Although I parried them as well as I could, there was no escaping the fact that something had to change. So I set out to rethink our performance management system. What was I really trying to achieve with it? What was the real value of the process I was trying to embed? And why did these experienced managers have such an aversion to it?

Instigating positive change in performance is challenging. Critically assessing an individual's performance and inspiring improvement is a complex human process that brings with it a cauldron of biases, motivations, and fears. Most managers lack the necessary skills to do it in a way that reenergizes the employee. Too often, the opposite happens, and the employee ends up demotivated.

And that's why the process is equally challenging for employees. Most tend to dread the performance appraisal as much as the manager. They're unsure how to receive and process feedback constructively.

My research led to the conclusion that the future of performance management lay in nothing more sophisticated than conversations. Allowing managers to focus on conversations with team members, and supporting them to make those conversations more meaningful and successful could be transformative.

Using a technology platform called BetterWorks (which we also used for managing our OKR system), we successfully implemented a straight-talking conversation model that promoted a healthy-challenge culture and allowed managers to drill down into the key behaviors that lead to higher performance. We gave our managers a tool kit of open-ended, thought-provoking, meaningful questions on topics known to impact personal performance: personal challenge, career progression, well-being, recognition, feedback, and goal setting. Rather than manage, managers were encouraged to coach.

Managers and employees had the freedom to trigger a conversation whenever they wanted; a series of questions was answered by both parties prior to the actual sit-down. This meant that when it came to the event itself, both parties could pay attention to each other's tone, facial expressions, body language, and all the other nonverbal ways in which we communicate.

Check-ins

To bring a lighter touch, we called these conversations check-ins. The rule of thumb is that they should take place often. Once or twice a year is not enough. A football coach doesn't wait until the end of the year to have a meaningful conversation with their players about a game that happened four months earlier. They don't even wait till the end of the game. Great quality conversations happen in the moment, on the sidelines, in the changing rooms, in the clubhouse, and on the training ground.

Football coaches continually help align players with team goals; they continually monitor effort and contribution. If you're hanging back and don't show up for your left midfielder as they pass you the ball, you'll know about it. Conversely, if you're playing your best game and put three goals in the back of the net, you'll know about that, too. You will be encouraged to keep doing what you're doing. A good football coach will observe and highlight your strengths, advise you on how to best use them, ensure you are learning from your mistakes, help you navigate that tricky opponent, and help you grow, both on and off the pitch.

You need to get the rhythm of these performance conversations right. Our mantra was, "Little, often, and all year round." Very often, however, the rhythm breaks down due to a lack of discipline, transparency, training, or the avoidance of tough discussions when things go off track. So many businesses struggle with their performance because individual problems are addressed too late or not at all. Many of us have been raised in a culture that preaches if you can't say something nice, don't say anything at all. So if we say something that's anything other than positive, it feels like we're being unkind.

Conversations about poor performance tend to get shared with the manager's peers instead of the employee themselves. So here's another rule to live by: Don't say anything about an employee that you wouldn't be prepared to tell them directly. One of the CEOs we coach includes this as one of his organizational values: "Feedback to the belly and not to the back." As a leader, don't tolerate backbiting from any team member. Encourage straight, direct, performance-improving conversations.

Over the years, I've worked with managers who have tried to spare the feelings of their team members, and eventually the decision to let the employee go was taken out of their hands. When the departing member asked, "Why didn't you tell me? Why didn't anyone tell me?" the manager had nothing to say.

Caring and Why It Matters

Twenty years after that heated performance management meeting, I still see situations in other companies where performance management is fraught with challenges and hostility. Thanks mainly to the emergence of things like ratings-free systems, employee-led conversations, and continuous coaching, we have seen many companies simplify their rigid, cumbersome review processes. Remember, however, that if your performance management systems are dysfunctional, they must be tackled at their core. If all you do is tinker around the edges without addressing the fear and discomfort that managers feel, nothing will change. Businesses need to create an environment where meaningful guidance is available to everyone, where managers can address problems up front and tell people clearly when they mess up. Encourage a system that balances challenge, compassionate candor, and support.

When someone is feeling challenged, it's often because they are being taken out of their comfort zone. This is essential for personal growth and improved performance. Maybe an employee is particularly nervous about presenting in front of a group of experts, or wounded by tough feedback. Perhaps they are delivering high-profile work for the first time. Whatever the circumstances, you must reaffirm the truth that nothing ever grows in the comfort zone and that by encouraging this feeling of healthy discomfort, we are enabling people to aim high and grow more.

At the same time, support comes through showing the employee that you're not just investing in them professionally but that you truly care about them. Your role as a leader is to encourage your team to constantly stretch and grow, leaning into their fears and supporting them in times of discomfort as they seek to take on new roles, new responsibilities, new projects, and so on.

Businesses that foster this type of environment and these types of relationships have a huge advantage in the marketplace. And there are plenty of examples of how this approach delivers. Much of GE's successful transformation under former CEO Jack Welch, for instance, was attributed to his ability to get the company's 250,000 employees "pulling in the same direction" and pulling to the best of their individual abilities. Over the past twenty-five years, the success of American Express has been predicated on the fact that they give equal weighting to goals *and* how they're achieved. They understand the importance of encouraging the right behaviors. In the Hyatt hotel group, the company's long-standing policy of employee development and promoting from within has been central to its high levels of retention in a sector notorious for staff churn.

6.6 ENCOURAGE OWNERSHIP

"People want guidance, not rhetoric. They need to know what the plan of action is and how it will be implemented. They want to be given responsibility to help solve the problem and the authority to act on it."
—**Howard Schultz, Starbucks**

You've set a clear vision. You know where the organization is going. You understand your purpose; all of your stakeholders know *why* you're doing what you do. The plan is set out and agreed; everyone knows *how* you're going to execute the agreed goals. Now it's about unleashing your people and encouraging ownership among the teams and individuals on those teams that will deliver success.

The global financial crisis was a great teacher. We discussed in P5 Process how it forced our business to think more creatively simply in order to survive. In addition, we urgently needed to reduce our overhead by at least £35,000 ($52,500) per month. The immediate, obvious way to do this was by reducing headcount. We really did not want to do this. But before I move to what we did next, I need to say that it is often critical in these situations to reduce your people costs as compassionately as possible, if you firmly believe that it is a necessary short-term measure to save the company and protect the remaining jobs. The hope is that a sacrifice now will, in time, lead to greater prosperity and those initially impacted may then stand to benefit.

So I placed the challenge before the senior team—£35,000 ($52,500) monthly savings. They asked for seven days to develop a plan. One week later, I sat with the board in the same room while the team presented Project 35. They proposed a range of innovations, which included a reduction in their salaries but did not include *any* reduction in headcount. No one lost their job.

Empowerment. Simply inviting the team to take the challenge, bringing them into the decision-making process proved exceptionally powerful. I was elated.

There's an important lesson here. You don't have to have all the answers. And as you scale and complexity builds, you most definitely won't have all the answers. Your team, however, operating on the front line, will have solutions to so many of the challenges that beset the scaling business. Ask for their ideas and insights. Don't feel the need to be the loudest or most-heard voice in the room (a mistake I made frequently). Not only will you discover unthought-of innovation and creativity, but you'll also unleash a powerful motivational force at the heart of your business.

New Sectors, New Markets

The recession turned out to be a catalyst for many profound changes, all of which facilitated our scaling journey. I mentioned earlier our overdependence on a single sector. To break that dependence, we examined our product set and explored how it might add value in other industries. This led to the establishment of a separate business unit, which enabled us to focus on a completely different sector—one that was less recession prone. We selected a small team and appointed a senior head from our existing business.

This was a great opportunity for those directly involved. It secured their jobs (for the near future at least) and created a wonderful, entrepreneurial, highly creative atmosphere, free from the restrictions of the parent. The team had a clear sense of ownership of agreed goals and hit the ground running. Established in 2008, this business grew quickly to deliver more than £10 million ($15 million) annual sales with a team of sixty in markets from North America to Australia.

The regional business we established in India was the most successful example of our strategic focus. The model—which we'll talk about in more detail in P8 Place—was simple. Establish regionally focused businesses empowered to take ownership of their region and develop in line with our vision. In addition, support the heck out of these businesses and use what we learn to incrementally improve that process everywhere else. In the early stages, this proved incredibly challenging, especially when it came to achieving quality standards in manufacturing. Our Indian engineering staff would often spend months at our Irish HQ immersing themselves in our behaviors and processes.

Thereafter, we empowered them to adapt the product and process for the needs of the local customer base. Again and again, we saw empowerment deliver success. Assigning responsibility for growth in each business unit gave opportunities to stretch and challenge individuals to optimize their own performance and that of their teams. As I write, the company employs almost 200 people in our Indian operation, which is managed by an all-Indian-executive team. In 2019, for the first time in our history, we brought in an external investor to help achieve a listing on the Bombay Stock Exchange.

Empowered teams with an agreed plan and clear line of sight to the company vision have been critical in our success. Within ten years of the global financial crisis, the company had grown exponentially and employed almost 700 people directly.

Although the world will continue to automate mundane, routine processes, the human touch will always be required to stir emotions and optimize performance. Empowering those you touch fuels growth like nothing else.

TAKE ACTION, IT'S SIMPLE!

Spotlight Cash. Put cash management at the heart of your growth ambitions. Cash is, was, and always will be king. Target at least six months' cash headroom throughout your scaling journey.

Implement Performance Metrics. Find a system that measures what matters and that resonates with everyone in the business.

Mentor for Performance. Mentoring and reverse mentoring yield peer-less results for everyone involved and fosters a growth and learning culture, which is vital in a scaling business.

Practice! It's as important in business as any other field of human endeavor. In particular, the leader of the scaling business needs to be a great communicator. Good quality, deliberate practice makes perfect.

Leverage Performance through Regular Check-ins. A conversational system of performance management, built on regular check-ins, keeps everyone on the message and engaged.

Encourage Ownership. Companies become increasingly complex as they scale. Encourage ownership to unleash innovation and solve the problems that you can't solve on your own.

Principle in Action—Enda McNulty

I followed Armagh Gaelic football passionately throughout my childhood and teenage years. This wasn't unusual given my dad's obsession with Armagh and the fact that my uncle played on the team in the seventies. The pinnacle of the county's success was reaching the All-Ireland Senior Football Championship final in 1953 and again in 1977. Both times, they lost. My uncle was on the team in 1977, when they failed miserably against Dublin.

The breakthrough came in 2002, in a packed stadium of 85,000 screaming fans, when Armagh finally secured a famous victory against Kerry, bringing them their first championship title ever. On that day, Enda McNulty played a pivotal role at cornerback, alongside his brother, Justin, in a team famed for its brand of football, physicality, and passion to win.

Enda's tenacity on the field was well known, but over the past few years, I've seen something of it off the field as well. Following a recommendation from a colleague, I invited Enda into our business to deliver a session on *Driving High Performance* during one of our strategy pit stops. His company, McNulty, specializes in "transforming human potential globally." By the end of that daylong event, he had our entire leadership and management team—more than forty in all—embraced in a huddle, calling out actions and behaviors that we admired in each other. The following day, we returned to all corners of the globe charged with enough energy and drive to run through brick walls, aligned, inspired, and hungry to tackle our 2020 Vision.

Enda's ability to hold the room that day was something I hadn't seen before. It was a masterclass in performance coaching. Like a great conductor, he made sure that everyone stayed focused and motivated throughout the day.

When I asked him to provide an interview for this book, he switched it up and suggested we precede our talk with a yoga session and a four-mile run through the Phoenix Park in Dublin. Throughout that engagement, he never stopped coaching me. Performance is always at the forefront of his mind—even to the point that when we finally sat down to talk, he suggested that we conduct our interview "as close as we can to a performance."

THE INNER GAME

Enda described the "secret ladders" to his success. He recalled with great fondness a list of coaches and mentors who had a huge impact on his life, both on and off the pitch. It turns out that three of the Armagh All-Ireland winning team in 2002 were also in Enda's class at school, while the great Kieran McGeeney, who captained the team, was a couple of years ahead of him. "It's so important," he says, "to surround yourself with strong, positive influences." His mother and father in particular had a huge impact on his coaching style. He talks about his mother's "amazing, compassionate candor" and how his father used to play psychology tapes by self-help guru Lou Tice in the car going to and coming from football matches. In the early days, Enda was embarrassed in front of his friends and resisted his father's messaging. Lou Tice's strongly accented Seattle twang waxing lyrical about potential and psychology was a world away from rural Armagh. What won him round was the discovery that Tice had successfully coached a range of famous American footballers and elite athletes.

"There must be something in this," was his conclusion.

He was only fourteen when he recognized that the mental game would be a vital component of his ambition to make it onto the first Armagh team to win the All Ireland. His dad gave him *The Inner Game of Tennis* by Tim Gallwey, an iconic book that had a huge influence on the young Enda.

When describing how he graduated from boy to All-Ireland winning, All-Star footballer to become the founder and CEO of a revered performance company, he is candid.

"A lot of failures, a lot of pivots. In business and sport and life, you're going to pivot multiple times. And I had a lot of luck and some great mentors along the way."

Enda's worked with a who's who of elite athletes, perform-ers, and corporate clients. When Jonathan Sexton was voted best rugby player in the world, Enda was his performance coach, while his client list includes Facebook, Amazon, Kel-logg's, Diageo, and Microsoft, to name a few. He's quick to say that he accepts no credit for the successes of the individuals he's worked with. Instead, he emphasizes what he has learned from them. Talk to the people he's coached, however, and you get a better sense of what it's like to have a world-class mentor on your side. I first became aware of Enda's achievements off the sporting field when I read an interview with another rugby star, Brian O'Driscoll. O'Driscoll revealed how he had considered giving up the Ireland captaincy before Enda's intervention in December 2008. The following year, Brian would enjoy his best-ever season, which saw him skipper Ireland to their first Grand Slam in sixty-one years and captain the British and Irish Lions in South Africa.

I asked Enda how he goes about drawing greater perfor-mance from world-class individuals. He says that you must become a "performance detective."

> You investigate. You become intensely curious about them. You must understand innately what their ambi-tions are. If they are already performing at the highest level, do they have another motive? What are their dreams for the future? How do they view past per-formance? You find out how they prepare. You look at pre-performance rituals, post-performance rituals... You explore everything.
>
> Once you know exactly where they are, you can both set your sights on where they need to be, and begin coaching them to achieve that high performance.

WHAT MAKES A HIGH PERFORMER?
Enda sets out a list of five characteristics shared by the high-est performers, no matter the performance crucible in which they operate.

1. Massive passion for what they do. They don't see it as a job or a career; it's their life. "You see the passion dance out of their eyes." What's more, they all want to get better. They are equally passionate about improvement.

2. Practice! "In business," he says, "we often forget this. If it's a pitch to win a new account, for example, then you need to put in hours of practice, and the quality of the practice is also extremely important here." He cites K. Anders Ericsson, whom we mentioned earlier and his theory of deliberate practice.

3. The highest performers bring a laser-like focus to what they do. It's never simply going through the motions.

4. They go above and beyond. They put in the discretionary effort when there's no one there to see. "An extra rep, when they don't have to, tells a lot about the person."

5. They have a proven ability to deliver significant results quarter on quarter, year on year, regardless of the economic terrain.

So what characterizes high performance in a CEO or senior leader?

"Firstly, the leader must understand what high performance looks like. They're always benchmarking, always looking for high-performance environments. They understand what great looks like.

"Next, understand who is going to be in your team. Who are the four or five key people who are going to help you win gold?"

We're talking at the Dublin Rowing Club, so Enda uses a rowing analogy. He says that you must have earned the right to be in the boat, and from my own experience, this is critical.

If there's any question around a person's eligibility, competence, attitude, commitment, or behaviors, they're not ready to take a seat among the crew.

He refers to the challenge of moving from an underperforming culture to a high-performance culture. "It will take two to three years of everyone pulling in the same direction, taking all parts of the organization with you. They must understand what it takes to transform; they must understand all of the milestones required to get there." In Enda's experience, less than 2 percent of people have this capacity (which, coincidentally, aligns to the percentage of SMEs who achieve scaling success).

Currently at an inflection point in the growth of his own business, which now earns seven-figure revenues, what lessons would he share or advice would he give to would-be SME scalers?

Ensure you're incredibly passionate about what you do. If you're not, you will get caught out somewhere down the line when things become tough, as they inevitably will. Spend time trying to understand what it is you are most passionate about regarding the professional track which you are now on.

Vision. Be crystal clear where it is you want to go.

Team. Be relentless and radical about getting the best team around you. An hour a month from a brilliant person will be worth much more than forty hours of an average one.

Mindset. Your own psychology, psyche, and mindset must be sound. Surround yourself with people who will challenge your performance and question the conditioning of your own mindset.

And ensure the mindset of those you surround yourself with is aligned and intact. How can you tell this? He gives an example of his time with an American football team, the Pittsburgh Steelers. In order to determine the mindset of their players, the coaches speak at length to the teachers that the perspective player has had throughout their school years. "Success leaves a lot of clues," Enda asserts. "Everyone who is successful has put in the hard yards. There's no skipping the fundamental milestones."

Strategy and plan. "If you have a world-class leader, a world-class team in world-class condition using world-class equipment, but you're following the wrong plan, you're going to be obliterated."

Reading

I asked Enda to recommend three books. A voracious reader, he suggested nine:

1. *The Brain That Changes Itself*—Norman Doidge

2. *Hail to the King of Sneakers*—Michael Jordan

3. *Winning!*—Clive Woodward

4. *Slaying the Dragon*—Michael Johnson

5. *The Inner Game of Tennis*—Tim Gallwey

6. *In Pursuit of Excellence*—Terry Orlick

7. *Hit Refresh*—Greg Shaw, Jill Tracie Nichols, and Satya Nadella

8. *Jonny: My Autobiography*—Jonny Wilkinson

9. *The Everything Store: Jeff Bezos and the Age of Amazon*—Brad Stone and Pete Larkin

To this list I would add Enda's bestseller: *Commit! Make Your Mind and Body Stronger and Unlock Your Full Potential.*

He adds a word of caution: "The answer is not the book. The answer is what you do with what you read in the book. Do you have the hunger to read it four times and pick out three principles that you are now going to practice relentlessly for ninety days? Then the book is of benefit. Otherwise, the book is just something you talk about at a dinner party."

P6 ACTIONS TO TAKE:

_____

_____

_____

_____

_____

_____

_____

_____

_____

_____

_____

_____

THEME 3

ACCELERATE

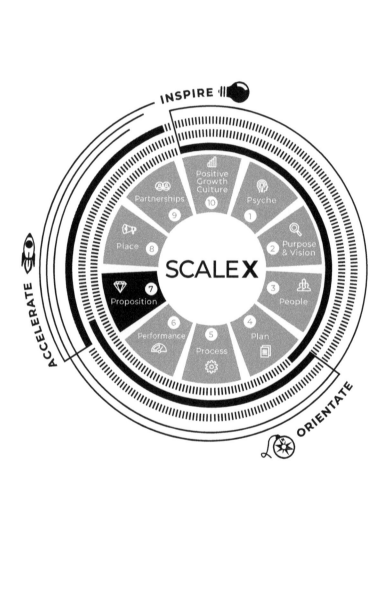

P7

PROPOSITION

"Successful companies create value by providing products or services their customers value more highly than available alternatives. They do this while consuming fewer resources, leaving more resources available to satisfy other needs in society. Value creation involves making people's lives better."

—Charles Koch

WHY DIDN'T WE PUT PROPOSITION AT THE START OF THE SCALEX 10 Principle Framework? Because scaling mode is fundamentally different to startup mode, where having something to sell in the first instance is of course critical. By now, however, you will have already proven the viability of your product or service. The next step is to clearly define and dial up a value proposition that allows you to aim high and grow more.

The first challenge is to decouple from your emotional attachment to the amazing product or service that you have either invented or brought to market. That wonderful feature that has taken months or even years of blood, sweat, toil, and tears to develop? It doesn't matter. Not to your customer, *not unless you can clearly demonstrate its value to them.* This is not an easy fact to accept. Time and again, I have seen founders fail to see their business through the eyes of their customers, which is why a value proposition remains one of the most overlooked and misunderstood elements of running a business. If you wish to scale successfully, you will have to shift your perception and bring that value proposition into razor-sharp focus.

A report commissioned by Barclays back in 2015 found that entrepreneurs aspiring to scale their organizations needed to "develop a clear articulation of their company's competitive strength in the eyes of the customers, and how this strength is related to internal processes and knowledge. This needs to drive an identification of the relevant growth path in a way that allows scaling without leading into a complexity trap."[59]

Let's begin by examining what a value proposition actually is.

7.1 "SO WHAT?" TEST FOR VALUE

"Your customers are the judge, jury, and executioner of your value proposition. They will be merciless if you don't find fit!"
—**Alexander Osterwalder**

There are many definitions of value proposition. One of my favorites comes from Michael Skok, entrepreneur in residence at the Harvard Business School: "In its simplest terms, a value proposition is a positioning statement that explains what benefit you provide for who and how you do it uniquely well. It describes your target buyer, the pain point you solve, and why you're distinctly better than the alternatives."[60]

You must understand what makes you unique. You must understand the gains you deliver to your customer and the pains you remove. A striking value proposition is a promise designed to convey how your brand stands apart from the competition, and why your target audience should choose you over the rest.

The "So What?" Test

A classic error is falling into the "Hey, Mr. Customer, look at these cool features" trap. Always apply the "So what?" test. The feature may be cool; there may be a lot of ego and pride invested in it. But if it doesn't add to the customer's gain or decrease their pain, then *so what?* Always, always look at it from the consumer's perspective.

Working with engineers across many disciplines over the last twenty years, I've often seen how focused they tend to be on product or service features, and how they struggle to convey the *value* of a particular feature to the customer. Again, always ask the question, "So what?"

Take the car industry. Whereas a mechanical engineer may marvel at the engine design, the cooling system, the valves, and camshaft, the vast majority of us simply don't care. Some of us can drive happily for a lifetime and never have a clue about what's happening under the hood. The problem is that companies frequently use these under-the-hood features to build an argument for why their company, product, or idea is better than another. In reality, this is merely *what* you do, as opposed to *why* you do it, and it's the why that speaks to the value of what you do for your customers. Don't expect them to value the double hexonated piston valve if you don't assign clear value to the double hexonated piston valve. Don't give them a half hour's presentation about why you're the biggest supplier of double hexonated piston valves in a "look at how wonderful we are" kind of way. Tell them instead that the car will get you there safely, using less fuel, in greater comfort, and so on.

Everyone at the front line of the business must understand the value your product or service delivers for the customer. The language that you use to develop and articulate your value proposition must reflect and connect with your customers or clients. It's that simple and that complicated.

VALUE Proposition Guidelines

Vagueness kills. Be clear and precise. How are you making your customer's life easier? What job does your product or service perform? Define what makes you different from your competition.

Alleviate the customer's pain. Quantify it and highlight it in your value proposition.

Leverage the gain. How will your product or service generate additional revenues for the customer?

Understand it from your customer's perspective. Immerse yourself in your customer's world to understand how you're helping them.

Engage with social media and display your value proposition prominently online. Make it easy for prospective customers to find you, using language they understand. Ask existing customers to extol your value through in-person, written, or video testimonials.

The best companies are particularly adept at framing their value proposition. Take the online video conferencing company Zoom, with which everyone became familiar during the COVID-19 pandemic. Their value proposition is front and center on their website: "In this together. Keeping you securely connected wherever you are." Scroll down and you see five reasons why you should choose their platform, all presented beneath the tagline "One Consistent Enterprise Experience." The value to the customer is clearly defined. Interestingly, the company highlights "security" as a central feature of their offering—a response to a perceived weakness at the early stages of the pandemic.

Tortuga is another great example. They make carry-on-sized travel backpacks, designed to take everything you need when you travel but without the hassle, delays, and risks of checking your baggage. At the front of their site, it says, "Pack light. Go further." Simple, clear, and unambiguously customer-centric.

Or Salesforce: "Manage and improve the relationships you have with your customers, prospects, and partners from one unified platform."

Or Canva: "Your secret weapon for stunning design."

Or Deliveroo: "Your favorite restaurants and takeaways, delivered to your door."

Remember, your value proposition is a declaration of intent that underpins your brand by letting your customers know what you stand for, how you operate, and why you deserve their business.

We will explore this in more detail a little later in the chapter.

7.2 INNOVATE

"You don't build it for yourself. You know what the people want and you build it for them."
—**Walt Disney**

Ambitious SMEs tend to have an awkward relationship with innovation. They long for the freedom of the old days, when they could do what they wanted, and yet they know that in order to scale successfully, they need to impose more discipline on how they innovate.

There's an entrepreneurial paradox typically pervasive in aspirational scale-ups. The creative talents of the founder, once the source of a company's success, can begin to impede progress. Here's the situation: The founding entrepreneur, full of nervous excitement, arrives at the desk of the product development engineer to talk about a new product that will revolutionize everything.

"What about the latest product? The one that we've been developing for the past six months?"

"No, forget about that; we're not doing that anymore."

Months of going back and forth between engineers and visionary follow, together with an explosion in related costs. The chosen few engineers work tirelessly under the guidance, enthusiasm, and pressure of the founder…until the next shiny new idea comes along, and then it's a case of abort and begin again.

Your company has arrived at scaling base camp thanks to the founder's energy and brilliance. These creators, ideators, and collaborators have a rare and wonderful mindset. But getting to the summit—scaling—requires a different mindset.

Redefining Innovation

"Every organization will have to learn to innovate—and innovation can now be organized and must be organized—as a systematic process."
—Peter Drucker

Innovation is now all about enabling the needs of your customers and widening the gap between you and your competitors. This means allocating resources—time, money, and people—in what was previously a discrete cost, in what was previously something that simply emanated from the head of the founder.

The innovation function will be like any other within the business, requiring discipline, structure, process, and an accountable owner. It will be characterized by a deep desire to forge strong links across the business and especially with those working at the front line, those directly in touch with your customers, those who are attuned to what constitutes value to the customer. In my experience, these frontline, customer-facing teams are a gold mine of ideas. You just need to create a process to mine them.

Remember, scaling success ultimately means that this wonderful business will survive beyond any one person, and that includes you.

This doesn't mean that your great ideas will no longer be fertilized; it simply means that all ideas will be systematically assessed, and if they meet the requirements, they will be progressed by the innovation function. In fact, embedding an innovation process will provide you with even more time to use your creative faculties. The difference is this: maturity comes in the scaling organization at the point when the founder can no longer pull rank and skip the innovation pipeline queue in an effort to fast-track their ideas.

Nor should innovation become the exclusive domain of the product development function. Rather, it should be enshrined in an organization's culture. Remembering P5 Process, encourage employees not only to innovate on the front line but also in the processes and systems that help enable smooth and effective customer delivery *at* the front line. As in every other part of the scaling business, innovation needs to be planned. Your approach to this key process should be aligned to your vision and purpose and targeted at the market you're operating in.

In my last business, we instilled discipline into the innovation function early, thanks in no small part to a research and development collaboration with a local university that was grant supported by a business development agency. Applications had to be processed and that required structure. We followed up by appointing a lead development person and a project sponsor—me. We also agreed on project milestones. Now, for the first time in our product development history, the accountability that came with grant support brought a rigor that we just hadn't had up to that point. No one could jump the queue.

It was uncomfortable at the start, but it worked. In time, that rigor was vital to our emergence as industry-leading innovators, to the point where we were revered globally for our product development. More about that later.

Innovation in DNA

We were fortunate in that most new projects required substantial elements of customization. Because we co-created naturally with our customers, innovation was in our DNA. As we scaled, we continued to forge strong relationships with key customers—those who were keen to push back the envelope and accept a level of risk in design. This dynamic yielded results time and time again. To give some idea of how deep this ran in the company, one of the business units we established during the global financial crisis set this as its purpose: *To Innovate against Convention.*

We also established a cold, hard metric (an OKR) to gauge the success of our innovation function. Our innovation ratio objective (IRO) required that 30 percent of revenue in the next twelve months be derived from products launched through our innovation process within the previous thirty-six months.

There is huge value to be gained from cultivating and encouraging innovation throughout your organization, and it's the process you establish to harvest those new ideas that makes all the difference. Everyone has ideas about how to improve the business, the processes, your product, the customer experience—just ask them! If ideas were the preserve of a chosen few, we wouldn't have seen the runaway success of crowdsourcing platforms. Imagination is one of the higher mental faculties that distinguishes us from all other mammals. Harness it!

In our company, we instituted what we called the World Beater series. Every single team member was assigned a group that was then given a project focused either on product development or addressing a challenge in the business. Friday afternoons were devoted to World Beater activity, and each group would present on their work at least once a year. This initiative, in addition to helping create a culture of collaborative innovation, generated a wide range of wonderful new ideas. The added bonus was that it gave the board an opportunity to interact with team members that we wouldn't normally meet. World Beater had an associated initiative which we called Dangermouse, named after the old cartoon. The designer—the one who wields the mouse—can come up with just about anything on the screen. Dangermouse was all about ensuring that whatever was designed could actually be built. In the drive to create something great, that pragmatism could not be forgotten.

Ten Ways to Add Value

If your product or service offering is the cheapest in the marketplace (like Southwest Airlines), then price is your value proposition and key differentiator. If it's not, then you must figure out why the customer is going to pay more for your product or service. CEOs have often told me, "We're different from our competitors," but when asked how, they struggled to respond meaningfully. Let's take a look at some of the ways you can innovate value in your offering.

1. PROVIDING EXPERT ADVICE AND A VERY HIGH LEVEL OF PROFESSIONALISM

This is something I saw done particularly well in my previous role. Professionalism was one of our unique selling points. We were the only company in our industry to recruit graduate engineers and provide training through to chartership level. At the project design stage, we held in-company workshops so that we could assess customer needs in order to deliver a bespoke solution. This became a key part of our selling process. We trained our sales team to provide value by giving the customer advice that was significantly better, more sophisticated, and consequently more valuable than that of the competition.

2. BUNDLING AND PACKAGING

This isn't solely about how your product or service looks; I'm also talking about putting together desirable packages and/or added benefits that together create a great deal more value than the product or service on its own.

One of the most innovative "bundlings" I witnessed in our business was the integration of two products we struggled to sell by themselves, because the competition simply had much more competitive offerings. Both were necessary for the same process, but they were often procured from different suppliers. By integrating them, our offering provided clear procurement efficiencies for our customers, who weren't slow to snap them up. That product was successfully patented and is now a market leader in the Indian market.

3. SERVICE LEVELS

Is it possible to differentiate your offering by providing a higher level of service? Or by adding different levels of service based on a customer's size, order frequency, or level of purchase? One of the reasons we were inspired initially to create a partner network in export regions was because we felt that the in-country partner could be more responsive to our customer's needs than we could (this was prior to establishing a direct presence in-market).

4. LOYALTY PROGRAMS

For frequent flyers. The more someone buys from you, the greater the service or pricing benefits that they receive. Having clocked up a lot of air miles over the years, there are airlines I have a strong preference for, not just for their service but also the strength of their loyalty program.

5. ONBOARDING

As new customers come on board, you may want to provide a transition team to help them make the most of the products or services that you sell. In one part of our business, we provided the customer with equipment operators during the setup and early-operation phase. This ensured the product was delivering value from the outset and mitigated the risk of easy-to-fix problems being needlessly escalated and damaging the brand. The more your customer is educated in your products or services, the greater their productivity. In the same vein, consider offering the customer staff training. Certification gives the customer the reassurance that operators are skilled in delivering the product or service.

6. REWARDS AND RECOGNITION

Go one better and formally recognize outstanding customers for their ability to realize the potential of your company's product or service, their commitment to you, or their ongoing promotion of your brand. Each year, we would host ten of our best customers at a two-day event to recognize their support over the previous twelve months. These events were a huge hit. Over those two days, our best customers reveled in the close attention they enjoyed from our senior directors. It proved a fantastic way of cementing relationships and boosting goodwill.

7. STRATEGIC PREFERENCE

Recognize a customer's strategic importance in a new region or market by providing higher quality products, a more sophisticated level of service, dedicated team members, or dedicated phone lines. We often established spare-parts-holding arrangements for strategically important clients. These extra parts were kept in storage on-site but only had to be paid for when used. As mentioned in P5 Process, this helped answer the question, "How are you going to support me from the UK if I'm based in Australia?"

8. DEDICATED TEAM MEMBERS

This works particularly well if you have a technical product or service, or one that requires ongoing support to maximize its value, and is typically found in B2B environments, such as software or cloud services. As an extension of the onboarding process, you assign dedicated people to handle your customers' accounts. Your customers' success with your product or service is critical to repeat business. Recognizing this, more companies are shifting responsibility for ongoing customer care and growth from an account manager to a customer success manager (CSM). A recent LinkedIn survey identified CSM as one of the most promising sales jobs for 2019.[61] A 2019 *Harvard Business Review* article meanwhile points out that with complex and evolving technology products, customers need ongoing help to adapt and realize value. "Customer value realization is the flywheel that keeps customers coming back. The CSM can be the power that accelerates the flywheel."[62]

9. SPEED OF SERVICE OR ENHANCED LEAD TIME FOR DELIVERY

In my own industry, it was quite common for customers to deliberate for years on a purchase. Once they decided to invest, however, lead time on delivery was often a critical factor in their product selection. Shaving a few weeks from delivery times in large projects was a critical factor in our favor on many occasions.

10. INFORMATION

Leverage your unique perspective on your industry and underpin your value proposition with a newsletter that updates your customers with timely and relevant information. We held webinars, in-company think tanks, among our customers and hosted conferences partnering with global authorities within our industry on the latest trends and challenges. Become a thought leader in your industry and provide real value amid the noise of social media.

Once again, the key thing to remember is that what got you here won't get you there. A clearly defined value proposition will be critical to achieving your strategy. Remember, too, that as you scale, you will loom ever larger on your competitors' radar. To maintain the value proposition that sets you apart, you will have to innovate continually. Your challenge? Do it before they do it.

7.3 MAXIMIZE STANDARDIZATION

"Quality in a product or service is not what the supplier puts in; it is what the customer gets out and is willing to pay for. A product is not quality because it is hard to make and costs a lot of money, as manufacturers typically believe."
—**Peter Drucker**

During the 2007 financial crisis, we learned that if we really wanted to scale up, we had to define our product offering very succinctly. Up to this point, we had relied heavily on a small number of talented engineers. These were design artisans, guys who combined technical brilliance and experience with real business development capability. This is a rare and wonderful combination. If you ever find it, cling to it! These individuals had the ability to sell large projects from a blank sheet and often did.

These people would listen carefully to the customer's needs and, like a street portrait artist, would bring the customer's vision to life before their eyes. The problem, however, was this: how do you scale that? Their genius was central to getting us to this point in our growth journey. The irony is that they had actually become the bottleneck. It was as if the bus that got us this far was now blocking the road ahead.

The challenge was how to convert their artistry into something a little less black magic—something repeatable, scientific, and most importantly, scalable. How do we extract years of artisanal knowledge and inject it into a team of frontline salespeople with no previous knowledge of our industry or the customers they were selling to? One of our unique selling points was the fact that we customized our solutions. Now, as the recession took hold, we had to retain the quality and functionality that was a hallmark of our larger bespoke projects but engender a solution that could be easily exported around the world. We had to deliver on our value proposition but in a more, well, standardized way.

The other issue with the genius engineer/bespoke approach is its complexity and consequent cost. Our designers, tasked with detailing the concepts, would take that napkin sketch and create an intricate network of pipework, walkways, handrails, and structures woven under and around solid chunks of heavily engineered equipment. Delivering on time was a serious challenge because each project was so different that there was little past experience to base schedules on. The same went for price. Almost every time, we saw projects go seriously over budget, and inevitably, we had to take the hit.

We had no shortage of ideas. Each new project came laden with innovation. What we desperately needed was a process for turning those ideas into real products and solutions for masses of other customers. The answer lay in productization.

Productization

Productization was our highly focused R&D initiative; R&D, in this case, standing for "Rip-off and Duplicate!" By examining the hundreds of projects we had already completed, we drew out the common elements that might be ripped off and duplicated in a more standard design. Our lead engineers, energized by this new target, quickly identified a host of common characteristics in equipment design—things like layouts, connection points, sizing, capacities, and so on. Armed with this information, they began to draw the first iteration of what would become our core product. Excitement grew among the engineering team as these embryonic designs began to develop arms and legs. Each new iteration would be presented, appraised, refined, and bettered. Eventually, our very first product was born. This would, in time, become a global industry leader, much replicated to this day.

The next step was to turn that productization process on our entire range. We identified commonalities that allowed us to develop modules, which we would use in turn to create customized solutions. So we had our scalable product but without losing the bespoke solutions that were central to our value proposition. We could now brand the modules and market their value. We became known as the company that introduced modularity across all of the sectors we operated in, and it was such a successful approach that it became the industry standard.

We assigned product and technical specialists within the engineering team to support new sales recruits; each region would have a sales manager and a technical support resource. This greatly facilitated scaling. We no longer had to find and recruit the unicorn salesperson, that person with a rare combination of commercial and technical abilities. The new sales team now could sell from a palette of standard modules to quickly configure a solution for a customer through the design process. No more blank sheets and no more design team trying to puzzle through a hand-drawn blueprint.

We also found that this approach drastically reduced quotation waste. Prior to productization, only 7 percent of inquired projects became confirmed orders, so a lot of time and energy went into scoping out projects that would never yield revenue. It was a shocking level of waste.

Now the sales team could quickly configure a customer solution from the modules available, giving much more clarity to design, technical layout, and pricing teams. No more customized drawings or elaborate quotations. Project cost was far easier to estimate, which ruled customers in or out much earlier in the process. This made the sales teams much more productive. Moreover, the removal of technical complexity reduced their dependence on those design, technical, and pricing teams. That independence was really empowering and was central to increasing our conversion rate to 20 percent. Only the *real* leads got through.

Processes obviously have a key role to play here, too. We talked in depth in P5 Process about the necessity of embedding a process culture. Once productization is established, you will also need to establish the processes that place it at the heart of what you do and to ensure that innovation is deployed to continually improve those systems.

7.4 PATENT OR NOT TO PATENT

"Intellectual property protection is critical to fostering innovation. Without protection of ideas, businesses and individuals would not reap the full benefits of their inventions and would focus less on research and development. Similarly, artists would not be fully compensated for their creations and cultural vitality would suffer as a result."
—STOPfakes.gov—a one-stop shop of US government tools and resources on intellectual property rights (IPR)

You've done all the hard work. After years of trial and terror (!), your latest innovation is ready for release. It is original, it embodies your value proposition, and it's the repository of all your hopes. Now, do you patent it or do you just promote it? It's a dilemma that most scale-ups face at some point in their journey. The answer, however, is rarely straightforward. Invest cash now to protect the potential benefit of an unproven product or preserve your cash, release your product, and hope that being first to market will offer enough protection.

If your whizzy-spinny doofer becomes hugely successful, competitors will at best lean heavily on your design. At worst, they'll copy it, add a few more features, and sell it for less—or both. They will make the same marketing statements and may even claim that this invention was the result of their toil, not yours. If they're a larger corporate—and larger corporates are not above these things—they will have the brand loyalty and deep pockets to push their version of your product as you never could. If you haven't protected it, there's nothing you can do about it.

So what to do?

I've seen all of the arguments for and against patenting, but in my experience, it works.

Following our productization strategy, we successfully launched our first modular product in 2010 at the world's largest construction expo. At the time, we were still trying to navigate a path out of the global financial crisis. Against this backdrop, preserving cash was a priority, so we decided to promote rather than patent. We reasoned that being first to market would offer some level of protection. So in an attempt to accelerate sales, all our eggs went into the promotion basket. I should say, too, that it wasn't a case of blindly picking promotion over patenting. Our marketing strategy was clearly aligned with our vision, which was that we would become number one in our industry. In order to exploit a global market opportunity, we would need to understand what we were going to sell and the channels through which we would sell it. The productization process had delivered the first part of that equation. In parallel, we had concluded that the optimum strategy was to do something we had never done before, which was to sell through an established equipment dealer network.

Our product launch met with huge excitement and admiration at the expo, and soon we had a list of renowned industry distributors queuing to speak with us. In the months that followed, we put a range of distributor agreements in place, covering areas as far apart as South Africa and Australia. Our competitors watched as our product lit up the market. So far so good.

But there was a problem.

Up to this point, we had been selling blank sheet, turnkey projects. Our value proposition largely resided in our ability to comprehend the many variations in a customer's requirements and turn that knowledge into a successful project. Now, all of a sudden, we found ourselves disconnected from the customer. Our dealers did not want us (the mere manufacturer) speaking with *their* customers.

"Just give us the brochures, the specs, and we'll do the rest," they said.

In the past, we had built to order. Now we found ourselves in this strange situation of building to stock and attempting to provide dealers with a product that would cover most technical eventualities, an impossible task.

It was a disaster. The dealers did not always fully understand the technical nuances of the customer's requirements and in any case, were conditioned to sell standardized products. They would only ever offer what they had in stock. When problems arose—as they quickly did—the dealer would put an arm around *their* customer and point toward the manufacturer. Us, in other words.

This was an alien place for us to be. We had lost the intimate relationship with our customers, which was the unique thing that underpinned our value. Worse, the dealer model pushed us *too far* into productization, to the point where we almost commoditized our offering. At the same time, we had made it easy for our much larger competitors (who were skilled designers and manufacturers of other equipment) to copy what we did. The magic was out of the box. In an industry well known for how heavily it leaned on the intellectual property of others, we had fallen into a trap. We had gifted a beautiful invention to the industry. Due to our lack of experience managing a dealer network, our first-mover advantage had been compromised.

It took some ten years, but in that time, almost every competitor in our industry brought out a version of our invention, and we were powerless to do anything to stop them.

Win or Learn

It was incredibly frustrating, but we couldn't allow ourselves to obsess about that failure. Our culture was "Win or Learn," and we knew that if our processes had delivered one great product, they could deliver another. So we focused forward and channeled our creative energies into developing new modules. This time, we made sure to protect our IP. In the years that followed, we were granted patents across many new products and processes. This strategy worked.

We were now able to ward off those who attempted to copy what we had done. The other advantage lay in the fact that the investment community assigned value to the patents that we had secured. We discovered that patents help give you credibility in the capital markets and provide a level of comfort to third-party investors. Our patents guaranteed that the market opportunity we had identified would not be lost to the competition.

In time, we made the strategic decision to unwind existing distributor relationships, simply because they prevented us from selling our unique value proposition. Instead, we established a regional infrastructure, which we'll talk about in more detail in P8 Place.

I strongly recommend that you take advice from your local patent agent early in the product development process. They will guide you through the maze, allowing you to achieve the optimum level of protection. Informing yourself early will allow you to make the best decision, and a good patent agent will help train your design team on this process so that much of the subsequent work can be done in-house. Remember, too, that once you have released your invention to the market, the game is over. You cannot secure a patent retrospectively.

7.5 LEARN TO SELL THE MAGIC, NOT THE METAL

"I've trained more than 2 million salespeople in seventy-five countries and I teach them all the same thing: Sell the value and the benefit of your product or service to your customer. Focus on explaining and expressing how it works for the customer. If you focus on the value, the price becomes less and less important. If you don't focus on value, the only thing you can talk about is price."
—Brian Tracy

I spent much of my career in what's usually described as the bulk materials handling industry. It is an incredibly competitive space. Two segments of that industry, rock crushing and aggregate screening (this simply means separating the crushed rock into different sizes), are now heavily commoditized and largely compete on price. We operated in the third segment of the broader industry, which was far more nuanced. To add to the pressure, 50 percent of the value of our annual project sales revenues came from just 10 percent of the volume of projects we sold. We were always reliant on closing three or four very large projects, which were very difficult to predict, to achieve our annual target. We couldn't help but envy the sheer volume of products sold in the other two segments, but that was not where our talents lay. Our value stemmed from an understanding of the customers' pain and associated gain, and an ability to reduce one and boost the other.

There's no doubt that our productization strategy made it easier for competitors to enter the industry, but their focus remained on the product's features as opposed to the customer's pain. This is what allowed us to enjoy a certain competitive advantage.

Our mantra to the sales team was always "Sell the magic, not the metal." The salespeople who understood this, who through their own initiative would obsess about their customers, spending time with them, seeking to understand their problems—these were the ones who enjoyed the most sales, the highest customer loyalty, and secured the best margins for our company.

Price

Price will always be an issue. The challenge is to keep the focus on value. If you cannot articulate the value of your product or service, you will find yourself plunging headlong toward the bottom of Margin Killer Canyon, like a bungee jumper without a bungee.

After twenty years in business, having met hundreds of customers, I have yet to hear one of them say, "Wow, that's cheap. I would have paid more!" The customer will always want you to play the price game. Regardless of your brilliant innovations—which put you miles ahead of the competition—they will continually compare you to the competition. Procurement departments will put your years of sweat and research tears into a spreadsheet and tell you, with all the warmth of the grim reaper, that you're simply too expensive. Less-experienced members of the sales team will harass you over the price target, and you'll start to doubt yourself: *Maybe we are too expensive.*

Stay strong! If you get drawn into the price game, you will not win. Hard-won margin can disappear in minutes.

It's simple.

If you find yourself competing on price, then you've failed to effectively articulate value.

Value

Okay, what is value, then? Value is the excess benefit your customer will get over and above the price he or she pays for your solution. If your solution costs $100,000, and when implemented is expected to earn $400,000 in incremental revenues, then the value attained is $300,000 ($400,000 less $100,000).

Value isn't more features for less money. Nor is it the cost of inputs. It is what your customer derives from your product or service.

Understanding value *to the customer* is critical. If you fail to understand and articulate value well, they will force you to negotiate the price based on what your product or service costs to bring to market. We found a particular difficulty here. Customers who understood the cost of manufacturing with steel would ask, "How much are you charging per kilo?"

To avoid being dragged into that blind alley, we used a return on investment (ROI) calculation tool and kept the discussion on the process of extracting the value that our solution promised. Communicating a clear path to positive ROI will distinguish the value of your product.

So how do you communicate value?

There are four steps in the value-communication framework. This was originally formulated by Justin Withers, now SVP Strategy and Corporate Development at ZoomInfo. It also draws on work done by Alex Osterwalder in his book *Value Proposition Design*.[63]

Step 1: Define the Problem—The Pain

Pain is anything that irritates your customers before, during, and after getting a job done. This could be undesired costs, unnecessary downtime, excessive maintenance, negative emotions, risks to health and well-being, etc.

We want to avoid pains because they are things we tend to FEAR. Pains can be:

- **Functional.** An existing solution doesn't work

- **Emotional.** I feel bad every time I do this

- **Ancillary.** I wish I didn't have to travel for this

- **Reputational (or Social).** I'll look bad doing this

We would spend time auditing our customer's operations (again, the most successful salespeople were really good at this). The goal, at this point, was to learn, not to sell. We would take time with their senior people, walking around their business, listening intently, and observing carefully, asking a series of well-crafted, open questions, all with the aim of developing a clear picture of their pains.

- Does it take a lot of time to perform operation X?

- How much does it cost?

- Is there a substantial effort required?

- What level of disruption does it cause the business?

- Does it take additional manpower?

- How do *your* customers perceive this operation?

- Is there a health and well-being cost associated with this? How does it make you feel when you have to do X? What are your frustrations, annoyances, the things that give you a headache?

- How are current solutions underperforming? What isn't working well? Which features are missing? Are there performance issues or common malfunctions?

- What are the big challenges you encounter? Do you understand how things work? Do you have difficulties getting certain things done, or do you resist certain jobs for specific reasons?

- What negative social consequences do you encounter? Are you afraid of a loss of face, power, trust, or status?

- What risks do you fear? Are you afraid of financial, social, or technical risks? What do you fear will go wrong?

- What's keeping you awake at night?

- Are common mistakes being made? Is a solution being used the wrong way?

- What are the barriers to adopting a solution? Are there up-front investment costs? Is there a steep learning curve?

Step 2: Show the Benefit of the Solution—The Gain

Sales reps love focusing on product features and taking the customer through glossy brochures on their corporate tablet. This makes sense in theory. After all, it's the features that deliver the value, and it's the features that you've spent the last year developing. Of course you want to tell the customer about them. But this is a mistake. The question is not how great is this dual max flux capacitor? It's this: What benefit does it actually provide?

Brochure selling does not work. The sales rep drops into the customer's office and leaves a brochure with the receptionist. Or if they're granted a meeting, they take the brochure out and spend precious customer face time talking endlessly about the dual max flux capacitor in all its shiny glory.

One of our products was a vibrating screen, used for sorting aggregate into different sizes. One of the key features of this product was that it was galvanized. Instead of a traditional paint finish, we applied a protective zinc coating to the steel. Sounds nice, but instead of talking about that, we talked about what it meant for the customer: a longer wear life, much better protection for the equipment in harsh marine environments, less downtime, lower total cost of ownership over the life of the product, and less frustration from operators because it was low maintenance.

Gains are classified into four separate types:

REQUIRED GAINS

These are gains without which a solution will not work. For example, at its most basic, a smartphone has to allow you to make a call.

EXPECTED GAINS

These are relatively basic gains that we expect from a solution, even if it could work without them. For example, since Apple launched the iPhone, we expect phones to be well designed and look good.

DESIRED GAINS

These are gains that go beyond basic expectations but that we would love to have if we could get them. These are usually gains that customers would come up with if you asked them. For example, we would like smartphones to seamlessly integrate with our other devices.

UNEXPECTED GAINS

These are gains that go beyond customer expectations. They wouldn't even come up if you asked them. Just think of the many unexpected gains a smartphone delivers through its apps: GPS navigation, file-sharing apps, fitness trackers, and so on. Before Apple brought touch screens and the app store to the mainstream, nobody really expected these things to be part of a phone.

THE GAIN QUESTIONS

- Which savings would you value most in terms of time, money, and effort?

- In a B2B environment, how would increases in quality impact value and the price you charge to *your* customer?

- What quality levels do your customers expect? What could you offer in excess of that?

- How do current solutions delight your customers? Which specific features do they enjoy particularly?

- Is there something your customers haven't identified that would make their jobs or lives easier? A flatter learning curve? More services? Lower costs of ownership?

- What positive social consequences do your customers desire? What makes them look good? What increases their power or their status?

- What do you value most? Good design? Guarantees? Additional features?

- What do you dream about? What do you aspire to?

- What would be a huge relief for you?

- How do your customers measure success and failure? How do they measure performance and cost?

Step 3: Articulate Your Value

To support our sales team, we constructed a simple return on investment (ROI) template which was subsequently adopted by our competitors. It was based on the discovery questions we asked about the customer's operations. The output was a one-page income statement highlighting the payback period and ROI relating to the investment in our proposed solution. At its most basic level, the concept is expressed like this:

$$\text{Simple ROI} = \frac{(\text{Gains-Investment Costs})}{(\text{Investment Costs})}$$

$$= \frac{(\$700{,}000\text{-}\$500{,}000)}{\$500{,}000}$$

$$= 40\%$$

Using these figures, we were able to create a compelling, unequivocal reason to buy. We often examined our target customer's strategic aims, as specified on their website, annual reports, or other corporate literature. If, for example, they explicitly stated their desire to achieve more output from their existing mineral resources, we could demonstrate how our offering facilitated that.

Learn to do the math, gather as much information as you can during the discovery exercise, quantifying the savings and additional revenues, and you'll make it so much easier for your prospects to understand your value proposition as it pertains to them. And there won't be a heated discussion about why your "premium price" is too expensive because the customer will understand why it's worth it.

Step 4: Bring It All Together with a Story

When you have delivered your solution to the customer and it does just what you said it would do, capturing *their* story and bringing it to the world is very powerful. It's the perfect way to showcase your value proposition. It will incorporate the three points: the problem, the solution, and the value. And if told using the customer's words, in the customer's voice, it will have much more impact on target customers than the best sales pitch in the world. This is especially important when selling in a new country, new market, or indeed both. Make your existing customers brand ambassadors. We have a herd mentality, and no one likes to be the guinea pig. So when you win that initial customer, treat them so well that they will tell everyone about the value you have delivered. We witnessed this phenomenon time and again in new markets.

Develop stories that include a situation (pain point), action (purchase of your product), and result (ROI), and include these in your sales collateral. Develop case studies, one for each industry or line of business you sell into. Go further. Ask for video testimonials, allowing the customer to tell the world the difference your solution has made to their business, to their lives, to the lives of their customers. You'll be surprised how willing they will be to share their story. Why? Because it demonstrates how clever they have been in evaluating and choosing the right solution, especially if they have moved ahead of their competition.

These testimonials will serve to strongly reinforce everything that you have articulated in relation to your value proposition and will become a powerful weapon in your selling arsenal.

7.6 EVOLVE YOUR VALUE WITH YOUR CUSTOMERS

"Strive not to be a success, but rather to be of value."
—**Albert Einstein**

Your role in the ongoing creation of value is this: make your customer the star. The mantra we used was, "Be the star maker, not the star."

We would always aim to deliver a solution that would make our customers (this was a B2B model) a star in front of *their* customers. We set out to build loyalty, to the point where our customers weren't names on an invoice but actually close friends and brand champions.

We set out to get our customers to feed into our innovation pipeline by emphasizing their needs each and every time. We made the customer the focus of our conversations and marketing messaging. We used every opportunity to get our team members in front of customers, to promote the understanding that we only existed because of those customers, and to encourage team members to form personal connections with them.

Customers and markets change over time. Your business needs to evolve with them. Rather than make assumptions about your community based on their past needs and buying behaviors, create feedback loops so you're always in the know. You do this by maintaining your relationships with customers, by making sure that decisions regarding your customers and the products that serve them are made in consultation with those who are closest to the customer. Your value proposition will need to evolve in line with your growing customer community.

We kept numerous channels of communication open with our customers: within our technical presales function, our project management delivery team, and when installed, our after-sales team. This policy was underpinned by internal processes that ensured valuable customer information about our products and services was continually fed back. In itself, this allowed us to keep our value proposition customer focused, but also, it operated as a powerful loyalty tool. We invited our customers to innovation workshops. Customers who feel they are being listened to, who are asked for their ideas and opinions don't tend to stray.

This is something that Jeremy Eakin of Eakin Healthcare understands. The company, which has grown rapidly over the past five years, plans to be the fastest growing global trusted partner for ostomates by providing innovative ostomy solutions. An ostomate is someone who has had an ostomy, which is a surgical procedure that creates an opening in the body for the discharge of wastes.

Part of Jeremy's strategy to ignite these ambitions centered on revolutionizing the way in which the company interacted with its customers. In the past, they had frequently brought nurses, who have a pivotal role in enabling sales, to their Belfast HQ to talk about their products.

"Now we completely restructured those visits," says Jeremy. "We asked them in advance to prepare case studies and discussion topics. Then we recorded those sessions and wrote up our findings.

"We started an online panel of consumers. Each month, they get a questionnaire and a topic like 'How is lockdown impacting your stoma change routine?' We created a website—completely unbranded—with videos from nurses giving patients advice, and a patients' forum that we mine to help boost our understanding of patient needs. We've got two people working full time on that site, using social media to build and promote it. In addition, we commissioned market research in the countries we targeted.

"None of this is rocket science," he admits. "We just hadn't been doing it properly before."

Watch the Market

When the market changes, start asking questions:

- How does this affect my customers?

- How will it change their behavior?

- For how long?

- Where would they go if not to us?

By continually interrogating your customer's motivations and re-actions, you will trigger new solutions and innovative ways of adding value as a result of external shocks and changes.

During the COVID-19 crisis, fitness centers closed overnight, but the creative ones stayed in close contact with their customers, renting out equipment, providing online fitness classes, motivational videos, and even recipes to support healthy eating.

Instead of traditional market research, send ten team members to talk with ten customers each month. Do this and your company's sensitivity to what is happening in the market will go through the roof. You'll win when you connect the dots faster than your competitors.

TAKE ACTION—IT'S SIMPLE!

"So What?" Test for Value. Don't proclaim your proposition's features from the rooftops. Proclaim its value to your customers and encourage them to extol its virtues. Distance yourself from your product or service. Put yourself in the customer's shoes and ask, "So what? Where is the value?"

Innovate. Scaling companies need to change how they innovate. An innovation process is all about enabling the needs of your customers and widening the gap between you and your competitors.

Maximize Standardization. To facilitate scaling, you need to harness innovation to create standardized products that embody the brilliance of your value proposition.

Patent or Not to Patent. The choice is to protect your IP or hope that being first to market is sufficient protection. Do your research carefully and take advice from your local patent agent.

Learn to Sell the Magic, Not the Metal. Price will always be an issue. The challenge is to keep the focus on value. If you find yourself competing on price, you've failed to effectively articulate value.

Evolve Your Value with Your Customers. Customers and markets change over time. Rather than make assumptions about your community based on their past needs and buying behaviors, create feedback loops so you're always in the know.

Principle in Action—BioTector

When Martin and Nancy Horan set up Pollution Control Systems in Cork, Ireland in 1995, their plan was as simple as it was compelling: to develop the best online TOC analyzer in the world. TOC stands for total organic carbon, which is one of the most important metrics in assessing water pollution. Online analyzers are deployed in factory settings and typically sit right at the end of the pipe, where they flag any contaminants before they enter the water course. At the time, the industry was dominated by several large, household-name corporations, all of which produced analyzers that relied on one of two technologies. The Horans had bought a new, fledgling technology that had one advantage over the traditional methods. BioTector, as it was called, was robust and self-cleaning. When contaminants flowed into either of the two traditional analyzers, they clogged up and had to be manually stripped and cleaned before they could be recommissioned. Not so with BioTector. That was the good news. The bad news was that it was not as accurate as either of the two traditional technologies. David Horan, son of Martin and Nancy, would eventually become CEO of the company. He takes up the story:

> There were other problems. TOC analyzers were a grudge buy—bought only because the regulator insisted upon it. Because regulation drove sales, BioTector's competitors could say, "Don't go buying BioTector; you need a tried-and-tested technology." It was easy to scaremonger.
> Cost was also an issue. These analyzers are essentially little factories, containing pumps, valves, reactor chambers, and pipe work. In the drive to create the best analyzer in the world, we systematically replaced every component with the very best, most robust that could be found. This meant that BioTector, in addition to being "nonstandard" was up to twice as expensive as its competitors.

Dad, already a successful entrepreneur, worked closely with his head of R&D, Seamus O'Mahony, on a project they called Get the Accuracy Right. Months of trial and error followed, until one Valentine's Day, Seamus discovered that adding manganese to the process catalyzed the chemical reaction, freeing up the last few atoms of carbon and finally delivering an accurate reading. Straightaway, Dad prepared the paperwork and patented the process. We now had the most robust analyzer in the world, and it was every bit as accurate as the legacy technologies.

So we had a great product. The next task was to build the great company that could deliver on its potential.

When I joined the company, the first thing we did was simplify things by changing our name to that of the product—BioTector. Then Dad and I got on the road and traveled extensively. Building on the great work that he had already done, we established a distribution network around the world. We spent a great deal of time with distributors, with customers, and at trade shows and conferences, establishing contacts and key influencers in a range of industries.

Everything we learned was fed back to the R&D team in Cork, who continued to develop the product. We set ourselves apart by doing what our competitors were really too big to do. If the customer said, "I need a system to deliver the sample to the analyzer," BioTector would say, "I can do that for you." If the customer said, "I need a house to put it in," BioTector would say, "I can do that for you."

Distributors would frequently push back on the price, but we refused to budge, even when that meant losing sales. We knew that our product offered something that no other product could offer. The difficulty lay in articulating that value more clearly.

As the company built partnerships with bigger and more influential distributors, we began establishing the processes and procedures necessary to enable scaling. In the beginning, each analyzer was built in its entirety by one engineer. Now a production process was initiated to standardize the product, reduce defects, and ensure timely delivery. Our head of production implemented lean manufacturing, and we overhauled and streamlined all of our processes.

In our early days, we had been an R&D-led company. Our engineers were given the freedom to try things out; many of them had pet projects on the go. That had to change. Our mantra became "Everyone is in sales," and R&D people were frequently redeployed to enable those sales. Though we were still a small company, we had begun to think and act like a big company.

Because of the system's unique abilities, we knew that focusing on end-of-pipe applications was underplaying BioTector's potential. So we began to think about the analyzer in new ways. What if you installed BioTector *before* rather than after waste management? If your analyzer could tell you that contaminant levels were low going into waste management, would that allow you to cut back on waste processing cost?

Or what if you installed BioTector right in the middle of your process? Could it help to flag product losses? Oil and gas plants, breweries, and dairy processors are made up of miles of piping, conducting valuable process material to different parts of the factory. If you could pinpoint losses early, would that help?

We realized that if you could create a product-loss argument for installing a BioTector, it would no longer be a grudge buy. The premium it commanded over competitor products would be eminently justifiable, *if* we could make it clear just how much installing a BioTector would save.

Some customers had already figured this out and were using BioTector in process control applications. Mars, for example, bought a BioTector, and word got back to us that the analyzer had paid for itself in three days. Three days! There had been a major malfunction in the factory, the analyzer had picked it up, an alarm had gone off, and a team was dispatched to fix the fault. If it had been missed, €70,000 ($80,500) worth of product would have been lost.

Sometimes a distributor would call us and say that a big malfunction had been caught by BioTector and that it had saved the company a fortune.

What's a fortune? That was the big question.

Part of the answer came through Andrew McDonald, who ran one of our local distribution companies, EASL. His focus was the dairy industry, and his brainwave was to install a BioTector in a Transit van. He would drive this into dairies and place the intake pipe in a drain. The following day, he would come back and show the plant manager how the TOC count had spiked during the day. These spikes clearly indicated events during which product had been lost. By checking the time stamps on these spikes, the plant manager was able to go back and see what had happened and make whatever changes were needed to stem the losses.

Andrew's presentations alone were often enough to generate sales, but without knowing exactly *how much* was being lost, the argument was only half won.

So we sourced an excellent marketing consultant, Mel Galloway, and asked her to help us come up with a story, a story about product loss that could demonstrate in clear, unambiguous terms the value of installing a BioTector at the heart of the production process.

Because there was so much existing information around the dairy industry, this is where she began.

Mel said to R&D, "Okay, I know when you sample stuff going down the drain, you're measuring total organic carbon, but is there any way of converting that to liters of milk?"

R&D developed software which could take the TOC data and apply a conversion factor for full-fat milk. When combined with a flow rate, we could then generate a reading for milk lost. Armed with this information, we were able to arrive at some pretty shocking conclusions. Most dairies were losing between 3 percent and 5 percent of everything they bought. This was huge. What's more, these losses were going down drains and ending up in the waste treatment plant. That meant that not only was product being lost, additional resources were needed to treat this waste.

This was the story we needed to fully unlock our value proposition.

We were now able to work out that if a typical dairy cut their losses by just 15 percent, they would save themselves €600,000 ($690,000) per year. Factor in the reduction in treatment costs as a result of that saving and that figure grew by €105,000 to €705,000 ($120,750 to $810,750). By contrast, a BioTector cost in the region of €40,000 ($46,000). Moreover, that 15 percent was conservative. Typically, we found that after BioTector was installed, dairies saved themselves anywhere between 25 percent and 40 percent.

In one dairy, they connected the analyzer to an alarm system. If the BioTector detected milk where milk should not be, there were flashing lights and sirens. In another dairy, they set up an auto-text system. Everybody knew that when the message came in, you dropped everything and ran. Process people began to understand their plants a little better. They saw where the issues were and addressed them by changing components or implementing new maintenance procedures. Huge savings were made.

And the great thing about it was that we had the entire market to ourselves. The two legacy technologies would become clogged when anything other than clear water passed through them. But BioTector was self-cleaning. We had designed it to be like a car: needing maintenance once every six months, regardless of what it was asked to process.

In the years that followed, we developed similar propositions around brewing, oil, gas, and the soft drinks industry. The company grew rapidly, and in 2012, we won a host of accolades, including a Frost and Sullivan product leadership award. Their analysis concluded that BioTector had become the market-leading technology in the US, with an estimated 25–30 percent share of the TOC water and wastewater analytical instrumentation market.

In 2014, Danaher acquired BioTector. Over the four years leading up to the acquisition, the value of the company rose by just under 1,600 percent.

P7 ACTIONS TO TAKE:

_____

_____

_____

_____

_____

_____

_____

_____

_____

_____

_____

_____

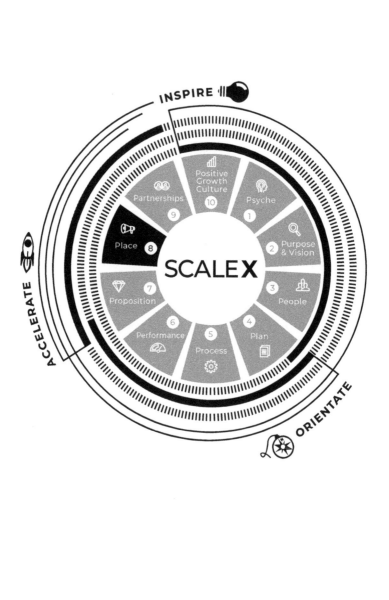

P8

PLACE

"In virtually every respect, the challenges you expose yourself to by accessing new markets will raise your game and enhance your own and your company's skills immeasurably."
—Brendan McGurgan

I'D LIKE TO TELL YOU THAT AS CEO OF A MANUFACTURING SME, our first experience of exporting came as a result of a well-thought-out strategy which was then expertly executed, but in reality, we almost stumbled into it. At the time, back in 2004, about 85 percent of our revenues were coming from within Ireland, with most of the remainder from the UK. We often spoke about establishing reference customers beyond our home market, but it wasn't until we received an email inquiry from Karachi, Pakistan that we took our first tentative steps into the wider world.

Up until this point, our deals were always very hands-on. We wrapped our arms around customers and worked very hard to make the sale happen.

But in this instance, six months after we received that email—without ever having met the customer—we crated up a sand-washing plant and sent it off. Our design manager booked a flight to Karachi to oversee commissioning on-site. He was met at the airport by a man driving an armored jeep, who told him to duck down in the back seat as he wove through the streets to a heavily guarded compound on the outskirts of the city. The design manager then spent a week in the compound commissioning the plant, before being put back into the jeep and returned to the airport. It was quite a surreal experience, but for us, the overwhelming lesson was this: If we can export to Pakistan, we can export anywhere.

8.1 SET YOUR SIGHTS ON NEW MARKETS

The board and I knew, too, that if you are serious about your scaling ambitions, you have little choice but to look beyond your home market. For US-based SMEs, that means moving outside your state. For everyone else, that means moving beyond national borders. Research demonstrates time and again that SMEs that export achieve higher growth and naturally create more jobs and innovate more. Research by Capital Economics for UK Export Finance, the UK's export credit agency, finds that firms trading internationally grow at a rate of over 15 percent compared to just 8.4 percent for those focusing on domestic markets alone. Forty-two percent of SMEs polled say that exporting has increased profits by up to 20 percent, while almost one in ten say it has increased profits by over 20 percent.[64]

We essentially had two reasons for developing an export strategy: one defensive, one offensive. Number one, it would mitigate the risk of a downturn in any one geographic region. Different markets tend to go through the economic cycle at different rates. If one is in recession, another may be emerging from it. And second, we realized that creating a global network, a global footprint, would give us the framework to scale the company.

At the beginning, we hadn't a clue what it took to send a plant to Pakistan. I remember the bank talking about getting a bill of lading once a letter of credit was in place. I said, "Surely, you mean 'loading'; there's no such word as 'lading.'"

We had so much to learn about the operational technicalities of exporting, and in particular exporting to a country with a radically different culture to our own. Our lack of knowledge around trade regulations, cultural differences, language, foreign exchange, and so on made everything harder. But we didn't know what we didn't know.

Not long after the Karachi adventure, an opportunity opened up in the tiny Gulf state of Qatar. We jumped at it, but once again, we had a great deal to learn about project delivery in the Middle East. At an installation in the desert, we discovered that part of the control panel we had shipped from Northern Ireland had actually melted, and we had to deliver a second unit that could stand up to the Qatari sun.

A subsequent project saw us deliver what remains as the world's largest sand-washing plant to the Middle East. The sale, worth about $10 million at the time, pulled most of our team's resources east. But owing to a lack of experience, weak processes, and some poor decision making on our part, we racked up costs of £1.4 million ($2.1 million) in the second year. This gave us an accounting loss in 2008 and stretched our little company in a variety of different ways. We emerged from that adventure battered and bruised…and yet confident. As we have continually asserted, everything comes back to psyche and how you respond. We could have said, "That's it, we're never doing that again. Let's stay close to home and focus on the markets we know." Instead, we chose to say, "Look at what we've achieved. Yes, it was tough, but we've learned a lot. Let's put those lessons to good use."

This was the point at which we allowed ourselves to dream.

Sacrifice

That first foray into Pakistan came as a result of a web inquiry, but it would be wrong to think that things were as easy as that. I can count on the fingers of one hand the number of internet inquiries that translated into a deal *without* a substantial level of travel back and forth. Almost every customer we won had to be nursed from inquiry to sales close, and that required a huge investment of time and resources.

Moving into new markets is always difficult and sometimes it's exceptionally difficult. So it's important to manage your own expectations. There is great reward, but these things take time and persistence. Creating capacity and freeing yourself from the day-to-day is critical to the development of export markets. There will be significant investment, and there will be low returns in the early stages. Because you have to spend so much time trying to gain traction in the market, be prepared to spend a great deal of time in the air.

As I write this in the early days of 2021, we have yet to see if the revolution in remote working and communication brought about by the COVID-19 pandemic will have a longer-term impact on international business travel. Although certain jobs may be more amenable to remote execution, I suspect that developing export markets will still require a certain amount of face-to-face contact.

Vision

"Lack of direction, not lack of time, is the problem. We all have twenty-four-hour days."
—**Zig Ziglar**

As always, the vision was critical. Our vision was that we would be a global company. You can't achieve that by stealth; you can't go under the radar. You've got to state it. It's got to be out there. It's got to be big and bold and clear and unambiguous. Communicating your intent publicly creates a sense of accountability. We would be a global company. Anyone joining the team knew that aspiration, and we made sure that there were daily reminders of it. In fact, in 2010, we changed our name simply to reflect that ambition. We became CDE Global.

Mindset goes hand in hand with vision. The vision acts like a magnet pulling you to where you want to go; it enshrined our desire to go global. This focused our mindset.

I'll talk about planning your exporting campaign a little later, but if you're waiting for the perfect export strategy, it'll never happen. You've got to find out as much as you can and then just get out there. You've got to make the mistakes and learn from them. And you will make mistakes. The trick lies in refusing to allow them to deflect your mindset or cloud your vision. Trust that the more you immerse yourself in export markets, the more doors you knock on, the more you learn what will or will not work for your company.

On one of our first Australian-bound projects, a piece of equipment brushed against a pine tree in our yard during pre-dispatch assembly. We thought nothing of it, but when the shipping containers arrived in Australia, a spot check by customs uncovered pine needles caught under the rubber of the conveyor belt. Importing organic material—unwittingly or not—is against the law in Australia. So our container was immediately impounded and quarantined. Between decontamination, delay, and scrutiny of all additional containers for the project, those pine needles cost us six figures.

Although we didn't see that coming, we didn't see it as waste. We recognized it for what it really was—an investment in our exporting capabilities.

All future containers bound for Australia were decontaminated pre-dispatch and sealed by specialists who provided certification that accompanied the cargo. As discussed in P5 Process, everything we learned was captured in project review meetings and fed back into our processes so that we didn't make the same mistake twice.

To be clear here, we didn't set out to make mistakes, and we didn't enjoy making them. We just couldn't let them put us off. The other point about mistake making is that we achieved a great deal of what we achieved because we were the first in our industry to do so many of the things that we did. As such, we had no one to learn from. We didn't have the benefit of seeing how others had done it.

Also, the concept of *win or learn* will work only if it's embedded in the culture. As a leader, think carefully about how you respond to learning of a costly mistake. People have to be open about the mistakes that they make; there has to be transparency. That will only happen if your response is measured, and if it prompts *positive* action. If there's blaming and cover-ups, the whole thing will fall apart. We go into more detail about establishing this kind of workplace in P10 Positive Growth Culture.

Exporting was once associated with large, long-established manufacturing companies. Today, 10 percent of all UK SMEs are exporters. These hungry, outward-thinking businesses, which operate across a wide range of sectors, are finding their place in the exporting world. Moreover, there is now ample private and public sector support for companies expanding into new markets.

8.2 INTERROGATE YOUR EXPERIENCE

Our first forays into exporting didn't begin with desktop research. Nor did we commission any market research. We were opportunity led, customer led. We received inquiries and we serviced them. That's how SMEs operate. This is their great strength: that positive aggression to get out there and win business. Once you've done that enough times, you start to build a portfolio. It's going to be varied and will probably have more failures than successes, but it's the teaching power of that experience that's important now. You need to stand back and see what you've learned.

Prior to the aforementioned Middle East project in 2006, most of our business was local and was exclusively focused on the construction sector. Ten years later, we operated in eight global regions across five separate sectors. Our export credentials extended to almost one hundred countries. It all began by chasing inquiries and picking through our history for clues about where the best export opportunities lay.

During the recession, we took a long hard look at our product set, and in particular our screens, which were designed to sort different-sized sand and aggregate particles. What we realized is that the screen doesn't care what it's sorting, which begged the question, are there other industries out there where our equipment could add value? Instead of sand, could it be used to screen iron ore, or construction and demolition waste, or maybe even other kinds of waste? As luck would have it, at around this time, we were approached by the waste management company Biffa. They were contracted into a UK local authority to handle sewage treatment. Without going into too much detail, this process requires the use of large digester tanks, which must be cleaned frequently, and whatever is extracted must be taken off to a landfill. Cleaning out digester tanks is expensive. Landfill is expensive. If you could screen out this waste *before* it clogs the tank, you would have quite a value proposition. We tested that proposition and found that we could divert 95 percent of this material away from landfill. During the recession, screened aggregate was being sold for around £4 ($6) per ton. Diverting sewage waste from landfill saved the customer between £80 and £90 ($120 and $135) per ton.

That first installation was subsequently awarded the Severn Trent Environmental Gold Award. But the real reward lay in the discovery of a whole new sector and one that wasn't half so recession-prone as construction. So we launched a separate business unit, CDEnviro, with financial support from the local enterprise support agency. At the time, we were faced with the prospect of making senior people redundant. Instead, we were able to move them across into this new entity. So here was the proof that we could take an existing technology, modify it, put a different wrapper on it, and dispatch it into a whole new market. Yes, there were new standards we had to understand and meet and all kinds of new things we had to learn, but with time and effort, we were able to uncover a hidden pathway toward our scaling vision. Six years after establishing that company, it was placed eleventh in the prestigious *Sunday Times* Lloyds SME Export Track 100.

It's about talking to the customer, understanding why they bought from you, and the value they're drawing from your product or service. It's all about looking for patterns in the data and fine-tuning that wonderful SME "we can do anything" mindset. Just last week, I was talking to a CEO of a window blind company who pivoted in the middle of the COVID pandemic and began making face shields for the retail industry. Another local company specializing in sportswear manufacturing became a leading supplier of medical garments. Once you've demonstrated that you can bring value to another sector, don't let that opportunity go cold. Don't be the window blinds guy who also does a few shields. Be the face shields guy as well. So many companies pivoted successfully during the pandemic because they were forced to think strategically. They conjured opportunities from the ashes of their existing businesses. Don't wait to be forced. Go for it now. Look for the threads that run through your offerings and explore how you can use them to bring value to other sectors.

Big companies often struggle to do this, but SMEs can turn on a dime.

What else?

Construction opportunities in Karachi led to an installation in India, not in a construction setting but in mining. We took a closer look at how this was working and saw that we could easily take that product and that skillset and apply it to other mining opportunities in areas like Australia and South America, which had thriving mining sectors.

The construction and demolition (C&D) waste business was a little more obvious, since it was that bit closer to quarrying. We developed technology that would divert between 80 percent and 90 percent of C&D waste from landfill and allow that to be reused in construction instead of natural and finite sand resources.

The key point is that you've got a different value proposition in each sector, and this returns us to the last principle—you've got to learn to sell the magic, not the metal. You've got to figure out what the magic is in each of these sectors. In the environmental industry, because we were bringing something different, we positioned ourselves as innovators, as disruptors. It was something similar in the mining industry. Mining projects were characterized by long lead times. Industry suppliers delivered what were effectively mini-villages—"stick-build" projects that could take years to install. We parachuted in with a modular format that could be deployed more rapidly without compromising quality.

In the recycling industry, we positioned ourselves as thought leaders. We drove innovation, pioneered new technology, and held global seminars with invited academics and industry experts.

It might be the same underlying technology, but everything depends on how it is applied to different sectors. Understanding your positioning is crucial. Are you low cost? Are you an innovator? Are you better at what you do than everyone else? The language that we used with the mining customer was different from the language we used in the sand and aggregates sector, which was different from the environmental sector.

It's about stopping and raising your head out of the business, looking back and analyzing what you've done. It's about seeing opportunities not as discrete events but signposts to the future. Success, then, lies in the difference between knowing and doing.

By 2012, as we faced one of the most important planning sessions in our history, we were busy colonizing five distinct sectors. Sand and aggregates, C&D waste recycling, mining, environmental, and specialist sands. Five sectors and five ways to realize our scaling ambitions.

8.3 MAKE SURE THAT EXPERIENCE CHIMES WITH RESEARCH

For me, research always started with "who," not "how." When we had an opportunity to expand into Brazil, my first call was to the local enterprise agency. I explained, "There's an opportunity for us here. We want to develop this market. I don't want to reinvent the wheel. I would love to talk to someone who's been there and done that."

As it happened, there was no one in Northern Ireland who could talk to us, so I asked them to cast a wider net and connect me with someone in Great Britain who might be able to help. They were very helpful.

And I got a book: *Doing Business in Brazil.* I found out about the legal requirements, the structures, the import rules. We engaged a legal company to help guide us, and we set up a local company in São Paulo. We immersed ourselves and learned on the hoof.

Don't get me wrong; we didn't dive in blindly. We did the research, but so much is learned by doing. You've got to get in there and test the water. You have to get a sense of the place. What's your gut telling you? Does the research support that?

Research began before the plane even touched down. At the beginning, our core business was the provision of industrial, wet-processing equipment to the construction sector. The number of cranes we could see from the airplane window as we came in to land was a rich source of data, testifying that there was a vibrant market.

Whenever there was downtime with a customer, we would go talk to other people operating in the market or talk to the local trade promotion agencies. Over time, the research we gleaned from the market gave us the confidence to make greater investments in those markets.

Desktop Research

Research won't guarantee a successful strategy, but without it, you will be blind to the plethora of cultural, regulatory, competition, and pricing issues that feed into good decision making. Moreover, good-quality research provides great learning for your leadership team. Encouraging everyone on the team to think about the global landscape prompts a mindset shift. You'll get much better engagement than if you simply present them with a strategy and aligned targets. After all, who will be leading this project for your business? Who will take ownership?

You need to be alive to the idiosyncrasies of each market.

In the Middle East, the workweek ends on a Thursday. Sunday is the first day of the week. You've got to account for the fact that during Ramadan, Muslim team members don't eat or drink.

Hierarchy is important in this part of the world. We had quite a flat structure, but we always respected the fact that in the final round of negotiations, our Middle Eastern clients would expect to deal with someone at the same perceived level in our company. In the United States or Australia, hierarchy was far less of an issue. Once there was a strong rapport with the local business development lead, the client was happy to deal with them without ever meeting the senior people.

In Northern Ireland, you can set up a new company in twenty-four hours. In Brazil, it takes six months.

The more thorough the research, the greater your confidence in breaking into a new market and establishing a growth strategy based around it. Well-researched and well-grounded demand projections make it easier to commit investment.

It's also important to inform yourself about the broader trading environment, and in particular, the tariff arrangements in place between your home country and your target markets. Tariffs inflate the price of imported products in order to protect local businesses and jobs. So they will undermine the competitiveness of your export offering. But there's an opportunity in this, too. India, with a population of more than one billion, was a market that we set our sights on. To overcome the tariff barrier, we established a manufacturing base in Calcutta, which in time proved highly successful. And while that business was finding its feet, the tariff barrier kept our foreign competition out. Know your markets. Who offers free trade and who offers less-favorable trading conditions? And keep an eye on international business news. In a volatile world, trading arrangements can change quite quickly, making some markets less attractive and others more so.

Understanding the different regulations in your target markets will ensure the first foray into exporting isn't one step forward and five steps back. Safety, production, quality, and more recently, GDPR regulations can differ from market to market and indeed from sector to sector within markets.

Even slight variations in product regulations will require production modifications which may be costly. Some of these modifications can mean that your modified product can be sold in only one market, generating risky up-front investment to facilitate those fledgling orders.

Consider:

- Is there an appetite for your product or service in your target market?

- Do local companies export there already?

- Who is your competition in the prospective market?

- Does your company have sufficient resources to do the necessary research and provide the additional people needed to meet increased demand?

- What are standard practices in your target market? Get local knowledge.

- How will you deal with exchange-rate risk?

- Is your product or service compliant with export market regulations?

- Do you need a license to export your product or service to the new jurisdiction?

- Do you have sufficient insurance coverage against damage or loss in transit and against credit, commercial, and political risks?

- Are you talking to the local enterprise promotion agency about the supports that are available?

Remember, too, that no amount of research will give you certainty. No one can predict the future. To lead a scaling company is to take calculated risks. External shocks—terrorist attacks, pandemics, regime change—will always be a risk, and you will have no choice but to respond to them.

Ambitious, determined, curious, open-minded leaders who push their thinking and stay vigilant to what is going on in the market will stand a better chance of navigating these changes and uncertainties than those who do not.

Finance

Most elements of the sales process are significantly prolonged when you operate across borders. This creates risk. The difference between profit and loss on a transaction can often depend on the time it takes to get paid. This is why it's a good idea to build export financing into your business infrastructure. It allows you to release working capital from overseas transactions—working capital that might otherwise remain tied up in invoices for long periods, constricting cash flow, and all that it entails.

Although there are numerous institutions that provide a variety of trade finance products, you should always talk to your bank first. As we became more experienced, we were able to discount letters of credit up front prior to delivering our projects. The aim was always to reduce risk and ensure our cash was safe regardless of the customer or country-risk profile. The size, cost, and terms of finance are broadly dictated by the source of capital as well as the institution's assessment of your operational risk.

Managing multiple currencies is another headache for novice exporters. In the first instance, we always tried to bypass the issue and do business in our local currency. In reality, however, that's going to run counter to the need to localize your offering (I'll go into more detail on this a little later). A key part of our strategy centered on being local in everything we did, just to make it easier for our customers to do business with us. That meant having a local presence and quoting prices in local currency. When it came to managing forex, we first sought to match exposures, to "naturally hedge" our currency risk. Our home currency was sterling, but if we had euro receivables, we examined our supply chain and tried to pair those off with euro payables. If that wasn't an option, we agreed forward currency sales with our forex provider. Remember, currencies can move suddenly and swiftly. You don't want to find your margin wiped out overnight. Most importantly, don't try to play the markets. Currency movements *can* work in your favor, but don't succumb to casino fever. Let those who speculate on foreign currency do that. That is not your job here. Your job is to make it easy for the customer to buy your goods or service. That's your focus.

8.4 PLAN YOUR CAMPAIGN

Over time, we developed a very strong presence in the Middle East and became the number one supplier in both Kuwait and Qatar. Redoubling our commitment to export led to growth. We created the aforementioned joint venture to develop the Indian market and then the wider Asian market. This was the first time we'd set up an autonomous business outside of Northern Ireland.

In addition to giving us a launchpad into Asia, it also provided a template for setting up future regional businesses. At the beginning, the Indian business was hugely challenging, and to be honest, it could have gone either way. I traveled to India a great deal and worked very hard with our joint venture partners to drive this part of the business forward. Today, it manufactures to the highest quality standards and exports to fifteen countries.

They say men make plans and God laughs. When I became CEO in 2007, myself, our business development director, and our founder went into a room and came out with our 2010 Vision, which was to build a nine-figure revenue company. Within six months, that plan had been torn up, and our only focus for the next four years was survival. It wasn't that we lacked ambition; it was simply that the plan was predicated on winning big projects across the globe. But when the global financial crisis took hold, there were no big projects anymore. It wasn't until late 2011 that we felt sufficiently confident to begin planning again. In January 2012, we created our Ready for Rio strategy, which, as before, aimed to achieve a $100 million revenue company by 2015. Why Rio? Because London was gearing up for the Olympics that year, and the positivity that surrounded it was infectious. The next Olympics would be in Rio in 2016, and we promised ourselves that by then, we would be the number one wet-processing company in the world and that our company would be earning revenues of +$100 million annually.

There were three pillars to our new vision: people, innovation, and productization—all of which we've discussed in earlier chapters. In P7 Proposition, we talked about productization and the failure of the distributor model. We discovered the hard way that although we might be able to create a modular product, we still needed ongoing interaction with customers to make that product work.

So we said okay, right, distribution won't work. Maybe a franchise model would make more sense. We suggested to distributors that they employ dedicated personnel, whom we would train before returning them to their markets. This failed because the distributors simply didn't comprehend the franchise model. It wasn't that they were bad people and we were good people, or vice versa. They simply had a business model that required the purchase of commodity products. Our equipment didn't work that way.

Everything came to a head when I got a call from one distributor.

"I've heard that one of your sales guys is over here."

"Yes," I said, "he's at a customer site, showcasing a piece of equipment to another customer. This was the closest site reference for him."

I was told, in no uncertain terms, that we had no right to be there, in *his* country without the distributor's knowledge. And as for talking to *his* customers? How dare we!

That's when the penny dropped. This was crazy. We'd created a straitjacket for ourselves. It was so liberating the day we decided, that's it, no more intermediaries. We're going direct.

It would take longer, it would take greater levels of investment, but it would liberate us and give us control of the customer relationship.

These first attempts to be strategic in our expansion planning may have failed, but they were central to helping us reveal who we really were. We were a boutique project solutions provider. We want to productize our offering to enable scale, but we could not pursue that strategy all the way through to commoditization. We still needed relationships with customers.

So, now, eighteen months into our Ready for Rio vision, we realized that we had to change course. We had to localize. I'm going to go into detail about how that worked in the next section. Before that, I want to talk about the next phase of our planning.

New Direction

I always talk about our distribution network and franchise adventures as our most successful failures. Why? Because of how much we learned and because they gave us some traction in important markets: Europe, Australia, South America, and indeed Africa. We were already number one in Ireland and the UK and well-established in the Middle East. This is why, despite the setbacks, by 2015, we became the number one wet-solutions equipment provider in the world and achieved our vision of becoming a $100 million revenue company.

Our next plan set 2020 in its sights. We called it 2020 Vision. Our moonshot, as we've discussed before, was that we would become number one, not just in the world, but in every country in the world. This sounds ludicrously ambitious, but hear me out.

Up to this point, determining Place—the regions we would sell into—had been haphazard. Now it was time to get strategic. We needed to be more logical, more *deliberate*.

We operated across five sectors, and we already had a substantial footprint in several key locations around the world. To make our vision achievable, we chunked out the world into bite-size parts. Ireland/UK was our first strategic region. North Africa was largely Arabic speaking and had an Arabic/Muslim population. That made it ethnically, linguistically, and culturally similar to the Middle Eastern market, where we already had a firm foothold. So we established Middle East North Africa—or MENA—as our second strategic region. Our joint venture in India had extended its remit to twenty-four countries in Asia—that was our third strategic region. Long story short, we broke the planet down into eight strategic regions. And it was at this point, when we still had so much to learn, that our global scaling vision really began to crystallize.

Strategic regions. What did the "strategic" prefix mean? It meant that these regions would command certain resources: their own premises, their own business development team, their own service team, their own stock on the ground. It also meant that we would need to gear up to support these regions centrally. We had to consider our logistics, finance, legal, marketing, IT, and so on and how we were going to protect our intellectual property once we took our products and services outside of the UK and Ireland.

Eight strategic regions. And in each one, we operated in five distinct sectors. This gave us a matrix, a framework for growth. Eight regions, five sectors: forty "boxes" as we called them.

I remember sitting in a US airport departure lounge with our global business development director when he posed the question, "Could we 10x our sales again?"

We had both been key members of the leadership team for the first 10x growth cycle, which took us from revenues of $10 million to +$100 million. The big question was whether we could go to $1 billion.

He took the napkin from beneath his coffee cup and started to draw it out. Take one strategic region—North America—and one sector—construction and demolition waste. Could we do $25 million there? Yes, that was doable—challenging, of course, but doable. Okay, so could we then target $25 million revenue growth in *each* box? If so, that would give us total revenue potential of $1 billion and another 10x vision.

Our 2020 Vision assembled a bigger, newly formed leadership team in Stuttgart, Germany in 2015 to kick it off. Simple techniques such as a SOAR (strengths, opportunities, aspirations, and results) analysis kick-started discussions. What we learned was shared as the team went about agreeing on a set of ambitious targets.

There was such great value wrapped up in our regular pit stops. Each one was carefully planned to keep the team focused on the vision and as a means of checking in on progress. In later years, external speakers were invited to stimulate ideas. Lively debate was encouraged and expected. As time went on, our newly appointed regional leaders shared their localization plans, which enabled the rest of the team to double-check their alignment. We analyzed how we delivered our work. We found new ways to collaborate. We learned best practice, and as time went on, we dedicated time to learn about ourselves and each other. We laughed a lot, built strong connections, and stronger confidence in each other.

8.5 LOCALIZE

When the distribution model and then the franchise model broke down, we realized that we needed to get boots on the ground and fast. We needed salespeople.

Despite the urgency with which we needed these resources, I did not want to cut corners. And I really liked the chartership model. In the company, we had chartered accountants, engineers, and marketers, but at the time, there was no such thing as chartered sales professionals.

So what do we do? How do we assemble a global sales team quickly and train them in what is a technically challenging sale? We talked in P3 People about the importance of having a talent champion in the business. I now turned to him for help, and together, we created our Stride Business Academy. We invited the Institute of Leadership and Management to help create a structured program that would produce qualified people. Yes, there were quicker ways to sell, but it was vital that the quality be right. To get that first cohort through the program, we tapped our network and pulled in a mix of former distributor employees, graduates, and salespeople. Most were based in the particular markets we had targeted and had the local knowledge that would become central to our strategy.

These, then, were the first people on the ground. As they began to gain traction, the next step was to bring in service engineers: people first and then infrastructure. Strategic means we are going to spend; these guys aren't going to work from home. We invested in offices. We registered local companies. The Stride Academy, together with a program of secondment from HQ, ensured that we maintained our culture, but now, in each of our strategic regions, that culture was given a local flavor.

As this program matured, we established relationships with universities in each of our strategic regions and recruited international students. They were brought to Northern Ireland where they were injected with the CDE serum—that is, our company culture. Then they returned to their home markets to work within local teams.

Here's a key point: Decisions should be made as close to the customer as possible. To make an export strategy work, you need to immerse yourself in the market, so key decisions about product development and talent development should emerge from those who are on the front line. The accountant sitting at their desk in HQ, whose worldview is mediated by spreadsheets, should not be the one making critical strategic decisions about the market.

They're "Parts," Not "Spares"

Nor is it just about putting local people on the ground. Our products, too, had to be adapted. Many of these modifications were simple terminology changes. In America, for example, instead of talking about "spares"—which is our shorthand for spare parts—we had to talk about "parts"—which is theirs. We made sure that we had local websites and that all of our promotion and marketing collateral had a local accent.

Other modifications were more involved. Electrical specifications had to be changed and motors had to be changed. Nor was it sufficient to simply convert meters to feet—you couldn't have a 7.2-meter (23.7-foot) conveyor; it had to be a whole number—twenty-five feet or whatever—and that held true for all parts: belts, screens, and so on.

The critical dynamic here was to make things as easy as possible for the customer. That could only be done by immersing ourselves in the market and understanding what we needed to do to make the customer's life as easy as possible. At this stage, it's critical to listen to your people on the ground. Over time, we created a standard for an American offering, for a South African offering, for an Australian offering, and so on.

Pilot testing a new product, service, or business model can help to minimize the cost of modifications and help you to refine your offering in international markets in a more controlled way. Of course, the risk of doing so may alert the competition to your strategy. But we were obsessed with our customers—not our competitors. We had a saying: "Winners focus on winning. Losers focus on winners." Your energy flows where your attention goes, and if your attention is firmly and squarely on your customer, you're doing it right.

Cultural Alignment

South America was one of the strategic regions that presented a lot of challenges at the beginning. For that reason, as CEO, I was heavily involved in getting things started. It took me a while to realize this, but part of the problem was that our approach to selling was out of kilter with the culture and atmosphere of the place. We brought a structured, disciplined—almost Germanic—mindset to sales. You would think that this was a very positive way to approach things, but the reality was that we weren't getting sufficient traction on sales.

During one of my early visits to Belo Horizonte in Brazil, I stayed in the Royal Savassi Hotel. The concierge there made an immediate impression on me. Juan spoke excellent English. He took a great interest in what we were doing, and at the end of each day, he would always ask how things had gone. Being local, he knew the city well, and he always offered to help out if there was anything he could do. In the course of our conversations, he explained that he had learned his English in New Jersey, where members of his family were still based. He had completed a business degree, and although he had taken the job in the hotel to cover his expenses, this wasn't where his heart was.

Lukas, who would take over the South American operation, was due to travel to the region to meet customers a few weeks later. So I made Juan an offer. Would he accompany Lukas for the duration of his stay to help with translation and to help us get the lay of the land? More particularly, we wanted him to help us understand the people, the atmosphere, and the way things worked here. He jumped at the offer.

I went back to Lukas and told him that I wanted to try this guy out. "See how he operates. See if he's good with customers. Watch how he handles himself."

Lukas reported very positively on the few days he spent with Juan, and on the basis of that, we offered him a business development role. A week later, Juan was on a plane to Northern Ireland, where he went through our Stride Academy. He would go on to develop a successful career in sales, and he was instrumental in proving the importance of having excellent local resources in place.

Of course, sourcing the right people wasn't always that straightforward. In the years that followed, our approach to finding high-caliber salespeople became more scientific. There are always risks involved in sourcing talent, but by making that process as scientific as possible, we increased the probability of getting it right.

Yeah, But

We hit the same problem in almost every market we entered. Customers would ask if we'd delivered a project in their country. We would proudly tell them that we'd delivered projects all around the world, but they'd always ask, "Yeah, but have you done it here?"

"Well, no, but come and see this project in Australia that's similar to yours, and you'll understand how we do things."

And they would say that they didn't want to go to Australia; their material was different from Australian material. It wouldn't matter that we'd tested their material and knew exactly what we were dealing with; the fact that we weren't local, that was the issue. They wanted to see our systems working in their backyard before they would commit. They wanted to know that we were there for the long haul. They wanted to know who would take care of servicing, who would pay for service and freight if parts had to be returned, and who would carry out training. These questions all had to be answered before we had any chance of securing the contract.

We determined early on that in order to be successful in these markets, you have to be local, because that's how you establish trust.

Trust is critical.

By having a local presence, by telling the customer that this was where we saw our future and that we were here for the long haul, that's what made all the difference.

"Yes, we only have three customers here, but did you know that your area is one of our strategic regions in our five-year plan? Our vision is to develop these regions, and that means feet on the ground here; that means investment right here where you're running your project."

Hiring locally was central to that strategy. By bringing in local people, we were able to demonstrate that this was not a quick hit and then we're out of here. It wasn't a case of someone flying in on Monday morning, working all week, and then flying home on Friday.

Our customers were investing significant capital sums in our products, so we had to prove to them that we would be there for service and support throughout their projects and beyond.

That trust was hard won, but once we had it, it paid off very well.

It always amazed me how small our industry was and how quickly word spread. It took us a long time to sell one compact plant in Poland, but when we eventually won the deal, five other companies bought the same plant immediately afterward. Before international sanctions were imposed in Iran, we had a customer who bought equipment from us and loved it so much that he became a distributor and went on to sell nearly fifty of these units. I should add that this was an exceptional case, in a country where having a distributor was critical to doing business.

If your first installation goes well, word spreads very, very quickly, particularly in this era of social media and connectivity. And conversely, if you fail to meet customer expectations, you will not get away with it for long.

8.6 ESTABLISH AN INTERNATIONAL CULTURE

"Talk like you've always done business in North America, in Asia, in Africa—wherever—even if you never have."
—Brendan McGurgan

I mentioned that we changed our name to CDE Global in 2010. This was in the depths of the recession, when we were still locked in survival mode, but it was a signal of intent. *When we get through this, we're going to grow. And fast.*

We saw it as critical to establish our global identity early and reaffirm it as often as possible: We are international. That's how we talk; that's how we walk. I believe that's vital for any company with scaling ambitions. Talk like you've always done business in North America, in Asia, in Africa—wherever—even if you never have.

It was also very important to agree on the right leader, the pioneer who would go out first to stick our flag in the ground and get things rolling, regional managers who could establish our customer-for-life process. Very soon after that, we would send out the support crew who would come in and begin building the infrastructure we needed to achieve the growth targets we had set for ourselves.

As the business grew, we began to appoint project managers in each country as well. These were usually a blend of Northern Irish team members on secondment and local representatives who knew the territory and the language, many of whom came from our earlier distributor network. We were always keen to find people who already knew the industry, who knew the market, and were aligned with our culture.

We made it very clear to everyone who applied to join our team that we were a global company, that we had a global export strategy, and that if you weren't up for a lot of travel, you should look elsewhere. That global dimension was enshrined in our vision, and we reminded ourselves of it every day.

It was important for all of our leaders—even those based at HQ—to travel regularly to our strategic regions in order to understand and appreciate what we were trying to do on the ground.

Anytime I had to base myself in one of our regions, I always took the time to get to know people and to immerse myself in the culture. Martial arts is one of my passions, and while in Qatar, I joined the local tae kwon do club. Because the sport is international in nature, the core of what they were teaching was exactly what I had been learning at home.

We observed all of the local holidays and traditions and even brought them back to Northern Ireland. When team members from the regions came in for one of our academies, we would pick a particular culture and celebrate it. So, for example, when Eduardo was here from Brazil, he cooked Brazilian food and delivered a presentation on life in his country. During Eid, we had another team member talk to us about Eid celebrations, and they brought in traditional Arabic sweets. Later, we earmarked weeks during the year when we would celebrate different cultures. And we also offered free language classes at lunchtime to anyone who wanted to take them. It helped people to feel more at home, it opened our eyes to different cultures, and it allowed them to bring a little piece of their country back to Northern Ireland. And the signal went out loud and clear. We are international. It's in our DNA.

TAKE ACTION—IT'S SIMPLE!

Set Your Sights on New Markets. You can't scale if you rely exclusively on your home market. A "win or learn" mentality is vital in going global.

Interrogate Your Experience. Take a closer look at where and to whom you sold in the past. This experience will provide you with clues about the best sectors and markets to target now.

Make Sure That Experience Chimes with Research. Tap your network and find the people who've been there before you. Do the necessary desktop research to validate your strategy.

Plan Your Campaign. Create the appropriate marketing strategy aligned to vision and values.

Localize. If you need to put local teams on the ground, make sure they understand your culture so that your company's ethos is maintained but now acquires a local flavor. To build trust with the customer, you must be seen to be putting down roots.

Establish an International Culture. Make it clear. You are a global company. Anyone who joins needs to keep their passport current.

Principle in Action—STATSports

STATSports began as a two-person enterprise in Newry, Northern Ireland in 2007. Today, the company has offices in London, Chicago, and Florida and is the world-leading provider of GPS player tracking and analysis equipment.

The STATSports APEX System is wearable tech that allows coaches to gather and analyze performance data and use it to get the very best out of the elite athletes with whom they work. Customizable across a range of sports, from soccer to basketball and rugby to American football and athletics, STATSports is the future of sport.

In 2019, the company signed a five-year deal with the US Soccer Federation, while Premiership footballers Raheem Sterling and Alex Oxlade-Chamberlain have both invested seven-figure sums in the company. STATSports' core business is B2B and focuses on elite sports partners and organizations, while the newer B2C element is also gaining traction rapidly. Co-founder and COO Seán O'Connor talks about how STATSports moved beyond their home shores and established a broad customer network, which now includes sales of consumer products in over one hundred countries.

Our key clients at the beginning were Leinster Rugby and then Ireland Rugby. Everyone knows everyone in the elite sports space in Ireland/UK. Once we got into that network, we were quickly able to establish a base of clients and could begin to build relationships with them. But we didn't have anything you could call a plan back then, other than to simply secure more teams. That was how we operated right up until maybe three years ago. We have since evolved and become more structured, which isn't the best word, but more methodical. We resisted that evolution for a long time because we didn't want to become too corporate or too rigid. We didn't want anything that would make us turn away from opportunity. So in those early stages, we found markets by following opportunities.

Our approach, which was to build a network of clients, was probably the best way to grow. If I was to have that time over again, I would still go that way, because the hardest thing to do in elite sport is to get face time with the person who makes the decision, the fitness coach of Manchester United or Liverpool or Arsenal or any of these teams. You could come up with a fantastic product tomorrow, but your biggest problem would be getting in front of the right people and having the credibility to say to one of the top clubs, "I've got something that can help you." The best way in is through that network.

We had people on the ground in the US seven years ago, but for an extended period, we didn't do much more than service existing clients and continue to build our network organically. We had never really gone out and said, "Right, we're going to knock on doors here and show people what we can do." We've only recently started to do that in a serious, grown-up way.

It was important that in seeking to crack the US market, we did not neglect existing clients. We rely on that human network. You can't lose sight of the fact that they're the ones who will move you into new areas. They're the ones who will give you the validation badges that get you meetings.

BARRIERS TO ENTRY
Every region is different; every region has its own unique barriers to entry and you need to adapt your strategy to take that into account. We pursued and signed a partnership with the Qatari FA because Qatar will host the next World Cup, so that gives us a world stage. We discovered that in that market, it was important to bring in local people who understood how Qatar worked. At the same time, these local team members needed to understand how the company worked. We found that local people, injected with our company know-how, was the way to gain traction.

In places like China, you need to go a step further. You need *to be* a Chinese organization to do business in China, or you need to partner with a Chinese organization. It's so far away, it's so culturally different, and trust is a huge issue.

We made two failed attempts to penetrate the US. We already had two young Irish guys there who were really more service than sales, so we hired a senior salesperson locally. He looked great on paper, but this approach did not work. Then we tried another guy. He, too, was well qualified and well connected in the places we felt we needed to be connected into. Again, however, it didn't work. So we rethought our strategy and decided to take Irish team members, people who knew our business really well, and move them to the US. The second element of the strategy was to grow a local team around them. Those we moved to the US understood our business, and the people they hired had the necessary local knowledge. That's what worked in this case, but the point is that no one solution works well across all regions.

There's one guy in Argentina who has been a stalwart for us. He's got the local knowledge, he's got the local black book, and crucially, he's got the people skills. That's what it comes down to again and again. No matter what your strategy, no matter what region or sector, you have to get the right person. Sometimes the hardest part is getting that right.

Five years ago, we did really well in Portugal, and not because of anyone actually working for us there, but thanks to a top division coach who just really liked the product and realized it was far superior to what was out there. He became an advocate for us, and that got us traction far more quickly than we ever would have managed alone. So we developed that relationship and made sure he had everything he needed to do his job to the best of his ability. I consider that guy a good friend to this day. That strategy wasn't preplanned but was simply an opportunity that arose and that we were flexible enough to be able to take advantage of.

And of course you must localize the product. You can't speak with an American football team and not talk in yards. If you want to be taken seriously in America, you need to tailor yourself to talk and walk American. You don't change who you are as a company, but you do tailor your approach to suit that.

DESKTOP RESEARCH

You've got to do your homework. If we're going somewhere or planning something, I like to know as much as I can about the people and the region. Take soccer in the US. It is so different to any other region in the world; it's even changed massively in the last twelve months. Understanding that is key to having any success in the US. Do your research and know who you are working with, who your customer is.

We found the export support agencies—in our case, Invest NI—extremely useful. The work we did in Qatar actually came through an Invest NI link. The point is that if you don't ask, you won't get. These people are there to help. You can get into your own wee bubble, where you think, "Nobody is going to understand what I'm trying to do," or "Nobody knows my business like I do," or "Our business is different." Then you have a simple conversation with someone and you realize that you're not that different and that these professionals can help you far more than you ever thought possible. They can connect you with people who've been down the road before and save you an inordinate amount of time by simply pointing you in the right direction.

P8 ACTIONS TO TAKE:

_____

_____

_____

_____

_____

_____

_____

_____

_____

_____

_____

_____

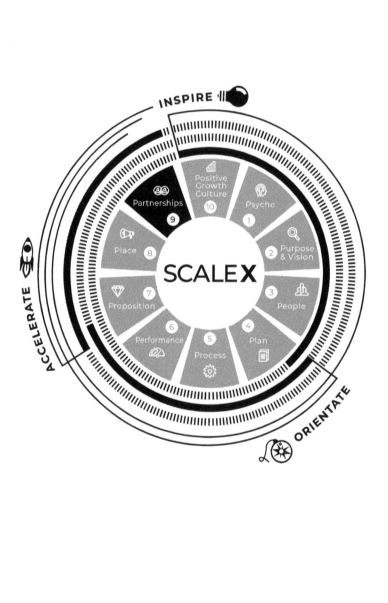

P9

PARTNERSHIPS

"A partnership is any person or organization with whom you intend to build a long-term relationship with the collective aim of attaining your vision."

—Brendan McGurgan

HOW DO WE GET OUR PRODUCT OR SERVICE TO MARKET IN THE quickest way possible without diluting our value proposition? That's the dilemma facing most scaling SMEs. It wouldn't be a problem if there was access to abundant cash, but there doesn't tend to be access to abundant cash. And this is why we need partnerships. Think of a partnership as a circuit breaker or a ladder in Snakes and Ladders. It can get you where you need to go much more quickly than you could ever manage on your own.

All of the partnerships we ever entered into—and there were many—were an attempt to accelerate progress toward our vision with the minimum amount of investment.

But there's a price, and that price is control. This is why founders—who don't like to surrender control—do not number partnerships among their favorite things. Getting comfortable with taking your hands off the steering wheel is an essential part of the partner development process, and developing partners is an essential part of scaling.

The good news is that we can guide you through the process so you can avoid making the kinds of mistakes we made and so you can recognize that some ladders are actually snakes in disguise.

Partnerships can help the business across the three, overarching functions of the customer-for-life process. Again, these are winning the business, delivering the business, and supporting the customer's success. In particular, partnerships are critical in the development of new markets, in the development of new sectors, and in the development of the supply chain.

9.1 SCALE INTO PLACE WITH PARTNERSHIPS

In 2019, market research company Forrester surveyed 454 companies in the United States, Europe, and APAC as part of an investigation into the role of partnerships in driving revenue. Seventy-seven percent said they saw partnership development as central to that year's sales and marketing strategy. Moreover, firms with the most mature partner programs drove 2x faster revenue growth than companies with less mature programs, and were up to 5x more likely to exceed expectations on a variety of business metrics.[65] When thinking about executing your vision, think about who you can get to support you.

Working with a known brand, for example, can get you to market a lot more quickly and more cheaply than flying solo. Tech companies like IBM, Google, Salesforce, and so on have built huge partner ecosystems that contribute significantly to their revenue streams. Microsoft and Workday Inc., for example, recently announced a strategic partnership that will, among other things, allow Workday customers to run software on the Microsoft cloud.[66] Kainos, our featured Principle in Action in P3 People, has also accelerated its scaling ambitions via a partnership with Workday.

Contemplating a strategic partnership is a monumental step for the founding team of any SME. We'll go into detail about how to make it work a little later, but here's the key point. Founder leaders who succeed in scaling their business learn how to collaborate well with others. They learn to build the broad and complementary skills required to scale their business without compromising their core competencies. Once again, what got you this far won't get you the rest of the way. You may have achieved a certain size by micromanaging the business, but without the processes and systems in place to break key-person dependence, you will not scale the business. It's not humanly possible.

Remember, every success arises from a dependence on others.

You do, however, have to be strategic about how you develop these partnerships. Some are more critical than others. You can't spend all day with the banker if the banker plays a small part in the overall enablement of the vision. Be intentional with your time. Back to strategy, which is all about the allocation of resources. The CEO's time is a critical resource. Spend it strategically. Like Bill Gates, Jeff Bezos, and Richard Branson, you've got twenty-four hours in the day. In allocating that time, be strategic in developing your network and prioritize the partnerships that enable the vision.

Franchising

Michael and Nikki McQuillan opened their first café in Belfast in 1999. Their vision was that The Streat would become the best-known café concept to emerge from the island of Ireland. When they sold the business eleven years later, there were fifty Streat cafés thriving in diverse locations across Britain and Ireland. At the outset, the couple ran the cafés themselves, growing organically and relying heavily on finance to expand. It's worth noting that the McQuillans always regarded their bank as an essential node in the ecosystem of relationships that would sustain them and fuel their growth.

"In the early stages of a business," says Nikki, "you get your initial support from the bank, whether it's a loan and an overdraft. Inevitably, halfway through year one, your forecasts turn out to be a little bit more optimistic, and you need to go back. The bank gets frightened, and you don't tend to get what you need. So we decided on the first month of Streat 1 [which is how they referred to their first café] to send a one-page report to the bank manager every month. When he got the first one, he asked why we were doing this. 'Because we want to keep you posted,' we told him."

By the time the McQuillans needed funding for Streat 2, the bank manager had twelve one-page reports.

"He knew our average revenue, our gross margin, and our wage percentages," says Michael. "And we included the soft element, too. We talked about the positive customer reviews, and how we'd just introduced a new Chinese chicken sandwich, and we delivered the report with a couple rounds of sandwiches."

This kept the bank fully engaged with the business. Michael recalls he was cutting the grass at home one Friday evening, not long after they'd opened Streat 4, when his phone rang. He pulled it out and it was his bank manager.

"I had that sinking feeling. Why is he phoning on a Friday evening?" But when I answered, he said, "Michael, I'm standing outside a unit here on Upper Arthur Street. I think it would be brilliant for the next Streat."

By the time Streat 5 was opened, the couple realized that the organic growth that had got them this far would not be sufficient to scale the business. They decided to try a franchising model, beginning with what they term a little pilot. If it worked, great; if not, no one would have to know about it.

It worked, and in preparation for the next phase of growth, the company began developing and documenting the range of processes that would be vital in making franchising work. Absolutely Streat was the name they gave this collection of processes.

Michael explains, "It was everything that you needed to know to work in or operate a Streat from ten feet outside the front door to ten feet outside the back door, half an hour before opening to half an hour after closing, and everything in between, down to the size of the dice of the onion."

It helped that Streat had always placed a huge emphasis on training and spent far more in this area than comparable hospitality businesses. Although a bone of contention with the bank in the early days, this emphasis paid dividends right from the beginning.

"We did it because we wanted the customer to get a consistent experience," Nikki explains, "and consistent food. But another benefit on the HR side was it meant staff could move between cafés. And we had very good retention because people could always see a vision for themselves within the company."

Their training policies were so good, in fact, that they won a suite of awards in this area.

Retaining their five "core cafés," the couple set up The Streat Franchising Ltd.

"We went looking for a certain type of person," says Michael, "someone who was enterprising but not necessarily an entrepreneur. It's that old cliché: you need a person who wants to be in business for themselves but not by themselves."

He goes on:

We told potential franchisees that we would help them develop their business plan; we would get them in front of a bank or funders. We would help with the premises search. We would help negotiate any planning issues. We would then work and manage a fit-out design and run a recruitment process for the whole team. We would work with them through the launch and the first week and provide ongoing support for that first month. By the time they got to month three, they were taken off intensive Streat care and handed over to our regional managers and business development team.

Thereafter, it was about supporting the franchisees and doing everything possible to make them successful. Streat provided tools like NOPC, net operating profit calculator, which allowed franchisees to measure their operating profit per hour, per half day, per day, and per lunchtime, compared to the same time the previous week.

Michael sums it up like this: "Franchising is about supporting, developing, and policing. Because it's your brand. And you work hard to build it."

He says, too, that you do get the odd "rogue" who will try to add their own slant to your brand. And sometimes, as you enter new regions, a certain amount of flexibility is necessary.

"We allowed a 5 percent deviation in order to go local," says Nikki. "Community integration was one of our values, so that worked well with guys who wanted to tweak it a little bit."

Once the franchising model was established, growth came rapidly. Within four years, an additional thirty-four new outlets joined those first five core cafés.

India

We didn't go looking for the company that would become one of our first and most important partners. They found us. They were based in India and had determined that there was a market opportunity for our solutions. They secured a customer, then approached us with the idea of partnership. We were always open eared when there was a new customer in the offing, and Asia was one of the strategic regions we had identified. So we entered into an arrangement that saw us win several small projects. The problem we discovered, however, was that exporting heavy engineering equipment from our manufacturing base in Northern Ireland to India was expensive. As a result of tariffs and associated costs, it was fully 40 percent more costly than manufacturing in-country. So despite the fact that the customer loved the product and despite the fact that we could see that the market was on the cusp of an infrastructural boom, we simply were not competitive.

In order to scale and to get over this barrier to entry, make inroads into the region, and move closer to our vision, we had to change our tactics. We determined that if we were going to be serious about the market, we had to establish a partnership, a joint venture. Again, it all comes back to vision. If we want to do as we committed to do and we do not have the resources to overcome the barrier to entry, our choices devolve down to one: partnership.

Partnership may overcome the lack-of-cash issue, but it will fail unless you're prepared to invest time—both your own and that of your senior team—in assessing prospective partners and building the relationship. That bears repeating. When you scale, those at the top of the organization MUST put in the time to make these critical relationships work.

Due Diligence

In assembling a short list of potential partners, you need to establish exactly what you want from them: an understanding of your vision, a willingness to grow together, a particular skillset, and access to a target market.

Once you know what you want, do the background work. Talk to them. Find out if they line up with your values. Do they get your vision? What is their reputation in the marketplace? Get references if you can. Find out if they've managed international partnership relationships before. How did they work out? If they failed, why? If they worked, how? Do they have the infrastructure to support what you're doing here? Do they have a clear understanding of your value proposition? Will their strategy enhance or suppress it? You've got to understand all of that before moving forward.

Critically, there must be alignment between your vision and the aims of your partners. In those early stages, your job is educating the partner about your unique value proposition. Although an element of localization will probably be necessary, it's vital to maintain the integrity of that proposition. Once you have satisfied yourself of the partner's alignment to your goals and their good faith in maintaining your value proposition, you've got to be prepared to take your hands off the wheel and allow the partnership to work.

Remember, too, that this cuts both ways. Manish Bhartia is MD of the Indian company with which we partnered. Just as we had to give up a certain level of control when we entered into the arrangement, so did they.

"You've got to let go of your ego," he says. "In order to grow our business, it made sense to partner with a UK company and to let go of our own name. You should be guided by what is right for the brand."

9.2 INFILTRATE NEW MARKETS WITH ALIGNED PARTNERS

We were manufacturers. Our business model centered on selling direct to customers. As we evolved and as our reputation grew, we were approached by potential customers who weren't in a position to buy from us, but they still needed access to the equipment we provided. Large corporates and publicly traded companies tend to have twelve-month budgeting cycles as a minimum. This can tie their hands if they have an urgent need, which requires a capital investment. We'd get calls from big companies saying, "We need this now, but we can't buy it because our budget is already planned. Can you help?"

We knew from the level of inquiries that there was a big opportunity here, so we tried to capitalize on it. But these projects always turned out to be far more trouble than they were worth, so with great reluctance, we decided to decline these opportunities. The scale of the equipment and the bespoke nature of projects meant that our business simply didn't lend itself to rental.

We were approached by a UK company that up to this point we had identified as a competitor because they represented a competitor's product. What we had missed, however, was that their business was all about rentals. That was their model in the same way that ours was about direct sales.

They said, "We use a competitor's product, but it lets us down all the time. We'd love to use your equipment."

We explained that we'd tried the rental market and that it didn't work for us. We told them that we only sold equipment.

"But we would like to be your rental partner in the UK. You sell *us* the equipment and we'll rent it out. All we need from you is backup and support."

This made a lot of sense, so they became our rental partner, and the relationship worked out wonderfully.

This was the sweet spot of partnership. It allowed them to lease the world's best wet-processing equipment solution, and it allowed us to access a market that had hitherto gone untapped. Everybody won.

Critically, our rental partner *got us*. They understood our values and our vision. The relationship was so mutually beneficial that we were able to innovate together, and that, as we were to learn, is the hallmark of a thriving partnership. We created a more mobile version of our flagship product, modifying it for rapid deployment and swift removal from a site.

In any relationship, you can never lose sight of your value proposition. Here, our partner saw it as clearly as we did, and their intervention only served to enhance it. It was a case of 1 + 1 = 3.

9.3 MAXIMIZE SUPPLY CHAIN ADVANTAGE WITH PARTNERS

In the early days, we didn't do any fabrication in-house. Our company sat in the middle of one of the world's biggest crushing, screening, and wet-processing equipment manufacturing clusters. This meant that we were able to lean on a manufacturing skillset that had been built up over sixty years. We concentrated on the front end of the business and established great partnerships within the supply chain. They took our designs and built them under contract. These fabricators became an extension of us, obviating the need to make the investment in full-scale manufacturing facilities.

In P5 Process, we talked about how our failure to create effective processes and lines of responsibility led to huge difficulties on delivery day. Component parts manufactured by various partners would arrive together for the first time at the client site, leading to confusion and stress when sub-assemblies didn't come together as designed. To prevent this, we built an assembly facility, where we could stage a dress rehearsal. We brought all of the equipment together, assembled it, completed all the quality checks, satisfied ourselves that all was well, and then crated it up to be dispatched to its destination.

Our relationships with our supply partners were so strong that if there were any challenges in assembly, we needed only to lift the phone and an engineer would arrive at our facility. They acted like an extension of our own team. They understood that our success contributed to their success. And just as we innovated with our rental partner, we also collaborated on projects within our supply chain. We could say, "Guys, we have a problem here. How do we develop a solution?"

Filtering Out the Wrong Partner

One of those suppliers was a European company that built filter presses for the wine industry. Over the years, they adapted their technology for use in other industries, and we were instrumental in helping them to become a leader in filtration for the sand and aggregates industry. Another great relationship, born on shared values, mutual benefit, and clear alignment with our vision. I can't emphasize enough the importance of investing time in partner relationships. Developing this particular one required many, many visits to their manufacturing facility in Central Europe. Moreover, the key person in this company didn't speak English. This made relationship development more challenging as a result.

Back to that definition again: A partnership is any person or organization with whom you intend to build a long-term relationship with the collective aim of attaining your vision. The long-term element isn't there by accident. You need to understand that your vision will determine not so much what you need today but what you need in two, three, five years' time.

The Internal Champion

Our partnership with the filter press company strengthened as we scaled, to the point where we became strategically important to the development of their business. In 2015, we established our 2020 Vision, which was to become the number one wet-processing equipment solutions provider in every country in the world. With this renewed vision before us, we turned a cold eye on our supply chain and asked, "Do all of our partners have the infrastructure and the capability to support us in bringing that vision to life?"

When it came to our friends in the filter press company, we discovered that they had preexisting relationships in strategic markets like North America and Australia. They were tied to these relationships, and that meant that if we remained with them, our planned expansion into these territories would be hampered and our value proposition impaired.

Six months of very difficult conversations followed. They tried to find a way of holding on to us and their other partners, but at the end of the day, we could not find a workaround. We felt we had no choice but to terminate a fifteen-year relationship with an excellent partner, one with whom we had developed a product that had catalyzed both our success and theirs.

When that relationship ended, we got lucky, or at least we thought we got lucky. We began a courtship with a multibillion-euro European company. Our engineers thoroughly investigated their filtration product and determined that it was a good fit. The company was well established in the municipal sector but not so much in sand and aggregates, and that meant there were no conflicts with preexisting relationships in those key markets. What's more, they had a strong brand, known the world over. So far so good.

But the relationship ran aground very quickly. Why? The company was a behemoth. Huge. After the partner contracts were signed, we discovered that there was no one within the company to champion us or to champion our products. Why did that matter? We delivered customized solutions to customers. We obsessed about our customers. We were always looking for ways to innovate and to go above and beyond what the customer wanted.

Our new supply partners didn't operate like that. As far as we could see, they simply dropped the product on-site and walked away. And they were entirely resistant to change.

Had we stood back and coldly assessed their values, their strategy, their alignment with our vision, we might have thought twice, but we didn't. We were overly focused on the one little thing that had brought down that first partnership.

So we terminated. Serendipitously, we met our old partner at an expo shortly afterward, and after a few conversations, we reignited the partnership. That interim experience proved a good teacher, and we were able to find a solution to the challenge that had prematurely ended the relationship.

9.4 PURSUE MUTUAL ADVANTAGE

We've had plenty of experience of partnerships that looked amazing on paper, but in real life, not so much.

Turkey offered an exciting market opportunity. At one point, construction was booming, to the point where the country was one of the top consumers of concrete globally. We began talking with a local company that was one of the biggest dealers in construction machinery in the world. We had four days of meetings in Istanbul, traveling around different sites and facilities. I remember being beside myself with excitement, thinking that our little company in Northern Ireland was going to have a relationship with this huge corporation. Their customer list was the size of the phone book. I thought it was going to be an overnight success.

Instead, it was an overnight failure. Their salespeople were selling hundreds of thousands of diggers a year. A digger is a digger, but as I've pointed out before, ours was a customized project solution, with long lead times and a need to have an in-depth knowledge of the customer's challenges. Why would a salesperson get involved in all that when it's so much easier to sell diggers? Short lead times, no need to know the customer's problems, and zero customization. It was an easy commission: roll it in, get paid, and onto the next customer. With nobody championing our products, there was no traction, and the relationship fizzled out.

The lesson here is this: When you're doing your partnership due diligence, ask, "What's in it for them?"

And not just the broad organization. If those who are charged with promoting your product or service on the ground have no incentive to do so, that anomaly will manifest itself very quickly, and it will not be pretty.

From this point on, we always made this a central part of our discussion with our partners: Tell us what's in it for you. How will our proposition boost your proposition? There has to be clarity about that on both sides. That's when you hit the sweet spot—when there is a double accentuation of your respective propositions, when the relationship is greater than the sum of its parts.

The Failed Distributors

We had similar challenges with many of our distributor relationships. We expected to lean on their local knowledge, their local infrastructure, and their relationship with the customer. We thought we would be able to get our product to the customer much more quickly. Too often, however, we found that sales teams had no interest in getting involved in a partially customized solution and would not give us sufficient access to their customers. This meant that installations ran into trouble on day one, damaging our brand, and diluting our value proposition.

The problem was, we didn't ask enough questions at the outset. The lesson here is that you need to ask the prospective partner to list everything they want from the partnership and everything they don't want. If we had got into those questions and sought to understand that in the early stages of developing those distributor networks, we would have saved ourselves a great deal of pain. We would have understood very quickly that the partner didn't want us speaking to their customers. We would have seen just how far removed from our values and vision they were. They wanted a standard product and standard pricing. They wanted us to act like a factory, not a business-to-business customized solution provider. If we had mapped that—what they want and don't want—we'd have seen the conflict immediately.

But no. We didn't look too hard because we were so flattered by their interest. We were a small company being courted by much larger, internationally established companies. So we were like, "Let's not ask the difficult questions in case we get found out here."

Ask the questions. Get found out. If you don't, you'll regret it.

Some Partners Are More Equal than Others

When Skyscanner started out, the idea of establishing strategic partnerships with key players in the industry was a fantasy. The flight aggregator had no revenue and an uncertain business model. Moreover, they had to deal with a stream of cease and desist letters from the airlines whose websites they scraped to generate their content. Despite this shaky beginning, the company would go on to scale rapidly. In the eighteen months to February 2015, they doubled their workforce to 600 people.

Mark Logan, former COO of the company, points out that not all partnerships are created equal. While working with other startups in the tech sector, he has seen large technology companies make excessive demands in exchange for a chance to work with them.

"You have to be careful when you're a small company with no market power. You can be abused in the name of partnership, because the other parties are so much more powerful than you in terms of what they bring. They are very well aware of that, and the price of getting access to them can be very high."

It's only when you gain power in the market that you can move away from these frequently antagonistic, often transactional relationships toward a more genuine partnership based on what you bring to the table.

He cautions all SMEs entering into partnership arrangements to go in with their eyes open.

What do scaling companies need? Sometimes you need expertise, sometimes you need more customers. Partnerships can give you both, but what is sold in partnerships is not always delivered in reality. You have to be very careful when you sign a strategic agreement. Are they really going to devote their resources to bringing *you* more customers? Are they really going to send their best engineers over to help you? Don't be surprised in the early days if everything that looks like partnership is basically you giving a lot more than you're getting back.

But just because the partnership is unequal doesn't mean that it's not beneficial. You may not get all you would hope for, but you may still benefit from brand association, or expertise, or a new path to market.

"The key moment," says Mark Logan, "was when we arrived at a point where Skyscanner could drop an airline from our website. Then the airline would notice a reduction in their sales."

The Two-Way Exchange

Now for the first time, the airlines realized that Skyscanner was a lot more than a pesky middleman, cannibalizing existing business. The penny had dropped and the move toward partnership had begun. The cease and desist letters stopped coming and conversations suddenly became warmer.

"We went from airlines paying us nothing for our work, to airlines beginning to establish a more equitable model. They began to talk about how things could be better integrated."

This changed attitude on one side was mirrored by a shift in Skyscanner's thinking, too.

"It's a two-way thing," says Mark. "We eventually realized that we couldn't treat airlines as participants. We couldn't just set out to charge them more money for the users we sent them. We caught on to the fact that for two-sided networks, the more suppliers you have and the better they are represented, the more travelers you will attract."

This was the penny dropping on the Skyscanner side, and a real partnership began to emerge. The company began building pricing and performance tools, which the airlines could use to monitor traffic and improve decision making. They also began thinking creatively around advertising formats and devising other ways of boosting traffic to the airlines.

There it is again: you know the partnership is working when you're able to innovate together.

"There came a point where it became a two-way exchange. They realized that we were actually bringing them more traffic. We realized that we had to help them be successful and that they weren't just people we needed to bill."

This is the key point: The secret to successful partnerships is pursuit of mutual advantage. When they're winning, we're winning, so let's do all we can to make sure they win.

This realization prompted the development of an application programming interface or API which allowed partner websites to view flight information and book flights.

"At that point, we started to see what I would call a much more genuine partnership, where there is a genuine value exchange, and where no party is benefiting disproportionately…Both parties are able to recognize that they are operating on a level playing field."

One great example of this was a partnership between Skyscanner and Microsoft, where Skyscanner powered both MSN's travel pages and Bing's flight search results. The relationship, grounded on mutual benefit and equality, continued harmoniously for years.

9.5 LOOK AFTER THE RELATIONSHIP

The conventional advice about managing partner relationships is consistent: agree on a shared vision, goals, and expectations, create a solid business plan, establish formal systems and structures, and define the results you want to see. All sensible and all worth pursuing.

The bad news, however, is that business partnership failure rates are alarmingly high—70 percent by some estimates.[67] Despite an abundance of advice on how to make strategic partnerships work, that dismal record hasn't improved in the past decade.[68]

Where does it all go wrong?

You sign the agreement, go for a nice meal together, toast the future, and then fly home where life continues as normal. However, unless both parties take steps to develop the new relationship, the celebrations can quickly fizzle out.

Much like a marriage, nobody wants or expects a partnership to fail at the beginning. Everyone starts out with enthusiasm and high expectations. Also like a marriage, partnerships must be able to navigate—and often to actively leverage—significant differences between their strengths and operating styles. Learning how to manage these business relationships in a way that releases their power, stretches their contribution, and adds to their value is the key to success.

Talk to veterans of broken partnerships and you won't hear about better business planning or better contracts. Instead, you'll hear the same thing: a breakdown in trust and a breakdown in communication—an inability to resolve disagreements.

If you want a better relationship with your partner, if you want their cooperation on something, take the time to understand what's important to them. Make an effort to get to know how they operate. Ask what they need. Understand how they make decisions, what they value, what motivates them. Look for quick wins. Think about the potential challenges that will arise as you work together. Establish a simple set of guidelines or shared protocols to help guide the relationship.

In his book *Global Challenge*, Humphrey Walters recounts his experience completing the BT Global Challenge, dubbed "The World's Toughest Round-the-World Yacht Race." Competitors sailed 42,280 kilometers (30,000 miles) eastward, against the prevailing winds, encountering huge waves and force ten gales. Each crew had two weeks together before they were due to set sail. Humphrey and his crew on *Ocean Rover* made a critical decision prior to the race. They decided that instead of taking this time to understand the vessel that would carry them around the world, they would take the time to get to know one another better. They would develop a mutual understanding. They would explore how they made decisions and how each crew member liked to receive information. By the time they were ready to embark, they had worked out a code of ethics and behavior, which they boiled down to these three key principles:

1. Strict punctuality; nobody would miss their stint on watch.

2. A willingness to apologize early if a mistake was made.

3. No gossip behind the backs of fellow crew members.[69]

Punctuality signals respect and a commitment. A willingness to apologize demonstrates humility. A refusal to gossip seeds trust. Humphrey cites the time the group spent consciously building their relationships and developing this code of conduct as critical to their subsequent success. *Ocean Rover* was one of the few yachts that returned home with the same crew that began the journey. Moreover, theirs was one of the happiest vessels that took part.

So here's an important lesson. Work on building the relationship *before* you encounter the high seas or roaring gales. Agree on basic commitments and rules of engagement up front, when your frame of mind is positive and is critical to creating a partnership that will hold up when the tough times come. Doing the groundwork will help to generate consistent behavior, speed up decision making, and reduce frustration in the fast-moving world in which we all now operate. A failure to discuss and agree how you will work together will end up sabotaging your relationship down the road. Don't let mixed messages, broken commitments, and unpredictable, inconsistent behavior become your default protocols.

When things go wrong in partnerships, we typically end up playing the blame game. Focus instead on what needs to be done to fix the situation.

Cognitive Empathy

Mark Logan doesn't hesitate when asked the main ingredient of any successful partnership.

Trust.

"We found that the way to create great partnerships was through cognitive empathy. We asked ourselves, what is it that our partners are worried about? How do they feel about us? What's top of their minds at the moment? How can we anticipate how their concerns will change over time?"

In order to generate trust in your partners, be up front about your offering. This is what's good about it; this is what's not so good. Ensure there are no surprises down the line because someone failed to mention a salient fact at the outset.

"That sets you off on the right foot because in the end, when the lawyers are finished working out the contract, it's engineers working with engineers, it's product people working with product people, and marketing people working with marketing people. The more you establish positive relationships between each party, the better the whole thing works."

Mark also believes that the fear of losing your IP in a partnership situation is overstated. The nature of partnership is such that you don't tend to partner with a direct competitor, and in any case, when you have a great product or service, the value is about much more than just the code.

"The more transparent we became, the more we empathized with our suppliers and our airline partners, the more tools we built for free, the more they appreciated us, the better the relationship, and indeed the better the business became."

Establish Regular Check-ins

In addition to conversations that occur naturally during the course of the day, more formal check-ins each week and strategic planning sessions every six to eight weeks give dedicated time and space to address matters that impact goal achievement. Even if your values, purpose, and strengths align, your partnership will struggle if you don't prioritize communication. Use this time to reflect on what the partnership has accomplished and what, if any, changes may be needed. Partners must feel comfortable talking about anything business related, and they must be willing to have difficult conversations if required.

Such measures may seem unnecessary, but they are important, and the simple act of defining them can help to highlight differing expectations of how you will work together. Frequent check-ins can reveal hidden problems and indeed opportunities to create more value on the scaling journey. By annually reviewing goals, seeking feedback from leaders, and measuring performance against lead metrics, successful partnerships put their business relationships through the paces no matter how old, how new, or how geographically dispersed.

Once the key lead metrics that are most relevant to evaluating the partnership's ability to fulfill its objectives have been agreed, a dashboard can act as a catalyst for any interventions needed. These can be anything from simplifying processes, to introducing a new set of reporting protocols, or to restructuring the entire operating model.

9.6 EMBRACE INTERNAL PARTNERSHIPS, TOO

Don't overlook the partners you have within your business. Is there a co-founder, a shareholder, or someone on the board whose skills or resources you can co-opt in order to draw the vision closer?

One CEO I mentored brought in an investor who became chairman of the board. Things became difficult very quickly, however. The CEO was highly innovative, highly creative, and by his own admission, he liked chasing the next shiny new opportunity, even if that didn't conform to the agreed strategy. The chairman, by contrast, was very analytical and very rational. He needed an abundance of cold, hard evidence before he would act. Instead of generating synergy, these differing mindsets created running battles, and the relationship deteriorated.

Sadly, this is not an uncommon situation. The 2019 research from Fuel Ventures found that no fewer than 43 percent of founders bought out their partners. Seventy-one percent of these attributed the split to differences of opinion on the company's direction. Eighteen percent laid the blame on a poor value fit.[70] The fact that 73 percent of founders said they would never look for a co-founder again gives some idea of the stresses that these issues can cause.[71]

In the case of the CEO I mentored, we spent a lot of time under the hood of his relationship with the chairman/investor, trying to understand how they could make it work.

As before, it all begins with vision. Were they both aligned on the vision for the company? Once it was established that they were, it was a case of taking the time to work on the relationship, taking the time to stand back from the conflicts that had flared up, and finding ways of solving them.

In our last company, the shareholder group consisted of myself, the founder, and the business development director. There were times during that sixteen-year relationship when things became very heated. We continually checked and rechecked alignment with the vision, and critically, we invested *time* in the relationship. The three of us would eat together regularly; we spent time traveling together on business trips and went skiing for a week in January every single year without fail. We talked about all that had happened over the year. We fought, we laughed, and we asked ourselves, "Are we good? Are we aligned? Are we ready to jump back in?" For years, there was a healthy respect for our differences and what each person brought to the business. It was always lots of fun, and we always came back energized, enthused, reset, and ready to go.

Regular check-ins between partners are essential. Once the relationship with our Indian partner was up and running, I usually traveled to Calcutta twice per year. I was always part of the strategic planning process so that we could ensure a confluence of values, strategies, and vision.

These were great sessions where I would showcase all we had done in the other parts of the business. They would do the same, and we would explore new ways to expand the partnership in the year ahead. The synergies were wonderful and resulted in some great innovations. There were challenges, too, of course. They wanted to take things in a direction that we felt might be damaging to the brand or disconnected from our values or vision.

When those conflicts happen, it's the strength or otherwise of the relationship that will determine whether you forge ahead or fall apart.

Manish Bhartia, MD of our Indian partner company, puts it like this: "Be open and transparent. Successful partnership boils down to a shared ambition and a strong relationship."

It helped also that I struck up a strong personal friendship with Manish. I shared meals with his family, and we embraced local customs and traditions. It's always easier when you get on with people.

Gestures are important, too. I suggested to the CEO I mentored that he should instigate a weekly call with the chairman to talk over the business and, in particular, to thank him for his input. Always find the opportunity to let someone know that you appreciate their contribution.

Sometimes you've got to separate the intent from the impact. A partner might do something that rubs you the wrong way or seems contrary to your agreement. If the relationship is fundamentally sound, you have to trust that the action was well intended and forgive the impact.

Writing this book is a very good example of the necessity of prioritizing the relationship. My co-author and I have regular, painfully honest conversations with each other, but that transparency and respect makes our differences work. The air is cleared and you're not bottling anything up. Trust levels stay high.

You need to understand the different paradigms, the different perspectives, the different lenses through which people look. You need to check in constantly. Are we on the right path here?

Twelve months on and the relationship between the CEO and his investor/chairman is much stronger. They both respect each other's viewpoints and celebrate each other's unique ability. They've now got a common way of dealing with each other, which is both functional and serves the vision.

TAKE ACTION—IT'S SIMPLE!

Scale into Place with Partnerships. Protecting cash is critical for a scaling SME. Creating joint ventures and partnerships break down barriers to entry and grant access to markets that would otherwise be off-limits.

Infiltrate New Markets with Aligned Partners. Similarly, finding a partner who shares your values and understands your value proposition will open up access to new markets.

Maximize Supply Chain Advantage with Partners. Supply chain partnerships improve your offering without the need for significant investment. These relationships are at their best when you can innovate together.

Pursue Mutual Advantage. Ask, "What's in it for them?" If you don't know or can't figure it out, it's likely the partnership will fail.

Look After the Relationship. Partnerships are long-term arrangements. You need to prioritize key relationships and nurture them, checking in regularly to ensure that everything is working as well as it should.

Embrace Internal Partnerships, Too. Leverage the differences within the leadership team to create synergies, and manage relationships maturely to ensure these differences don't pull you apart.

Principle in Action—Gymshark

Founded by nineteen-year-old Ben Francis in his parents' garage back in 2012, fitness apparel brand Gymshark has become one of the coolest brands on the block, while the business that powers it has scaled to a 2020 valuation in excess of £1 billion ($1.5 billion). At a trade show at the Birmingham NEC in 2013, the company sold out of all its stock in the first day. In the aftermath of that success, Gymshark's Luxe tracksuit went viral on Facebook, generating £30,000 ($45,000) of sales within half an hour. Partnerships have been a huge part of Gymshark's scaling story. Engaging the right strategic partners at the back end of the business and connecting the right people to the brand has powered the company's explosion into the mainstream over the last three years. Gymshark's Global Partnerships Director, Calum Watson, takes up the story.

Having a clear purpose has been really important in keeping us focused through the exceptional growth over the last few years. Our purpose? To unite the conditioning community. Conditioning is anything you do today that prepares you for tomorrow. So it goes beyond just lifting weights or running miles. Conditioning could be changing your routine to get up an hour earlier every morning, trying to drink more water every day, going to the gym to lose a few pounds, or increasing your squat by ten kilos. We want to unite everyone who's taking action in this space. That one red thread, that one commonality is that everyone in our community is trying to improve themselves day by day. It doesn't matter if your focus is yoga, powerlifting, elite sports, or mental wellness. It is that mindset that links us all. We know to go further; we go together. Gymshark isn't a business; it's a belonging.

My focus is on front-end partnerships, so I sit within the brand function. For us, partnerships mean the network that surrounds the Gymshark brand. That could include influencers, athletes, celebrities, the press, media platforms, or anyone we choose to partner with on the front end.

Our founder, Ben Francis, is one of the pioneers of influencer marketing. He would send products out to his favorite fitness YouTubers—Matt Ogus, Chris Lavado, and Lex Griffin back in the day—asking them to try on the products and give him feedback. In time, they would become advocates and introduce Gymshark to their own communities. There was a real authenticity about what Ben was trying to do.

Our vision is to create one of the biggest brands in the world—to build Gymshark into what Nike is to the US and Adidas is to Germany. For that to happen, we realized that we would have to take the brand to lots of other communities. This thinking brought us to the idea that no matter who you are or where you come from, you should always feel like you have permission to wear Gymshark. That's how we've evolved.

To Recap:

Vision: To become one of the biggest brands in the world.
Purpose: To unite the conditioning community.

WHO ARE WE?

As a brand-led business, we listen to our community. We ask them questions. What types of exercises do they do? What type of sports do they play? What's their training style? We are always learning from them, and that helps to inform our strategy and direction. For example, which areas to focus on: from bodybuilding to cross-training to powerlifting and boxing.

And of course, too, you have to be aware of what's happening in the world. We got into combat sports in the run-up to the McGregor-Mayweather fight. At the time, it was all anyone was talking about. We wanted to be part of the conversation, but we weren't in a position to spend millions trying to sponsor Conor or Floyd. We noticed that Conor's striking coach, Owen Roddy, featured consistently in his content. The striking coach is the guy who wears the pads to help fighters train in the ring and improve on their striking skills. Owen is a former Irish featherweight champion and is highly regarded for his coaching ability.

We got in touch with him and ended up doing a deal together. One of the most-liked posts in the lead-up to that iconic fight is Conor about to hit the pad and Owen standing there in front of him in a Gymshark T-shirt.

Our partnership with Owen began as a one-off campaign, but the more time we spent with him and the better we got to know him, the more we saw how closely he aligned to our brand and our values. As a result, we ended up forming a much longer partnership—one that's been brilliant for him and for us.

So what do we look for in a partner? There is no set list or criteria. We ask: Are they genuinely interested in the brand? Do they have a community that supports and engages with them? There needs to be a strong level of credibility and authenticity.

We are a direct consumer and a social native brand, so that element needs to be there. We look for a strong understanding of content creation, so they would be active on their social media channels.

The person has your brand on their chest. That's your reputation and your value, so it doesn't matter how big they are in the world, if they're not a genuine, humble person, we don't tend to work with them.

B2B PARTNERSHIPS

My remit is the front-end partnerships. However, when it comes to B2B, we have some amazing partners that support our vision. Shopify is a key partner. Both parties have invested a lot into the relationship. They've been amazing in helping us to scale, and they genuinely want to help us grow and create the best customer experience possible on our .com site. Our teams speak frequently with each other. That relationship element is key.

Our partnerships with our supply chain solutions have also been very important. They have been excellent in enabling our scaling vision. Every forecast that we've ever created has ended up getting thrown out the window after a few weeks purely because of how rapidly we're growing. Having a partner means we can rely on them to scale with us, and that has been really beneficial.

TARGETS

Do less, better. There is no point in us trying to go after every single market, every single country, or every single subcommunity. We've focused on a number of key territories. Our focus is on entering these territories and building a strong, authentic brand presence there.

It takes time and commitment to be seen as an authentic brand within a space. It's all about choosing communities that have a strong affinity with your brand and then focusing on building that credibility so you can become a brand that resonates with those communities. As that takes root, you can start exploring new territories.

FINDING THE RIGHT PARTNERS

How do we find the right brand partners? In the early days, if I'm honest, it was gut feel. You did your research online to see who people were talking about. You looked across social media. Competitor brands would ask, "Who is the best athlete in the world? Who is going to win the gold medals? Who is going to win all the titles?" That's not our focus. We try to identify the right person within the conditioning community.

We're very much a human brand. We have a really strong emotional connection with our consumer. If I was to draw a pie chart on interaction with the brand, 10 percent would be via our social media accounts. The other 90 percent is sliced up between Ben, our employees, the athletes, and other talent who represent our brand. The common theme here is that your interaction with Gymshark is going to come through a human; it's going to come through one of our partners.

When we're choosing a partner, yes, they need to get social media and create good content, but the final box they need to tick is this: Do they align with our values? Do they genuinely believe in what we're trying to do here?

Most businesses say, "We pay you X, you need to do Y." For us, it's like, "Let's work together on this. We will put in as much as you need and go above and beyond for you. We ask that you meet us halfway." It's all about mutually beneficial partnerships where the core focus is on building the relationship, not focusing on what the output is.

CALUM'S FINAL THOUGHTS ON PARTNERSHIPS

1. Both sides need to buy into the overarching purpose. It needs to be mutual.

2. Balance the art and science. Data can be so powerful. It can enable you to gather insights and help to inform your decisions, but you can't ignore the human elements that are more difficult to measure.

3. Purpose, plan, and patience—Have a plan in place that ties back into your purpose, and if executed right, over time you'll see the return you were looking for. It takes time to build trust and an affinity with an audience. Be patient.

4. If you are new to this space, start small and build on it. From speaking to other industry people, I've seen and heard of several brands that have dived in, spent lots of money without a plan, and as a result, they don't see the immediate return on investment that they had expected, and it's deemed a failure. Start somewhere. Don't be afraid to fail. If you do fail, fail fast and take the learnings on to the next thing.

P9 ACTIONS TO TAKE:

_____

_____

_____

_____

_____

_____

_____

_____

_____

_____

_____

THEME 1
RE-INSPIRE

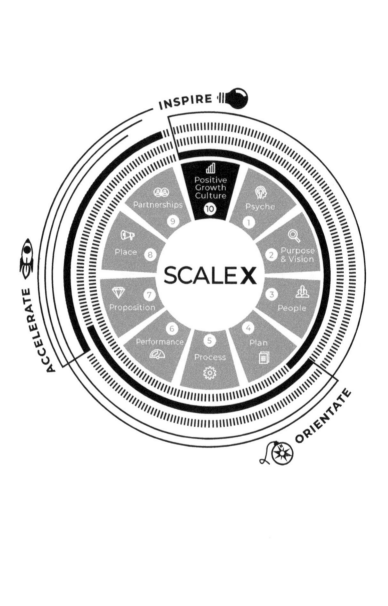

P10
POSITIVE GROWTH CULTURE

"I never lose. I either win or I learn."
—Nelson Mandela

WE'VE TALKED BEFORE ABOUT OUR COMPANY'S BIANNUAL PIT STOPS at which the leadership team reviewed strategy and checked confidence levels for the challenges ahead. My joining the company coincided with one of these pit stops and gave me my first taste of actually working in the organization. It was a fascinating beginning.

The event ran over two days at a local hotel and was attended by about thirty people in total: shareholders, the board, senior managers, and a handful of leaders flown in from around the world. This was the global leadership team in a single room. I learned so much from each person as they presented on their area of expertise. But it wasn't the company's global reach, or the caliber of the speakers, or the ambitious targets that impressed me most.

It was the culture.

First and foremost, the team was hugely respectful, and that's not to say that they were in any way afraid to ask each other the hard questions—far from it. This was an exceptionally competitive group of people. Over those two days, they challenged each other time and again, but they did so with tremendous respect. There was no whispering behind anyone's back. There were no attempts to undermine anyone. They let each other speak without butting in. Further, they invited contrary views and challenging opinions, and they genuinely appeared to value these contributions. There was real humility in the room; there was a real sense of common purpose. This team was clearing the path ahead and building up their collective knowledge so they would feel energized to tackle obstacles and grasp the right opportunities in the coming six months.

The second thing that struck me was how well mannered everyone was. I was raised by parents who placed a huge emphasis on good manners, and that grounding has stayed with me all my life. Saying "please" and "thank you," holding the door open for others, not speaking over them, and so on—these little habits are hardwired into my DNA. Civility and well-mannered interactions can go a long way toward making our working lives that much easier. In fact, I'd go so far as to say that good manners is the foundation of positive relations. In the hotel that day, I was so gratified to see that this tribe I had joined were on my wavelength and displayed manners their mothers would have been proud of!

The third thing that impressed me was the role that humor played in the room. They poked fun at each other and laughed hard. Don't underestimate how humor can bring a team together and make a workplace both industrious and harmonious. You only see humor flourish in places where people are allowed to be themselves, where the hierarchy is absent or understated, and great relationships dominate. It was Eisenhower who said that a well-placed sense of humor was part of the art of leadership, of getting along with people, of getting things done.

So my first impression of the culture was very positive—it just remained to be seen whether that positive impression would be borne out by actually working there.

10.1 SET HIGH STANDARDS AND STICK TO THEM

Words don't build a culture. Nor do prominent displays of company values in the reception area, or on mugs or mousepads. Leadership sets the standards. The behavior of the leaders creates the culture: what we do, whom we recruit, how we dismiss, whom we listen to and emulate, where we spend our time, how we talk, *what* we talk about—in meetings in particular—what we permit, what we measure, and how we invest the firm's money. Leadership behavior sets the tone.

Long story short, I wasn't disappointed. On my first morning at the office, I couldn't help but notice the general hustle about the place. Everyone had somewhere to go or something to do, and they weren't hanging around. The soundtrack was footsteps moving quickly across the car park from office to office or down the wooden staircase at speed. And despite the high energy vibe, people regularly took the time to greet and interact with one another. Within the first couple of days at company HQ, I saw the behavior I had witnessed during that pit stop replicated again and again: the same competitive but respectful interactions, the same good manners, the same sense of humor.

We spend a great deal of time talking about culture these days. Sound bites about culture fill our social media feeds and magazines are crammed with articles about culture, but what does it really mean? What impact does it really have on the growth and sustainability of our businesses?

It boils down to this: Business strategy determines what you do. Culture tells you how well you're going to do it.

Culture is created through the unspoken messages people receive about what is valued in your business. It tells people, "This is how we do things around here," or sometimes, "This is NOT how we do things around here."

A healthy culture will drive business success, so take the time to understand it, to nurture it, to build it, and most importantly, to protect it. Over the years, I've heard too many people refer to this as the "soft stuff" (other terms aren't quite as polite). The truth, however, is that there is extensive peer-reviewed research that supports the thesis that culture provides the real spark, that a healthy culture will have a huge, positive bearing on how you do business. A 2012 Deloitte study found 94 percent of executives and 88 percent of employees believe a distinct workplace culture is important to business success.[72] And yet, over the years, I've seen business leaders balk at anything that relates to how we think and feel about the people with whom we work. A leader who decides that culture just isn't their thing means that at best, their business will fail to derive the benefits of a great culture. At worst, they'll suffer the consequences of having a bad one.

Culture is much more than a shiny new office space or a statement of noble purpose. Culture tells your team the value you place on their happiness and how you will support them to realize their potential, motivate them, and ensure that they are fully productive.

Nor is it just about motivating your people. Your customers want to experience brands that mean something and resonate with them. Young consumers, in particular, want to interact with brands in the same way they interact with their friends.

When you have a positive growth culture, you can't hide it. It will flow out from and fill every interaction: with customers, with suppliers, with media, with all stakeholders. The very furniture seems to exude energy. Invest in creating a positive growth culture, and when you have it, protect it fiercely.

The Key Differentiators

In the weeks that followed my arrival into the company, I was able to see exactly what we were doing that made the culture so vibrant and so healthy.

First—just as had been apparent in the leadership strategy session—this was a highly motivated, highly competitive group of people. My colleagues challenged themselves as hard as they challenged each other. This level of competition meant that a huge amount of effort went into winning business, and there was an undeniable sense of shame when a contract was lost to a competitor. Over time, the company had cultivated the "win or learn" mentality. Implicit in that principle is that although one mistake might be acceptable, making the same error twice is not. That high level of competition fed through to a high level of performance and the rapid growth that the company was sustaining month on month and year on year.

The big risk with a highly competitive culture is that with everyone striving for higher and higher performance, the company ends up being dragged in different directions, or they trample over each other to get there. That didn't happen here. Why? Because the company vision was meaningful and ubiquitous, and it was underpinned by an equally meaningful purpose.

The second key attribute of this culture was the fact that people were given a high level of freedom. They were encouraged to find their own genius. One of the first things I was asked to do on joining the team was to come up with a people plan that would lead us to our destination. I recall the excitement of being presented with a blank sheet of paper and given the freedom to create. The flip side, of course, was the consequent trepidation at having such an alarming amount of trust invested in me. In the end, however, that autonomy allowed me to deliver some of the most creative and meaningful work of my career. Giving people more space and freedom than you feel comfortable with can be nerve wracking for the scaling leader, but given that freedom, a good team will return with results that you can't even imagine.

The third key attribute of the culture was *togetherness*. I was going to term this "investment in people," but that suggests earmarking money in a budget, and in any case, it misses the point entirely. "Togetherness" describes how the leadership values its people. The company invested a lot of time and effort into bringing its people together, strengthening relationships, building connections, and making people feel like they belonged. There were well-being events, social events, volunteering events, and countless opportunities for people to come together to learn from each other and have fun. Moreover, everyone took part, regardless of where they sat on the organizational chart. This was the clincher and sent an unambiguous signal: We *all* do these things because these things are important to *all* of us.

It was this great culture that gave the team a competitive edge and enabled them to win in a highly competitive environment. It was this great culture that ensured that each person delivered on their customer promises, despite the fact that teams were growing rapidly and were frequently divided by vast geographical distances. It was this great culture that attracted great people and inspired them to do the best work of their careers. It was this great culture that enabled the rampant growth of the business.

10.2 INSTILL A CULTURE THAT BRINGS OUT THE BEST IN EVERYONE

"The culture of an organization is shaped by the worst behavior the leader is willing to tolerate."
—Gruenert and Whitaker

You can't hide a great culture, nor can you hide a dysfunctional one. What's more, cultures are fragile things and can change overnight. Unfortunately, subtly toxic cultures are common. So many of us work in businesses where appreciation is absent, accountability is elusive at best, celebration is avoided for fear of sending out the wrong signal, and everyone's browsing the internet all the time. Worst of all, when meetings are held to address issues, no one is prepared to say anything. No one will express their concerns. No one feels safe giving feedback. And yet, when the meeting is over, people gather in small groups to say what they *really* think.

We've all worked in places where we felt stifled and blocked, where politics dominated and conflicts were allowed to fester. It's no surprise that a recent study from HR company BreatheHR in the UK found that toxic cultures cost UK economy £15.7 billion ($23.5 billion) per year and that poor culture was the reason that one in five UK workers quit.[73]

In the same way that a high-energy, fun work environment is instantly apparent, you can't miss the signs of a low-energy, no-fun place to work. There are few smiles and no laughing. There's zero banter in the breakroom, just edgy silence every time the door opens. Gossip, too, is a clear sign that all isn't well. If people allow each other to speak negatively about those who are not present, it gives license for this kind of behavior to spread through the organization.

Recognize the signs of a failing culture.

In a healthy culture, it's the relationships that oil the wheels, that keep things moving and ensure high productivity. When a culture turns, people increasingly fall back on formality and rely on written policies and procedures to negotiate the day. It becomes about dodging blame, keeping your head down, and staying out of trouble. When a culture is thriving, you'll never hear anyone say, "That's not my job." When culture fails, there's no sense of community and no sense of shared purpose or common bonds.

Good people don't stay in toxic workplaces.

Tackle It Head-on

Be the custodian of your culture. It's easy to call out and reinforce great behavior, and there's great satisfaction in doing so.

And it's equally important to be able to give someone a discrete tap on the shoulder and let them know, "That's not how we do things around here." A single person with clarity of conscience and a willingness to speak up can make a huge difference in protecting your culture. Support them. Don't underestimate any chance you have, no matter how small, to challenge the status quo for the greater good.

This is your responsibility as a business leader. It's way too easy to decide that it's a side issue or that you'll tackle it when you get the chance. Tough challenges will gradually slide out of focus, and the energy to tackle them soon dissipates. Then, over time, the unacceptable becomes the norm. Remember, poor cultures don't improve on their own. Action will be needed.

On one occasion, a suggested change in how overtime and bonus payments would be calculated caused a stir among the team, and in particular among two, hard-working, intelligent guys who felt aggrieved by the change. Instead of addressing the issue with their manager, however, they engaged a lawyer, and an issue that could have been resolved quite easily quickly got out of hand. In the weeks that followed, attitudes hardened and an attempt to brush it under the carpet only served to make matters worse.

When the problem eventually came to light, we encouraged the line manager to have an open, compassionate conversation with the team members. We asked him to affirm that we thought highly of these people but that we believed there was a better way to resolve the issue. Within hours of having that conversation—in which both parties were allowed to share their thoughts—the matter was resolved.

10.3 MAKE CULTURE FROM VALUES

"In most cases anyone can imitate your business. But nobody can imitate your business if it's built based on YOUR STORY. When your values infuse your business, you've given a special life to your creation."
—**Vishen Lakhiani**

Whether you've defined it or not, every business has a culture. The good news is, if it's not the one you want, you can change it. A culture isn't a set of rules that magically transforms how people act. It's simply a set of behaviors that you must intentionally cultivate. It is how you would like your people to behave when no one is looking, how you would like them to make decisions and resolve problems day in, day out, whether you're there to oversee them or not. If you don't seek to build a healthy culture, the team will work from their own values and act in ways that may or may not create an environment that you are proud of, let alone give you the advantage that you need to scale your business.

Once you have complete clarity about your company's purpose and vision, only then can you start to consider what is important to you as you set about achieving your goals.

For example:

- If your vision is to be leading edge and highly innovative, then your culture must encourage risk taking, experimentation, and curiosity.

- If you've set your sights on being a brand leader, then you need to infuse your culture with design expertise and creativity.

- As a scaling business, you must be customer-centric, so encourage a culture that cultivates strong relationships with your customers.

Culture begins by deciding what you value most: your company values. These must be drafted with purpose and vision clearly in view. Company values, also sometimes referred to as corporate values or core values, are commonly defined as the fundamental beliefs on which your business and the behavior of its people are based. They are the guiding principles that your business relies on to manage its affairs and its relationship with customers.

Common examples include integrity, boldness, honesty, fairness, trustworthiness, accountability, learning, and so on. Although these are clearly worthy, they have, over time, become hackneyed and meaningless. This is part of the reason why they tend to fail as values. The other reason is that they are focused on *belief* rather than *action*. What's more, they've been dragged through the mud over the years. And anyway, aren't integrity or honesty a given in your team? Do you really need to ask someone to be honest?

We Are What We Do

Take a look at this list of corporate values: communication, respect, integrity, excellence. They sound pretty good, yes? They are strong, concise, and unambiguous. They may even resemble your own company's values. If so, you should be nervous. These are the corporate values of Enron, as stated in the company's 2000 annual report.[74]

Generic values like integrity, trust, and transparency do matter, but what we *do* is more important. We are what we do. This is why, when values are communicated, not as a set of concepts but as calls to action, they are much more powerful. The CALM model is a tool parents are encouraged to use in interacting with children: communicate, advise, listen, and model. Of the four, modeling behavior is always the most impactful. Children may listen to only a fraction of what you say, but they will almost always model what you do. Screaming at them to stop shouting at their sibling gives them permission to keep shouting. Don't remonstrate with them for sitting on the couch all the time if that's where you spend your evenings.

It's just the same in your company. If you value a flat structure, then there should be no director-only parking spaces. If you truly value your customers, then reserve those parking spaces for them. It's all common sense, but as someone once remarked, common sense doesn't seem that common anymore.

In our company, we ran a series of facilitated workshops, bringing in our entire team to help identify what we valued most and what would help us to achieve our goals. These goals were, as we've discussed before, highly ambitious. We had identified eight strategic regions around the world in which we would set up business entities, then build a profile and a customer base in order to establish roots and grow the business globally.

The values we settled on were simply:

- Do It Safe

- Do It Right

- Do It Now

- Do It Together

I loved the rawness and the simplicity of these values. I loved how the whole team had been involved in creating them. I loved how they called for action. I loved how memorable they were. These values accurately reflected what was truly important to this team as they set about delivering their ambitious goals. Regardless of what was going on, the values stood tall. They were on everybody's lips: the service engineers, the project managers, the CEO, and the leadership team spread around the world. These values were as relevant in North America as in South America, Austral-Asia, Europe, and sub-Saharan Africa. They held on to their meaning and power on customer sites, in our offices, in the factory, and in the boardroom. This is how we do things around here, pure and simple.

Keep It Real

Good values call unambiguously for a particular kind of behavior, but for them to work, everyone needs to hold each other accountable. If you or your team either can't or won't follow through on the values you claim to hold, you can't expect that hypocrisy to go unnoticed. One thing people are brilliant at is sensing the gap between theory and practice.

I'm writing this in a hotel restaurant, and as I look around, the conclusion I'm drawing about the prevailing culture here is that it is lethargic and it is uncaring. Waitstaff are leaning against the wall and they're chatting to each other. Customers are being ignored. In fact, for the hour I've been here, no one has come anywhere near me. The breakfast buffet I've just visited is messy and half-empty, and the atmosphere is dreary and gray. I won't be back, but I honestly don't think they'll care.

It's unlikely, of course, their corporate values include lethargy or apathy, so I do a quick search, and their home page is emblazoned with this: "*Putting the customer at the heart of everything we do!*" I certainly wasn't at the heart of the few interactions I've had with the team on duty this morning.

Now, I know we can't blame poor customer service exclusively on poorly articulated values, but this little experience helps to highlight the fact that saying that the customer is at the heart of all you do does not put the customer at the heart of all you do.

If your team doesn't exhibit the behaviors that reflect your values and deliver against your customer promises, then they are meaningless. Your productivity suffers, and the sustainability of your business will be adversely impacted. What you say you do (your external brand) and what you actually do (your culture) must be fully integrated and aligned if they are to positively impact your scaling ambitions.

You can't have any ambiguity in shaping your values. You need to be sure that your team interprets them in the same way that you do.

10.4 PUT THOSE VALUES TO WORK

The injunction "Do It Safe" conjures up the familiar health and safety advice. As a minimum, we all deserve to work in a safe place. But what about psychological safety? What about providing your team with a safe environment to speak up if they feel something is wrong? Research shows that the highest performing teams have one thing in common: the understanding that they won't be punished when they make a mistake. An environment of "safe candor" is the holy grail. This is what we should all strive to achieve, where feedback is completely free of recrimination and where it only seeks to empower improved performance.

We wanted to ensure that our culture would encourage people to speak their minds and to be creative and stick their necks out without fear of retribution. In her book *Brave Learner*, Julie Bogart argues that being practical and logical is important, but it's not always the answer.[75] She focuses on encouraging ideas, creativity, and learning in children, but in my experience, her principles can be applied equally in the workplace. When someone comes to you with an idea, it is like a burning flame. You can either be the wind that fans that flame and helps it grow, or the bucket of water that douses and extinguishes the flame. Be the wind for your team. Provide them with the necessary guidance and safe boundaries—as opposed to strict rules and instructions—and invest your energy in fanning the flame.

To ensure that your values become real, establish a framework that identifies three to five desired behaviors associated with that value.

You don't want to tie your team down to a restrictive list of things they must do. It's also critical that you have an empowered, creative team acting on their own initiative. However, offering broad guidance and the occasional "nudge" in the right direction always helps to set your team up for success. Additionally, it's important to spend some time making your values real; translate them into something of genuine, practical value.

To that end, I often take teams through an exercise in which we go through corporate values forensically.

Suppose "Teamwork" is a value. We dive into that and we ask:

- What does teamwork mean to you?

- Why is it important?

- Who is an exemplar of teamwork in your business?

- What do they do really well that you'd like to see more of?

That last question is important. By calling out the names of those who exemplify the particular value, by identifying particular actions as wholly aligned to that value, it's far easier to see how that value might become embedded in *all* team activities. You call out behaviors that you want to see more of in the business and, conversely, those you'd like to see less of.

An investigation like this gets a great little discussion going, one that puts flesh on the bones of your values and allows everyone in the team to see what behaviors will work and what behaviors won't. It also helps to transform simple, one-word "belief" values into something far more powerful.

As Professor Damian Hughes recently said to me in a podcast interview, your aim in building a strong culture should be to catch people in, NOT catch people out. Always call out positive, value-aligned behaviors when you see them in your team. Always look for the ABCD behaviors, those that go above and beyond the call of duty, and then tell the rest of the organization. There's a quote from Italian poet Cesare Pavese that says simply, "We do not remember days; we remember moments." What we want to do when we call out positive behavior is to give the recipient a moment, one that they will remember. Make it a weekly habit to spot moments that are aligned to our values and to celebrate them.

10.5 LOCK YOUR VALUES INTO YOUR PEOPLE SYSTEMS

Cultural change takes time. One single event won't do it.

In one of my earlier roles, I saw very clearly how counterproductive this approach can be. When two large companies merged, the new entity set about defining their new culture. With the involvement of the wider team, a new set of core values was created. Between design, testing, and workshops, a huge amount of effort went into the launch event.

Then, one morning, everyone arrived into the office to find a beautiful white box on every desk. Intrigued, they immediately rifled through the contents of the box. There was a beautifully produced pocket guide to the company's values, together with a few novelty gifts, and a branded bar of chocolate.

Great so far, but that was more or less it. Everyone polished off the chocolate, flipped briefly through the guide, lost interest, and went on with their day. Nothing changed. A great opportunity to instigate sustainable change was lost.

Making real change happen takes continual effort. You need to integrate your values and behaviors into every aspect of your business—from employee benefit packages to marketing strategies, and customer service. Every single process that is created, every system installed, every technology that is used, every structure that is designed, every job title that is given should reinforce your values and behaviors. During our weekly Good News Friday updates, we always took the opportunity to acknowledge behaviors aligned to our values. This was a simple and effective way of acknowledging—again—this is the way we do things around here.

Getting Values into Your Performance Management System

If you want to create sustainable cultural change, your performance and reward system is a great place to start. Whenever a manager assesses someone on the team—be it positively or negatively—that assessment typically relates to behavior. It could be how helpful someone was, or the effort they put into making an event run smoothly, or getting a piece of work to a customer before a deadline. And conversely, it may be blaming someone else for things going wrong, not showing their support for colleagues, not communicating in a timely fashion, and so on.

A framework that defines the behaviors associated with the team achieving their goals gives managers a tool kit to have better quality conversations with their team members. The framework can provide a set of positive indicators so that managers can recognize the right behaviors and encourage more of the same. Similarly, it could identify negative indicators to help managers articulate the behaviors they do not want to see. And it provides a reference point for managers to question and challenge their team.

For example, the person who consistently points the finger at others—does this amount to a positive challenge? Is it consistent with the company's core value of "Do It Together"? Asking these questions opens up a deeper conversation that leads to something that the manager can act on.

Integrating your values and related behaviors into your performance management system breathes life into them, enabling much greater performance. It is the key to moving from that ephemeral feeling that things are improving to the real and sustainable traction which is the hallmark of a positive growth culture. It helps individuals see a connection between the ways they're asked to act—which might feel uncomfortable for some—and the overall growth of the business. Critically, it shows everyone that the leadership team is making a determined effort to move in the right direction. So much of your cultural success will be determined by what gets rewarded at your company. Every time an employee is recognized or rewarded for pushing the company forward, the culture strengthens.

Try Nudging

I've always been fascinated by what makes people tick. By paying attention to how we act and interact, by trying to understand emotions, you develop an understanding of human behavior, and this is crucial in dealing with sensitive situations, navigating difficult conversations, and negotiating the best results. Most businesses run at about one-third of their human potential because they don't pay enough attention to this. And yet, productivity is one of the biggest challenges we face. That's why enlightened companies are taking creative measures to unleash the energy of positive human behavior.

Nudge management, for example, has become increasingly popular. This is all about the subtle encouragement of small behavioral changes that, when taken together, generate big results. It's not about forcing people to do what you want. It's about encouraging them to make better decisions.

The idea gained popularity following the establishment of the Behavioral Insights Team by the British government in 2010. Known more generally as the Nudge Unit, it was derided at the start as being slightly eccentric, but this changed when it began to rack up a raft of successes. Simply changing the wording on a tax arrears letter increased compliance from 33 percent to 39 percent.[76] It may not sound like much, but that 6 percent change brought in millions that would otherwise have gone uncollected. Other governments and local authorities sat up and took notice. In 2015, Louisville, Kentucky doubled the collection of outstanding parking fines when it sent drivers a letter that said, "The majority of drivers who receive a parking fine in Louisville pay it within thirteen days."[77] To date, legislatures around the world have generated positive changes in areas as diverse as charity giving, electoral participation, and organ donation.

Not everyone is a fan of nudge management. Detractors argue that the practice amounts to coercion and that running behavioral trials is akin to doing experiments on people. This critique is in retreat, however, as the practice becomes more popular and more successful. Moreover, the fact that the world's most successful data company, Google, is an enthusiastic advocate and has been an influential factor. The management system at Google uses data to understand team behavior and introduce simple nudges that reset default rules, improving productivity, decision making, and perceived freedom.

These ideas are the brainchild of Economics Nobel Laureate Richard Thaler and Cass R. Sunstein and are showcased in their 2008 book *Nudge: Improving Decisions about Health, Wealth and Happiness*. They offer this definition of a nudge: "Any aspect of the choice architecture that alters people's behavior in a predictable way without forbidding any options or significantly changing their economic incentives…To count as a mere nudge, the intervention must be easy and cheap to avoid. Nudges are not mandates. Putting the fruit at eye level counts as a nudge. Banning junk food does not."[78]

Thaler stipulates three principles for nudging:

- All nudges should be transparent and never misleading.

- It should be as easy as possible to opt out of the nudge.

- There should be good reason to believe that the behavior being encouraged will improve the welfare of those being nudged.[79]

In Google, they altered the office architecture in order to encourage collaboration and the sharing of information. Food in the cafeteria was laid out in a way that subtly encouraged healthy eating.

A slightly more sophisticated example relates to the amount of time we spend in meetings. In many businesses, more than half of the working day is spent sharing information in meeting rooms and on virtual platforms. All too often, these are among the most unproductive hours of the day. Changing the default meeting time from sixty to thirty minutes automatically changes expectations, allowing a new social norm to take hold. This can be a very powerful, simple, and unobtrusive strategy to increase efficiency and deliver thousands of saved working hours.

Of course, changes do not have to be as subtle as this. Any effort to demonstrate the behaviors that are expected in your business will help to create the right growth culture. As you and your team set about pulling together to build something bigger than yourselves, understanding and implementing the core elements of that culture is critical. Again, those core elements are the things that say, "This is how we do things around here." Only you, together with your team, can determine what they are.

The key thing to remember here is that it's not about you, or at least, it's not all about you. Although you play a fundamental role in motivating your team and leading the way, a sustainable positive growth culture will only emerge when the right mindset and behaviors are ingrained in the whole team.

I'd like to highlight a key differentiator that emerges time and again in successfully scaling businesses: the use of positive language. Setting the right internal dialogue for your team is like turning the dial toward a positive growth culture. Deploying positivity will encourage your team to seek possibility, to find magic in the unknown, and generate a burning desire to succeed.

10.6 ENCOURAGE POSITIVITY

"The chief task in life is simply this: to identify and separate matters so that I can say clearly to myself which are externals not under my control, and which have to do with the choices I actually control. Where do I look for good and evil? Not to uncontrollable externals, but within myself to the choices that are my own."
—Epictetus

We are writing our book in the middle of a global pandemic. The news seems to get worse with each passing day. Circumstances are changing rapidly, forcing people to react with unprecedented speed. Millions of people around the world have lost loved ones. So many of us have been unable to mourn them as we would like, while millions of others are suffering terrible anxiety as a result of the way we have to live. It is a time when I believe that messages of hope and encouragement are more important than ever, and yet, they are largely absent from public discourse. Yes, we need to know and understand what's happening in the world, but I've never seen the level of negativity and pessimism that I'm seeing right now.

I choose to take a different perspective, a more positive one that will give me what I need right now.

COVID-19 has made me appreciate the privileges I have—my freedom, my health, my family. I had been taking these for granted. I had been getting lost in the busyness of my life and had stopped making time for the simple things. The crisis has put my problems in perspective and shown me what is most important: family, friends, love, and community.

It is vital to be able to identify the things that we can control. And words are the building blocks of the world we create every day. They touch our mood centers and color our emotions. Yes, we need to hear about the suffering that COVID-19 has unleashed, but why not share the stories of the millions who have come through it and survived? I think that we have overlooked the opportunity to tell these stories, to appreciate what is good, if only to protect our mental health during the crisis.

Choosing to speak about the challenges we face in a different way is, I believe, central to feeling more positive about our ability to overcome them. Understand what is both within our control and doesn't serve us (a diet of continual bad news, for example). Nothing spurs a team on like a healthy dose of positivity. Time and again, I've seen workplace challenges made less daunting by changing the perspective and seeing things in a more positive light. It is this that differentiates our ability to address problems.

I first started to notice how positivity in the workplace can act as a cultural differentiator back in 1995 while on student placement with the Marriot Hotel Group in Florida. My shift began at 5:45 a.m. It was a daunting start time for a student, but I found that within a couple of weeks, instead of dragging myself reluctantly into work each morning, I was almost skipping in. Why? Because every morning I was greeted by a great group of people who would put a smile on the grumpiest of faces. Their cheeriness and positivity was so infectious that you couldn't help but join in. And it wasn't just a surface thing. A "can do" attitude permeated everything that they did. It was my first lesson, but not my last, in the foundational value of positivity in creating a positive growth culture. The team's use of positive language not only rubbed off on everyone else (including me), but it also sparked a remarkable energy that led inevitably toward taking positive action.

We talked in P1 Psyche about how we banned the phrase "Not too bad" from the workplace. This is the standard Northern Irish response to "How are you?" and one I used for years without thinking too much about it. But my colleagues in Florida took me to task, pointing out that the implication of my unthinking response was that I was marginally better than "bad." The truth, of course—and they recognized this—was that I felt great. The smile on my face told them so. But why didn't I just say that? It was a revelatory moment. If you feel good, don't downplay it. Say it!

When we change how we describe a situation or challenge, it can open up new avenues for dealing with it. Perhaps you have a lot on your plate, so here is a great opportunity to learn how to delegate more effectively, to improve your prioritization skills, and increase efficiency. Perhaps you have a particularly tricky boss, but what a great opportunity to learn to manage upward. Perhaps you're addressing the risk of burnout in the business, so maybe it's a great opportunity to coach others toward achieving peak performance.

When you're trying to scale a business, you are constantly taking calculated risks: opening a new market, refinancing a debt, hiring a senior leader…At each juncture, you're either drawing closer to your objective or rethinking your plan. When you take a risk and it doesn't pay off, teams with a positive growth culture don't look at it as failure. They use it as a learning opportunity.

So be a champion of positive language and learning. This concept becomes challenging for those companies that value compliance with the rules over risk taking, or blaming people for failures rather than viewing it as a learning opportunity. Use words like "world class" and "number one." Why not? Although there's always a time and a place to reality-check your direction, when you're dreaming, running, and building quickly, make sure the positive champions in your room vastly outnumber the glass-half-empty crowd. Stand up and be the Chief Encouragement Officer!

TAKE ACTION—IT'S SIMPLE!

Set High Standards and Stick to Them. A great culture will only take root if it is the lived experience of company leaders and if every interaction with team, customers, and stakeholders embodies that culture.

Instill a Culture that Brings Out the Best in Everyone. Recognize the signs of culture decay: poor relationships, a lack of accountability, gossip, a reliance on formal structures to get work done, high turnover. Be a custodian of your culture. Call out good behaviors and redirect negative ones.

Make Culture from Values. Take the time to establish a set of values that accurately reflect what you do. Aim to be precise and clear, but avoid hackneyed terms; make your values calls to action and work hard to ensure you and your team live them every day.

Put Those Values to Work. Draw up the kinds of behaviors that your values require and infuse your organization with them. Make everybody accountable to each other. Encourage actions consistent with values and redirect actions that are not.

Lock Your Values into Your People Systems. A framework that managers can use to identify and encourage/discourage culturally consistent/inconsistent behavior makes it much easier to make values a reality in the workplace.

Encourage Positivity. Using positive language not only lifts your mood, but it also generates a more positive assessment of the challenges you face. You can't have a positive growth culture without positivity.

Principle in Action—
Jevon "JT" McCormick, Scribe Media

Scribe Media has helped over 1,700 authors to publish their books—among them ex-Navy SEAL and ultra athlete David Goggins. His memoir, *Can't Hurt Me*, was the second bestselling book in America in 2020. In 2018, *Entrepreneur* magazine named Scribe Media's culture the best in the United States. That's why we asked CEO JT McCormick to talk us through what it is that makes Scribe Media special.

> One of my first sales jobs was with a software company, and I was very good at it. As far as I was concerned, it was all about me as a salesperson. I didn't care about the rest of the organization. I remember saying to the software engineers, "Look, I don't care if you can launch a space shuttle from your phone. If I don't bring you a space shuttle to launch, you can't do shit." I should have been fired seventy-one different times. Instead, I got promoted to executive vice president of sales and marketing, and soon after that, I got promoted to president of the company. I remember my first day as president. I got to the office early and stood there alone, thinking, *Holy shit, I'm responsible for all of this now. Not just sales, not sales and marketing, but the whole damn thing?* That's when it hit me. I can't do this unless I'm surrounded by great people. That was the day that I said, "Okay, people first."
>
> In Scribe, our number one value used to be results. Not anymore. People first, then process, then profits. My argument is that you can have a flawless process, but if you put bad people there, they will wreck that process. If you have the right people, you can build the right process, and *then* you can make profits.
>
> What about the customer, you ask? If you have great people, they'll want to drive great results. They

will want to perform incredibly and provide incredible results for our authors. If you take care of the people, they take care of the customer. That's why even though we're a fifty-person company, we provide *Fortune* 100 benefits. We have excellent healthcare, so you don't have to worry about that. We have paternity and maternity leave, so you don't have to worry about that. We have an interest-free $1,500 emergency fund, a safety net for anyone who needs it.

And let me say this: I don't know why companies say customer satisfaction is their number one goal. Who the hell wants to be satisfied? If my wife is on a girls' night out and someone asks, "Hey, how's your husband?" I'm going to be pretty pissed if she says, "He's satisfactory."

THE CULTURE BIBLE

With most companies, you don't know what their culture consists of until you join. That's ass-backward. You should know who we are before you get here. That way, you can decide if it's for you or not. It works both ways. If you don't like what we stand for, we don't want you here. If you like what we stand for, please apply. That's why our *Culture Bible* is one of the first things you see on our site. It's a public document; anyone can add comments. It sets out our mission, purpose, and values, and the principles that flow from them. We live by those principles and values.

I say to people all the time, "No one works *for* me. People work *with* me." I'm no one's boss. If you're in leadership, you have one role: to support the people you work with. So for us, it's not about your direct *reports*; it's about your direct *supports.* I am here to serve and support. I clear obstacles; I move things out of the way for people to be successful in their careers. And it's careers, not jobs. I've heard so many people in leadership say that they have an open-door policy. I always think that if you didn't sit in an office, there would be no need for an open-door policy. So I sit out in the middle of the floor. People know that they are free to walk up to my desk anytime they want.

Asking questions—or learning—is a big part of our culture, too. If you are too prideful to ask a question because you think it will make you look dumb, you can't be in this culture, because asking questions is how you learn. I never graduated high school, and I'm surrounded by people who have gone to Harvard, to Duke Law School, to the University of Chicago. If I don't understand a particular word, I'll ask for a definition. I want the tribe members to see that the CEO will stop a meeting if he doesn't know what a word means.

That's the other thing: We're not a team; we're a tribe.

Optimism is another value. I do not do negativity. I don't wear rose-colored glasses—it's not as if there are no issues or problems. But the way to look at it is this: "Okay, how can we overcome the obstacle? How can we achieve the goal?"

We don't do quarterly reviews. You make a mistake the first week of January, and we're not going to talk about it until the first week in April? That's ridiculous. So we're all about feedback early and often. Let people know where they stand. I've often heard it said that no one should be surprised when they are being exited from the company. Equally, no one should be surprised when they're doing a good job! We do check-ins every thirty days.

If things aren't going well, we put a thirty-day plan in place to coach you up to where you should be performing. If we can't get you there, we're going to talk about coaching you out. Or we find a new seat for you. We've got at least ten people that started in a different part of the company and then struggled. We found the right seat for them and they flourished. In corporate America, you'll often see someone promoted and promoted, then they struggle and they're fired. Hold on a minute. You just fired eleven years of company knowledge? Why not try to find a better seat for them?

One of our principles is that you bring your whole self to work. We reject the idea that people should have different selves for work and life. Work is an integral part of life, and the idea that you can't share every part of who you are with all parts of your life is toxic.

How do you maintain this culture as you scale? It's consistency. It's constantly talking about your principles and values. If we win an award or get some great author feedback, we celebrate that. But every celebration has to tie back to a principle or value. So when you celebrate it, you've got to list the principle or value it represents in that celebration. So it's about constantly keeping the culture at top of mind.

When we put out a career description, we'll get 1,500 applicants for that one role. We've run the percentages, and it's actually easier to get into an Ivy League school than it is to get into Scribe.

Why? Because our culture is real. Because we put people first.

P10 ACTIONS TO TAKE:

_____

_____

_____

_____

_____

_____

_____

_____

_____

_____

_____

Joining Our Tribe

If you have successfully scaled a business and want to bring this experience to multiple companies, please consider joining us at Simple Scaling. Simple Scaling is a movement—one that exists to enable the success of would-be scalers, to allow them to deliver immense value to themselves, their shareholders, their team, their communities, and to society at large. Due to a rising demand for our services, we are actively recruiting hosts across the globe. If you want to learn more about becoming a Simple Scaling Host, please visit our website at simplescaling.com.

ACKNOWLEDGMENTS

WHEN CLAIRE AND I MET FOR LUNCH BACK IN LATE 2019, WE SHARED our respective visions for the next chapter in our lives. We both wanted to write a book to support business leaders in their growth aspirations, and we also knew intuitively that to write it together was the right way to go. What a journey it's been so far!

We are critical friends, truth tellers, and champions of each other. Writing this book together has served to cement a unique and precious partnership for which we will always be grateful. We look forward with great excitement to the road ahead.

No book, certainly no book worth reading, is ever completed through the efforts of one person or even two people. There are many others we would like to thank for helping to get the book across the finish line.

Our sincere gratitude goes to our amazing editor, John Hearne who, in his discreet, gentle, and professional way, erected some guiderails and kept us between the hedges. There is much of this book that befell the editor's scissors, but it is massively better as a result. Thank you, John!

Next, we would like to thank our publisher, Scribe. Little did we know as first-time authors that we were far from finished when we presented our manuscript! Thank you for all the gentle nudges and guidance toward the finish line.

Clare Patterson of Reason Why deserves huge praise. Clare brought the inspiration for our front cover design with a "Steve Jobs" eye for design detail. She continues to lead our branding, including the final design of our ScaleX™ Framework, and has become a close friend to both of us and to the wider ScaleX™ Tribe.

We'd also like to give a shout-out to everyone who contributed to the book, as well as those who gave their time to share their insightful scaling stories. You have helped bring more color and life to our principles, making them so much more powerful and real for our readers.

Thanks also to those whom we coerced into reading what we had written at various junctures along the way (you know who you are). Your feedback gave us the confidence and reassurance to persist. Thank you!

To the many people whom we have had the pleasure and honor to work with throughout our careers:

Brendan: As a young (and not easily managed) accountant in Coopers & Lybrand, I journeyed through the industry with various companies, most notably Amacis during the dot-com boom and bust, and later, CDE. There, I had the opportunity to lead a company to become a global Scale Up, which wasn't even a thing at the time. I had the great fortune to see the world and learned much about business, life, people, and myself along the way.

Claire: As a young woman entering the world of work, I developed into a trusted partner to a number of exceptional CEOs who greatly inspired me, most notably David Mawhinney, OBE. Thank you for providing leadership that nurtured my strengths, for giving me the freedom to pursue my interests, and for helping me to believe in myself.

On a personal note, huge thanks to our families: Colleen, Marty, Aine, Cara, Erin, Eoin, and Max for your support at each stage. You have been humble and honest cheerleaders at every juncture, and for that, we are immensely grateful.

To our parents—you inspire us. We hope that in some small way we have shown you all that we have listened, we have learned, and we have come to the realization that life is full of possibility. If we have one piece of advice to pass on to all the readers of this book, it's that limitations are often self-imposed, your qualification or profession do not have to define you, and most importantly, you can turn your challenges into great opportunities.

ABOUT THE AUTHORS

BRENDAN McGURGAN

Brendan is a global business leader skilled at building profitable, scalable businesses by delivering on his strong personal belief that anything is possible.

He began his professional career at twenty-one as a chartered accountant with Coopers & Lybrand (PwC). He qualified at twenty-four and joined the leadership team of a scaling software company. After four years in that role, he joined CDE Ireland as finance director. At the time, this was a small, locally focused Northern Irish engineering company. He became Group CEO at age thirty-two, and in his twelve-year tenure in the post, he led the company's scaling vision, transforming it into a large exporting business employing almost 700 people and achieving 25x revenue growth. During his time as CEO, the company delivered almost £500 million ($750 million) cumulative revenue and £50 million ($75 million) cumulative profit from more than ninety countries. The company also generated considerable cash reserves and became a revered leader in its industry.

After retiring from CDE after seventeen years, driven by his own purpose to inspire, connect, and enable ambitious leaders of SMEs to scale with purpose, he co-founded Simple Scaling with coauthor Claire Colvin.

Brendan currently acts as a Non-Executive Director to CDE Asia (part of the CDE Group), a company he co-promoted in 2006. In

2019, he co-led the successful private equity funding round, which secured investment from IIFL, India's leading integrated financial services group, to support the company's future growth ambitions throughout the Asia region.

In 2016, he was awarded the Institute of Directors UK Young Director of the Year and Overall Director of the Year. An avid sportsman and advocate of self-leadership through good well-being practices, Brendan is also a Wim Hof Method instructor.

CLAIRE COLVIN

Claire is a global talent and organizational development leader who graduated from the University of Ulster with a master's in human resource management. In her twenty-three-year career, she has worked alongside leaders, entrepreneurs, and founders, helping them to enable rapid business growth through people.

She is deeply fascinated by and expert in the powerful role of team dynamics in achieving business success. Defining herself as "a business leader with expertise in people," Claire understands the challenges facing SMEs, in particular the skills and solutions needed to scale. These skills have been honed by her time as global talent director on the board of a highly successful scaling SME. Prior to that, she spent fifteen years with an award-winning, indigenous technology SME that operated in a highly competitive environment and achieved 30 percent growth year on year.

Claire is a co-founder of Simple Scaling. She helps her customers optimize their business growth through their people. With a strong focus on humanizing the workplace through effective leadership, Claire helps her customers create people-centric structures and built environments to enable them to build world-class teams inspired and fueled by a shared vision.

REFERENCES

P0

1   "The Scale-up Challenge," Deloitte, November, 2014, https://www2.deloitte.com/content/dam/Deloitte/uk/Documents/strategy/deloitte-uk-scale-up-challenge.pdf.

P1

2   Scale Up UK: Growing Businesses, Growing Our Economy—A report from the business schools at the University of Cambridge and the University of Oxford, convened by Barclays.

3   "Enabling SMEs to Scale Up: Plenary Session 1," OECD, February 22, 2018, https://www.oecd.org/cfe/smes/ministerial/documents/2018-SME-Ministerial-Conference-Plenary-Session-1.pdf.

4   Jim Loehr, "Dr. Jim Loehr on Mental Toughness, Energy, Management, the Power of Journaling, and Olympic Gold Medals (#490)," *The Tim Ferriss Show*, December 28, 2020, https://tim.blog/2020/12/28/jim-loehr-2/.

5   Danny Pnemna, "Mindfulness Enhances the Performance of Elite US Special Forces," Mindfulness: Finding Peace in a Frantic World, January 11, 2019, http://franticworld.com/mindfulness-enhances-the-performance-of-elite-us-special-forces.

6   Nicole Spector, "Smiling Can Trick Your Brain into Happiness—and Boost Your Health," NBC News, November 28, 2017, https://www.nbcnews.com/better/health/smiling-can-trick-your-brain-happiness-boost-your-health-ncna822591.

7   Christopher N. Cascio, Matthew B. O'Donnell, Francis J. Tinney, Matthew D. Lieberman, and Shelley D. Taylor, "Self-Affirmation Activates Brain

Systems Associated with Self-Related Processing and Reward and Is Reinforced by Future Orientation," *Social Cognitive and Affective Neuroscience* 11, no. 4 (2015): 621–29, https://repository.upenn.edu/cgi/viewcontent.cgi?article=1571&context=asc_papers.

8   Joshua Brown and Joel Wong, "How Gratitude Changes You and Your Brain," *Greater Good Magazine*, June 6, 2017, https://greatergood.berkeley.edu/article/item/how_gratitude_changes_you_and_your_brain.

9   Kevin Roberts, *64 Shots: Leadership in a Crazy World* (New York: PowerHouse Books, 2016).

10   Neal H. Kissel and Patrick Foley, "The 3 Challenges Every New CEO Faces," *Harvard Business Review*, January 23, 2019, https://hbr.org/2019/01/the-3-challenges-every-new-ceo-faces.

11   Jim Rohn, "Jim Rohn: 'The Formula for Success in a Few Simple Disciplines Practiced Every Day,'" The Quote of the Day, June 18, 2020, YouTube Video, 13:03, https://www.youtube.com/watch?v=ilKQnEH33Po.

12   "Want to Learn a New Skill? Take Some Breaks," National Institute of Neurological Disorders and Stroke, April 12, 2019, https://www.ninds.nih.gov/News-Events/News-and-Press-Releases/Press-Releases/Want-learn-new-skill-Take-some-short-breaks.

13   Rangan Chatterjee, *The Four Pillar Plan: How to Relax, Eat, Move and Sleep Your Way to a Longer, Healthier Life* (London: Penguin Life, 2017).

14   "The Curse of Knowledge: Why Experts Struggle to Explain Their Work," MIT Management Executive Education, July 20, 2021, https://executive.mit.edu/blog/sleeping-your-way-to-the-top#:~:text=Sleep percent20deprivation percent20will percent20negatively percent20impact,deviation percent20loss percent20on percent20your percent20IQ.

P2

15   Cascio, "Self-Affirmation Activates Brain Systems."

16   A report from the business schools at the University of Cambridge and the University of Oxford, convened by Barclays. See "The Scale-up Challenge" by Deloitte.

17 "The Crisis of Purpose," PwC, 2019, https://www.strategyand.pwc.com/gx/
    en/unique-solutions/cds/approach/research-motivation/the-crisis-of-purpose-
    infographic.pdf.

18 "More than a Mission Statement: How the 5Ps Embed Purpose to
    Deliver Value," McKinsey, November 5, 2020, https://www.mckinsey.
    com/business-functions/strategy-and-corporate-finance/our-insights/
    more-than-a-mission-statement-how-the-5ps-embed-purpose-to-deliver-value#.

19 Greg McKeown, *Essentialism: The Disciplined Pursuit of Less* (Redfern, Australia:
    Currency Press, 2014).

20 Myriam Sidibe, "Marketing Meets Mission: Learning from Brands That Have
    Taken on Global Health Challenges," *Harvard Business Review*, May–June, 2020,
    https://hbr.org/2020/05/marketing-meets-mission.

21 Ibid.

22 Andrew Ross Sorkin, "BlackRock CEO Larry Fink: Climate Crisis Will
    Reshape Finance," *The New York Times*, January 14, 2020, https://www.nytimes.
    com/2020/01/14/business/dealbook/larry-fink-blackrock-climate-change.html.

23 *Accountancy Ireland Magazine*, June 2020.

24 Bruce Simpson, "Leading with Purpose and Humanity: A Conversation
    with Hubert Joly," McKinsey & Company, June 18, 2020, https://www.
    mckinsey.com/business-functions/strategy-and-corporate-finance/our-insights/
    leading-with-purpose-and-humanity-a-conversation-with-hubert-joly?cid=eml-web.

25 Ibid.

26 Ana Swanson, "How China Used More Cement in 3 Years than the US Did in the
    20th Century," *The Washington Post*, May 24, 2015, https://www.washingtonpost.
    com/news/wonk/wp/2015/03/24/how-china-used-more-cement-in-3-years-than-
    the-u-s-did-in-the-entire-20th-century/.

27 "World Is Running Out of Sand, Here's Why You Should Be Worried," *India Today*,
    July 7, 2019, https://www.indiatoday.in/education-today/latest-studies/story/
    world-running-out-of-sand-illegal-sand-mining-extraction-1563910-2019-07-07.

28 Sara Lira, "Illegal Sand Mining in the World: A Billion Dollar Business,"
    ACCAMTAS, 2020, http://www.accamtas.com.br/p/illegal-sand-mining-in-world-
    billion.html.

29 Marga Hoek, *The Trillion Dollar Shift* (London: Routledge, 2018).

30 Graham Kenny, "Your Company's Purpose Is Not Its Vision, Mission, or Values," *Harvard Business Review*, September 3, 2014, https://hbr.org/2014/09/your-companys-purpose-is-not-its-vision-mission-or-values.

31 "Purpose," EY, accessed August 2021, https://www.ey.com/en_gl/purpose.

32 Craig Kielburger, Holly Branson, and Marc Kielburger, *WEcomony: You Can Find Meaning, Make a Living, and Change the World* (Hoboken, NJ: Wiley, 2018).

33 "Moonshot," X, August 2021, https://x.company/moonshot/.

34 Jim Collins, *Built to Last: Successful Habits of Visionary Companies (Good to Great, 2)* (New York: Harper Business, 1994).

35 Simon Sinek, *Start with Why: How Great Leaders Inspire Everyone to Take Action* (London: Penguin, 2009).

36 Ken Blanchard and Jesse Lyn Stoner, *Full Steam Ahead: Unleash the Power of Vision in Your Work and Your Life* (Oakland, CA: Berrett-Koehler, 2011).

37 Brett Steenbarger, "Cultivating the Essential Ingredient in Leadership: Energy," *Forbes*, January 21, 2018, https://www.forbes.com/sites/brettsteenbarger/2018/01/21/cultivating-the-essential-ingredient-in-leadership-energy/?sh=3bf54788de1e.

P3

38 Tomas Chamorro-Premuzic, "Talent Matters Even More than People Think," *Harvard Business Review*, October 4, 2016, https://hbr.org/2016/10/talent-matters-even-more-than-people-think.

39 "Viewpoint: Was CIA 'Too White' to Spot 9/11 Clues?" BBC, September 10, 2019, https://www.bbc.com/news/world-us-canada-49582852.

40 Michael Ewens and Matt Marx, "Research: What Happens to a Startup When Venture Capitalists Replace the Founder," *Harvard Business Review*, February 14, 2018, https://hbr.org/2018/02/research-what-happens-to-a-startup-when-venture-capitalists-replace-the-founder.

41 Margaret Heffernan, *A Bigger Prize: How We Can Do Better than the Competition* (London: Simon & Schuster, 2014).

42 Ibid.

43 Naz Beheshti, "10 Timely Statistics about the Connection between Employee Engagement and Wellness," *Forbes*, January 16, 2019, https://www.forbes.com/sites/nazbeheshti/2019/01/16/10-timely-statistics-about-the-connection-between-employee-engagement-and-wellness/?sh=39b723f722a0.

P4

44 Richard Foster, *Creative Destruction: Why Companies that Are Built to Last Underperform the Market—and How to Successfully Transform Them* (Redfern, Australia: Currency Press, 2014).

45 Elizabeth Haas Edersheim, "Alan Mulally, Ford, and the 6Cs," Brookings, June 28, 2016, https://www.brookings.edu/blog/education-plus-development/2016/06/28/alan-mulally-ford-and-the-6cs/.

46 Ibid.

47 EJ Masicampo and Roy F. Baumeister, "Consider It Done! Plan Making Can Eliminate the Cognitive Effects of Unfulfilled Goals," *Journal of Personality and Social Psychology* 101, no. 4 (2011;): 667–83.

48 Jack Welch, "Five Questions that Make Strategy Real," LinkedIn, March 28, 2016, https://www.linkedin.com/pulse/five-questions-make-strategy-real-jack-welch/.

P5

49 "GoPro Cuts Second-Half Outlook Citing Hero8 Shipment Issues," Reuters, October 2, 2019, https://www.reuters.com/article/us-gopro-outlook-idUSKBN1WH2IJ.

50 Charlie Osborne, "This Is the Impact of a Data Breach on Enterprise Share Prices," Zero Day, November 6, 2019, https://www.zdnet.com/article/this-is-how-a-data-breach-at-your-company-can-hit-share-prices/.

51 Parija Kavilanz, "Mattel Fined $2.3 Million over Lead in Toys," CNN Money, June 5, 2009, https://money.cnn.com/2009/06/05/news/companies/cpsc/.

52 David Jenyns, *SYSTEMology: Create Time, Reduce Errors and Scale Your Profits with Proven Business Systems* (Prahran, Australia: SYSTEMology, 2020).

53 Carol Kinsey Goman, "Leading without Authority, 3 Crucial Skills for Leading without Authority," Susan Duggan Associates, May 25, 2017, http://susanduggan. ie/blog/2017/5/25/zw1iimebz1xklv4mmv7v3w6j7o7h19.

P6

54 John Doerr, *Measure That Matters: How Google, Bono, and the Gates Foundation Rock the World with OKRs* (London: Portfolio, 2018).

55 Ibid.

56 Ibid.

57 "Becoming Irresistible: A New Model for Employee Engagement," Deloitte, January 27, 2015, https://www2.deloitte.com/us/en/insights/deloitte-review/issue-16/employee-engagement-strategies.html.

58 K. Anders Ericsson, Michael J. Prietula, and Edward T. Cokely, "The Making of an Expert," *Harvard Business Review*, July–August 2007, https://hbr.org/2007/07/the-making-of-an-expert.

P7

59 *Scale-Up UK: Growing Businesses, Growing Our Economy.* A report from the business schools at the University of Cambridge and the University of Oxford, convened by Barclays.

60 Michael Skok, "4 Steps to Building a Compelling Value Proposition," *Forbes*, June 14, 2013, https://www.forbes.com/sites/michaelskok/2013/06/14/4-steps-to-building-a-compelling-value-proposition/?sh=7cd6e3d34695.

61 Kumaresh Pattabiraman, "The Most Promising Jobs of 2019," LinkedIn, January 10, 2019, https://blog.linkedin.com/2019/january/10/linkedins-most-promising-jobs-of-2019.

62 Andris A. Zoltners, PK Sinha, and Sally E. Lrimer, "What Is a Customer Success Manager?" *Harvard Business Review*, November 18, 2019, https://hbr.org/2019/11/what-is-a-customer-success-manager.

63 Alexander Osterwalder, Yves Pigneur, Gregory Bernarda, Alan Smith, and Trish Papadakos, *Value Proposition Design: How to Create Products and Services Customers Want* (Hoboken: Wiley, 2015).

P8

64 Barney Cotton, "Do Export Businesses Grow Faster than Other Businesses?" Business Leader, October 21, 2019, https://www.businessleader.co.uk/do-export-businesses-grow-faster-than-other-businesses/.

P9

65 "Forrester Study Takeaways: 'Invest in Partnerships to Drive Growth and Competitive Advantage,'" CoSell.io, March 2, 2020, https://medium.com/@cosell/forrester-study-takeaways-invest-in-partnerships-to-drive-growth-and-competitive-advantage-ab84c1abd447.

66 "Microsoft, Workday Announce Strategic Partnership to Accelerate Planning for Today's World," Microsoft News Center, May 27, 2020, https://news.microsoft.com/2020/05/27/microsoft-workday-announce-strategic-partnership-to-accelerate-planning-for-todays-world/.

67 Jonathan Hughes and Jeff Weiss, "Simple Rules for Making Alliances Work," *Harvard Business Review*, November 2007, https://hbr.org/2007/11/simple-rules-for-making-alliances-work.

68 "Why 70% of Partnerships Fail," LGC, October 5, 2008, https://www.lgcplus.com/archive/why-70-of-partnerships-fail-05-10-2008/.

69 Humphrey Walters, *Global Challenge: Leadership Lessons from the World's Toughest Yacht Race* (Leicester, UK: The Book Guild, 2011).

70   "What Do You Do When Founders Fall Out," Up and To the Right, August 2021, https://u2r.co/insights/founders-fall-out.

71   Ibid.

P10

72   "Core Beliefs and Culture: Chairman's Survey Findings," Deloitte, 2012, https://www2.deloitte.com/content/dam/Deloitte/global/Documents/About-Deloitte/gx-core-beliefs-and-culture.pdf.

73   "The Culture Economy Report 2020," Breathe, 2020, https://www.breathehr.com/en-gb/resources/culture-economy-report-2020.

74   "Enron Annual Report 2000," Enron, 2001, https://picker.uchicago.edu/Enron/EnronAnnualReport2000.pdf.

75   Julie Bogart, *The Brave Learner: Finding Everyday Magic in Homeschool Learning, and Life* (London: Penguin, 2019).

76   Menaka Doshi, "How the British Government Got More Citizens to Pay Their Taxes on Time," Bloomberg, June 10, 2017, https://www.bloombergquint.com/politics/uk-the-nudge-unit-uses-behavioural-science-to-influence-policy-outcomes-such-as-improved-tax-collections-and-pension-enrolment.

77   Martin Sweeney and Owen Philips, "How Can a Letter Encourage Us to Pay Our Parking Fines," The Behavioural Insights Team, March 4, 2016, https://www.bi.team/blogs/how-can-a-letter-encourage-us-to-pay-our-parking-fines/.

78   Richard H. Thaler and Cass R. Sunstein, *Nudge: Improving Decisions about Health, Wealth, and Happiness* (London: Penguin, 2008).

79   Ibid.

Lightning Source UK Ltd.
Milton Keynes UK
UKHW012130060322
399669UK00002B/42

9 781544 525